THE AMERICAN
JURY ON TRIAL

THE AMERICAN JURY ON TRIAL
Psychological Perspectives

Saul M. Kassin
Department of Psychology
Williams College
Williamstown, Massachusetts

Lawrence S. Wrightsman
Department of Psychology
University of Kansas, Lawrence

● HEMISPHERE PUBLISHING CORPORATION
A member of the Taylor & Francis Group

Washington   Philadelphia   London

THE AMERICAN JURY ON TRIAL: PSYCHOLOGICAL PERSPECTIVES

    3 4 5 6 7 8 9 0   E B E B   9 8 7 6 5 4 3 2

This book was set in Press Roman by Sheridan Press. The editor was Barbara A. Bodling. Edwards Brothers, Inc. was printer and binder.

Library of Congress Cataloging in Publication Data

Kassin, Saul M.
  The American jury on trial.

  Bibliography: p.
  Includes index.
  1. Jury—United States. I. Wrightsman, Lawrence S.
II. Title.
KF8972.K37 1988   347.73'752   8735245
                        347.307752
ISBN 0-89116-737-4 (cloth)
ISBN 0-89116-856-7 (paper)

CONTENTS

PREFACE

Trial by jury conjures up many images. The classic is an image of the jury that stands tall "for the people" as a bulwark against government oppression. This image has as its American birth a jury's defiance of the British in the 1735 acquittal of John Peter Zenger. But this is not the image that comes to mind for most of us. Our guess is that, with very little thought, most people would portray the jury in much less flattering terms.

There is, for example, a view of the jury as a conduit for community *prejudice*. This is an image that is all too familiar in our culture. The pages of history provide many trials, too numerous to mention, involving crimes with racial overtones in which jury verdicts appear to be driven more by bigotry than by the facts. This is the image depicted in *To Kill a Mockingbird*, where a black man, unjustly tried for the rape of a white woman, is convicted and sentenced to death by an all-white jury. Deserved or not, this image reared its ugly head again in the 1987 acquittal of Bernhard Goetz, the New York City subway vigilante.

There is a second, very different but also popular image of the jury as a *bleeding heart*. Many trial lawyers say that to be successful, you must appeal to juries through the heart rather than the mind. It doesn't matter if your case is flimsy. The idea is that jurors are sentimentalists. They are gullible, easily aroused by feelings of sympathy, and handily manipulated by the skillful orator. The 1982 verdict in the trial of John Hinckley, Jr., brought this image to the forefront: an "insult to hard-nosed common sense," as one commentator put it.

And then there is the *runaway jury*. It is fashionable, especially among insurance companies, to say that we have become a litigious society and that the jury is partly responsible. Jury awards in civil cases are out of control, we are told. Former Chief Justice Warren Burger (whose distaste for the civil jury is no secret) is fond of telling stories to foster that image. And certainly the 1985 verdict in the Pennzoil suit against Texaco added to it. In a case that sent shock waves through the business community, a Houston jury awarded its hometown company $10.53 *billion* plus interest—the largest award ever by a factor of six.

Prejudice, bleeding hearts, and runaway juries: What these portraits have in common, of course, is the idea that the jury, composed after all of ordinary people, amateurs, is an error-prone decision-making body. We do not intend to dispel these images—not entirely, anyway. There is at least a kernel of truth, and a kernel of fiction, in each of them. Besides, we are convinced that the best way to understand jury verdicts is to shift one's natural focus of attention away from juries per se and onto the stuff on which their decisions are based. What matters most, we think, is the content and conduct of *jury trials,* that is, the weight of the evidence and the procedures through which that evidence is presented. This conclusion, we will see, carries with it important implications. We read all the time about unjust convictions, unjust acquittals, and inflated awards in frivolous civil suits. What follows is the question, to what do we attribute the jury's failures, however frequent or infrequent they may be? Should we blame *juries* or *jury trials*?

With that question as a backdrop, this book explores a hidden world exposed by recent developments in psychology. In doing so, we draw heavily on current empirical research, including our own. We also take the liberty of speculating about possible ways to improve the system. By bringing psychology to bear on the courts' visions of how the jury should function, we believe certain modifications in trial practice and procedure become self-evident.

Saul M. Kassin
Lawrence S. Wrightsman

ACKNOWLEDGMENTS

No book is possible without an extensive support system. We want to extend our thanks to the many people and places who are ours.

We begin on the homefront: Carol, Briana, and Marc; their love and patience were tried on a daily basis. And then there are Mom, Dad, Sari, Cheryl, and Robin; their love and patience were tried on a weekly basis.

Moving into the workplace: Those judges and lawyers who so generously shared stories of their trial experiences with us; Lynn Porter, Angie Giusti, and their word processors; Williams College, for making time available through a sabbatical to the first author; the Psychology Department at Stanford University, for filling that time with a psychology-and-law postdoctoral fellowship; and the University of Kansas, for providing General Research Funds to the second author.

Turning inward: Ten years ago, the two of us met for the first time in Lawrence, Kansas. When we weren't talking about baseball, we were talking about juries. We have this book to show for that decade of friendship and conversation.

THE AMERICAN JURY ON TRIAL

1

OPENING STATEMENTS

On March 30, 1981, John W. Hinckley, Jr. shot and wounded President Reagan outside the Hilton Hotel in Washington, D.C. Three others were also hit by Hinckley's gunfire. The shooting was observed not only by scores of live witnesses but also by millions of TV viewers. Hinckley was immediately apprehended, charged with 13 crimes, and tried about a year later. The trial lasted for 7 weeks and included a parade of 6 psychiatric experts who testified about his state of mind prior to the shooting. Then on June 21, after deliberating for 25 hours, the jury returned a verdict of not guilty by reason of insanity. Did that verdict reflect favorably or unfavorably on the American trial jury?

On November 19, 1985, a Texas jury awarded Houston's Pennzoil Company a staggering $10.53 *billion* plus interest in its suit against Texaco. In a trial that lasted 17 weeks, Pennzoil charged that, in a bitter takeover fight in 1984, it had reached an "agreement in principle" to purchase 43 percent of the Getty Oil Company at $110 per share. Aware of the deal, Texaco then violated commercial contract laws by secretly outbidding them and acquiring the same stock at $128 per share. Texaco's defense was based, essentially, on the idea that in the business world an agreement in principle is not considered to be binding. The jury's award was the largest ever in legal history by a factor of six. It even exceeded the figure in damages estimated by Pennzoil. Again, we ask, did that verdict reflect favorably or unfavorably on the American trial jury?

THE TRIAL JURY: AMBIVALENCE, CONTROVERSY, AND CONFUSION

More than 3 million Americans are called for jury duty every year. Their reactions to it vary considerably. To some, serving on a jury means sacrifices of income, time, and energy. Like paying taxes, it is a duty compelled by the forces of government. To others, it provides a welcome disruption from their daily routine, a source of temporary employment, and even a unique opportunity to exert control over decisions that could determine the fate of individuals, corporations, the government, and society as a whole. For most people, jury service arouses both feelings. It is, at the same time, both a personal sacrifice and a source of excitement.

The ambivalence people feel about serving on juries is matched by a steady flow of mixed reviews about how effectively the system works. Juries now decide more than 300,000 cases every year. Inevitably, they sometimes reach difficult and unpopular decisions while in clear view of the public eye. Look at the John Hinckley jury, for example. The moment its decision was announced, the courtroom full of spectators, journalists, and trial participants fell silent before erupting with noise. They were stunned. Likewise, the public reacted immediately to the verdict with anger and disbelief. In an ABC News poll conducted within 24 hours of the verdict, 75 percent of the viewers sampled felt strongly that it was unjust. Media commentators too were critical, referring to the jury's acquittal as a "dismaying spectacle," a "travesty of justice," and an "insult to common sense."[1] One writer noted that in the days following their unexpected and unpopular verdict "the jurors might well have felt like Vietnam veterans returning to a country whose distaste for the long war came out as contempt for the soldiers."[2]

Was the Hinckley jury's verdict in error? Were they prejudiced against the government? Did they fail to understand the facts of the case, the expert psychiatric testimony, or the applicable law? As it turned out, those who blamed the jury for their unsatisfying decision were misdirected in their anger. Thus when reporters asked one juror why they had not pronounced Hinckley "guilty but insane," that juror had to remind them that the jurors were not lawmakers, that they were not provided with that option, and that "not guilty by reason of insanity" was the only available alternative to conviction. On the question of expert testimony, the courtroom battle of psychiatrists revealed a lack of consensus on how Hinckley should be diagnosed, much less the extent of his criminal responsibility. Finally, it turned out that, in compliance with federal law, the judge instructed the jury that the burden was on the government to prove beyond a reasonable doubt that Hinckley was sane. As one juror commented afterward, "we felt locked in by the law." Another said, "My conscience had me voting one way, but the law would not allow me to vote that way."[3] Even President Reagan came to understand the jury's dilemma. In Hollywood, soon after the trial, he commented on the burden of proof by saying, "If you start thinking about even a lot of your friends, you would have to say, 'Gee, if I had to prove they were sane, I would have a hard job.' "[4]

The Pennzoil verdict also added fuel to the controversy about juries. When it was first announced, the jury's $10.53 billion award against Texaco sent shock waves through the business community. The verdict was by far the largest ever. The initial explanations for it varied, but they all had in common the theme that the jury must have failed: It was a "runaway" jury, a jury biased in favor of a home-grown company victimized by a New York–based corporate giant, a jury determined to teach a straight-shooting, Western-style lesson about ethics, and a jury simply unable to understand the complications and nuances of business contract law.[5] Were these charges valid? Did the Texas jury base its recordbreaking award on factors extraneous to the evidence and the law? The story surrounding this case continues to unfold, so a final evaluation is premature at this point. But it is becoming apparent that this was not just a story about the failures of a civil jury. To be sure, the initial charges are not completely without merit. Posttrial interviews with the jurors revealed that they did show signs of regional bias. But were they biased before the trial or as a result of it? According to at least one observer's report, Pennzoil's lawyers were quite effective in their portrayal of the defendant as an outsider. Also, it has since been reported that the first of two judges who managed the trial before becoming ill did not have a sophisticated grasp of the case and made several rulings on the evidence that undermined Texaco's position. Then it turned out that the second judge admitted, months later, that he may have misinterpreted the law governing the case when he instructed the jury before its deliberations. As he put it, "that can happen to any judge. I mean, none of us are infallible, and that can happen."[6]

Public criticism of the jury, as in the Hinckley and Pennzoil cases, is nothing new. But it is often like blaming the messenger who delivers the bad news. That is probably to be expected. The jury is an exceptional institution. Where else, after all, is a group of ordinary citizens, strangers to one another, and naive about a case, empowered to make decisions of such consequence on behalf of their community? We would argue that precisely because juries consist of ordinary people brought in on an ad hoc basis, and because they are politically unorganized, without spokespersons, and unrepresented by a machinery of special interest groups, they provide a convenient, though misplaced, target for the frustrations resulting from unpopular decisions. It is all too easy to blame the jury for the failings of lawmakers, prosecutors, defense counsel, judges, court administrators, and the like.

Scholarly debate over juries can be traced about as far back in history as juries themselves. Two sets of arguments motivate the debate. The first is one of simple pragmatics. Critics maintain that the system is a very costly anachronism, consuming human resources and government expenditures in massive doses, that it is burdensome to those called into service, and that it is largely responsible for congestion and delay in the civil courts. Former Chief Justice Warren Burger was especially mindful of these kinds of administrative issues. He is also a particularly vocal critic of juries.

The second set of arguments concerns the more important question of how effective juries are at what they do. Critics contend that the jury, composed, after all, of amateurs, is a decision-making body prone to error. This argument surfaces in two distinct charges. The first is intellectual. It is said that the average person is not smart enough or educated enough to understand, much less decide, technically complex civil cases such as antitrust suits. Jurors are thus unable to follow not only the facts but also the letter of the law as described by the judge. These failures, of course, result in an administration of justice that is uneven and unpredictable. The second charge is related to temperament. Jurors are sentimentalists with bleeding hearts. They are gullible creatures, too often driven by emotion and too easily motivated by prejudice, anger, and pity. In even the flimsiest of cases, it is said, jurors are handily manipulated by appeals for leniency and inflated awards. As one lawyer put it, "Remember those twelve jurors facing you are sons and daughters, brothers and sisters, and mothers and fathers, before they were jurors."[7] Based on these arguments, juries are blamed for such evils as the litigiousness of American society, the increased cost of liability insurance, and the failure of the criminal justice apparatus to deter criminals. Mark Twain summarized these criticisms succinctly when he said, "The jury system puts a ban on intelligence and honesty, and a premium upon ignorance, stupidity."[8]

In response to the various charges, advocates of the institution argue that 12 heads are better than one and that a collective wisdom emerges from the process of deliberation. Also, it is argued that precisely because they are naive and uninformed, jurors—unlike their counterparts on the bench—can approach each trial with a fresh outlook. In a related vein, advocates maintain that it is desirable that juries do not adhere blindly to the letter of the law, that their flexibility is an asset. Rules should be shaped by the idiosyncrasies of the individual case. Besides, part of the jury's mandate is to represent its community's social conscience even when it is at odds with the law. As far as the problems of judicial administration are concerned, it is argued that the institution is inherently too valuable for policy to be based on the price tag. Especially in criminal matters, trial by a group of one's peers is like having a citizen review board that serves as a safeguard against oppressive government and arbitrary law enforcement. Finally, it is argued that jury duty is an important as well as symbolic civic experience. It educates the public and it reinforces its faith in the legitimacy with which justice is achieved in American courtrooms.

With juries arousing so much ambivalence and controversy, it should come as no surprise to learn that the legal system is often thoroughly confused about how they act and, in turn, how they should be treated. As we will see in the coming chapters, juries are viewed simultaneously as partial and impartial, brilliant and stupid, active and passive, compliant and rebellious, conscientious and expedient. These assumptions are not without consequence. Following from them are numerous policy questions: Should jurors be selected on a perfectly random basis or should certain segments of the population be systematically included while others are excluded? How should prospective jurors be questioned in order to determine their suitability for service? Should jurors be encouraged to watch a trial as spectators or as participants? That is, should they be permitted to ask questions or take notes? How should the proceedings be structured in order to ensure that jurors maintain an open mind? Should they be instructed before or after the evidence is presented? What should jurors be told in cases where their values might conflict with the law? And when it comes time to deliberate as a group, should they be guided or left to their own devices? What if they are deadlocked? Again, the court's answers to these kinds of questions depends on what they assume about human behavior in the jury box. And as we will see, the assumptions they make are often confusing, internally inconsistent, and contrary to psychological theory and research. Often they are just plain wrong.

A PREVIEW: PSYCHOLOGY, LAW, AND THE IDEAL JURY

We tend to think of the jury as a stable, never-changing institution. That is only partly true. To be sure, the right to a trial by jury is protected by the Sixth (criminal) and Seventh (civil) Amendments to the Constitution. But how that jury is defined is another matter altogether. More than ever, through a series of Supreme Court opinions, the character of the American jury is changing.

In a 1970 opinion the Court broke with a 700-year tradition and upheld a Florida defendant's conviction of robbery by a six-person jury.[9] Now nearly half of the states' courts permit the use of smaller juries as a way to cut trial costs. Two years later, the Supreme Court upheld a Louisiana defendant's conviction on similar charges by a nonunanimous jury whose final guilty vote was 9 to 3. In this unprecedented case the Court declared that states could accept verdicts from previously hung juries based on a three-quarters majority rule.[10] Then in a third major development, in 1969, the Supreme Court hinted that certain civil cases may be too complex to be decided by a group of laypeople.[11] Several judges have since used that suggestion to deny otherwise legitimate requests for a jury.[12] Finally, in 1986 the Court resolved two controversial questions concerning how juries are to be selected. It ruled, for the first time, that lawyers could not exclude prospective jurors in a way that systematically discriminates along racial lines.[13] Then it ruled that prospective jurors *could* be excluded from capital cases if they indicate an unwillingness to vote for the death penalty — even if they could be impartial when deciding on the defendant's guilt or innocence.[14] As we discuss in Chapter 2, both of these decisions will have a marked effect on the composition of juries in future cases.

Amidst the persistent debates, mounting cost-related pressures, and the flurry of recent changes, the time is ripe for us to take a long, hard look at this unique institution. Thus we ask the following trilogy of questions: What, specifically, does the legal system expect from its juries, are these expectations met, and, if not, can the courts do anything to improve their performance? In this book we take as a point of departure a simple thesis: that evaluating how juries actually function is a strictly empirical matter. We search for answers not in abstract legal theory and not in trial stories told by judges, lawyers, and journalists, but in the results of systematic research. The various methods through which these research data are gathered and the conclusions they enable us to draw are described later in this chapter.

On a substantive level, we have written this book with three goals in mind. The first is to define and articulate how the legal community thinks its juries should conduct themselves, that is, how it envisions the decision-making process in its ideal state. Litigants are entitled, in abstract terms, to a fair trial. But what does the concept of a fair trial mean in concrete behavioral terms? That is, how must juries perform in order to satisfy that criterion? By looking at Supreme Court opinions, case law, judges' manuals on trial management, the rules of evidence, and jury instructions, we were able to identify four general sets of ideals. These are described below. Our second objective is to evaluate the extent to which juries can be expected to achieve these goals *in an American court-room*. Over the years the legal system has established a complex network of rules designed to keep a harness on the jury. Jury trials are very carefully controlled, well-orchestrated events that are based on numerous assumptions about human behavior. What are these assumptions, how valid are they, and how does it all affect the jury? To answer these questions, we review relevant psychological theory and research. Third, we explore possible ways to improve how juries function. By bringing psychology to bear on the courts' ideals, we speculate on several possible reforms in trial practice and procedure.

The Impartial Juror

A fundamental ideal of the trial by jury is that cases be tried by an impartial tribunal, one that is not predisposed to favor a particular outcome. As we will see, that ideal is based on the assumption that at least one of the following conditions is met: (a) that jurors appear in court with a blank slate, neutral and untainted by life experiences or pretrial publicity; (b) that jurors can overcome their biases, making fair and objective judgments despite their predispositions; or (c) that those candidates for jury service who are irrevocably prejudiced will be detected and eliminated at some point during the selection process. How well is this ideal achieved? What kinds of people fail in a test of their impartiality? How are juries chosen and is the selection process, as we know it, an effective safeguard?

As antiwar protests and draft resistance spread across the country during the late 1960s and early 1970s, the Nixon Administration and the FBI sought to stifle and punish the more visible leaders of the movement. Among them were several Roman Catholic priests and nuns, including Father Philip Berrigan and Sister Elizabeth McAlister. Their group, known as the Harrisburg Seven, was charged by the federal government with conspiring to raid draft boards, destroy selective service records, kidnap Henry Kissinger, and blow up underground heating tunnels in Washington, D.C. The government selected as a trial site Harrisburg, Pennsylvania, a politically conservative area where Republicans outnumbered Democrats and where several fundamentalist churches and military installations were located. This trial is distinctive for another reason. It was the first of many highly publicized cases in which social scientists assisted defense lawyers in the selection of a jury. More will be said about this controversial enterprise in Chapter 2. But for now we note that one of the fringe benefits of such interventions is that it provides us with a bird's eye view of the jury in certain notable trials.[15]

Back to the Harrisburg Seven. In this very conservative community the defense team developed an interesting strategy, dubbed scientific jury selection. As we will see later, their methods are an improvement over what lawyers do on their own. But consider the following story. Among the prospective jurors was a man in his 50s who owned two grocery stores. When questioned by the lawyers, he said that he "couldn't be against hippies because I have some sons who look like that." On the war, he stated that "More could be done and should be done to end the war. . . . I don't know whether we should be there or not." A Lutheran, he felt that priests and nuns *should* oppose the war. Would you have chosen this juror? As one would expect, the defense team believed that he would provide a sympathetic ear. His selection for the jury was thus greeted with enthusiasm by both the defense lawyers and their consulting psychologists.

Skipping over the trial itself and into the jury room, it turned out that the jury deliberated for 7 full days before declaring itself hung, with a final vote of 2 guilty, 10 not guilty. Apparently, this grocery store owner was one of the two jurors who forced the deadlock by holding out for conviction. In fact, we know from interviews with the other jurors that right from the start of the deliberations he pronounced the defendants "guilty by the will of God," and shouted that it was necessary to convict them "to satisfy God's will and to save the children and grandchildren of America." In his ranting and raving, this juror banged on the table so hard that the Marshall stationed outside the door came in to check on the noise. What are we to conclude about this particular juror? One possibility is that he presented himself accurately before the trial, but was then converted in his views by the evidence. If so, then he personifies the impartiality ideal perfectly. An alternative possibility, however, is that he was prejudiced against the defendants all along and had deliberately misrepresented himself before the trial in order to gain entrance into the jury box. If that is true, then this juror's conduct personifies the serious violation of that ideal.

Pretrial bias among jurors is sometimes an inevitable fact of life, a force to be reckoned with. That being the case, it is incumbent upon the legal system to screen its candidates for jury service effectively. Are current practices consistent with that objective? And if they are, can lawyers detect bias well enough to capitalize on that opportunity? These questions are addressed in Chapters 2 and 3.

Evidence and Nonevidence

A direct implication of the impartiality ideal is that jurors are expected to base their verdicts on an accurate appraisal of the evidence presented in court while disregarding all facts, information, and personal sources of knowledge not for-

mally admitted into evidence. There are two rather clear components to this
ideal that verdicts be driven by the evidence. The first is that jurors can make
sense of the evidence, distinguish that which is credible from that which is not,
and, through their common sense, detect truth and deception on the witness
stand. The second is that jurors are able to exclude from their decision-making
process whatever they may have heard about the case, whatever lawyers might
have claimed during their opening statements, whatever inadmissible testimony
might have made its way into the trial (the "strike it from the record" phenomenon), and so on.

Kay Simmons was a senior 3 weeks away from graduating from Augusta
High School in Butler County, Kansas. She worked part-time as a waitress. On
Wednesday, May 8, 1979, she left work at about 10 p.m., stopped to buy ciga-
rettes, and then drove to the apartment of her boyfriend, Mike Roberts. When
she arrived at about 10:15, Mike was not there. He returned 2½ hours later and
found that his door was unlocked and the apartment was dark. Nervous upon
entering, he discovered Kay's nude body on the bed. Her throat had been slit
and she was dead.

After a police investigation, two men were arrested and charged with rape,
aggravated burglary, and murder. The suspects, Allen Jordan and Douglas Williams, lived (along with their women friends and two children) in the second-
floor apartment across from Mike Roberts. Both men were well known in this
small community as proverbial troublemakers. Although there were no eyewitnesses to the crime, there was other evidence pointing in their direction. To
begin with, Jordan's fingerprints were positively identified on the victim's eye-
glasses. When confronted by the police, he conceded that he had spoken to Kay
outside the apartment that night but insisted that he then returned home without
further incident. Having already served time for a robbery conviction, Jordan
was on parole at the time. Months earlier he had also been accused of raping a
14-year-old girl, but he was never prosecuted because the victim was unwilling
to testify. Needless to say, he was well known in this small community.

But why were *two* men arrested? Because of the manner in which Kay's
body was found, with her arms parallel to her sides, and with no signs of a
struggle, the police speculated that she must have been held on the bed by one
man while another slashed her throat. Also an autopsy revealed an abrasion on
the victim's left shoulder, which the police thought might have been caused by a
metal watch band—like the one worn by Williams. Since Williams had been
with Jordan earlier that day, he was the obvious choice as a partner. Jordan and
Williams were tried and found guilty by separate juries. Only Jordan was convicted of rape. But both were convicted of aggravated burglary and felony
murder. Both appealed their respective verdicts.

Essentially, Williams protested that there was insufficient evidence to support his conviction. His testimony was consistent with Jordan's, up to a point.
They agreed that between 10:00 and 10:15 p.m. Jordan shouted at Kay, then left
his apartment to talk to her. When he returned a few minutes later, Williams

claimed that Jordan commented "about how good looking the girl was next door; that he would sure like to get in her pants." According to Williams, Jordan then left for Roberts' apartment, at which point he stretched out on the couch and fell asleep. He did not know when Jordan returned, waking up only when their women friends returned at midnight. Strengthening Williams' appeal was the prosecutor's failure to introduce evidence about the victim's shoulder bruise or the defendant's metal wrist watch. Although the police had speculated that these were linked, the coroner did not mention this injury in his testimony. In short, *based on the evidence presented at trial*, the jury did not have firm grounds upon which to conclude that Williams was present, much less involved, at the scene of the crime. The case against him was based only on the theory that a second person was involved and that he was the most likely candidate. The jury accepted the logic in whole, probably because of the defendant's reputation in the community. But the Supreme Court of Kansas refused to, finding that there was insufficient evidence to support the jury's conviction. Williams was set free.

Was he guilty? It depends on who you ask. The jury obviously believed he was, but—according to the state supreme court—not based on the evidence presented at the trial. In the end, it is possible that Williams was guilty and escaped imprisonment only because of the failures of his prosecuting attorney. What is relevant here, however, is the fact that the jury strayed far beyond the information presented in the courtroom to reach its verdict. Ordinarily, we have no way of establishing the extent to which jury verdicts are driven by the evidence. Jurors need not explain or justify their actions. Often they are not even permitted to testify about improprieties that may have taken place during their group's deliberations. In this case, however, when their verdict was overturned, several outraged jurors publicly defended their thinking. Two of them went so far as to write letters of protest to the Kansas Supreme Court. One of these letters was particularly instructive. It revealed that its author inferred Williams' involvement on the basis of nonevidentiary sources of information.

The Douglas Williams trial is not typical. Nor do we report it to suggest that jury verdicts are necessarily based on legally extraneous factors. But it does illustrate that, on their own, jurors may not draw sharp lines between evidence and nonevidence and that their decisions can be substantially affected by the latter. In Chapters 4 and 5 we describe this problem in greater detail. We look at the psychology of evidence and at how effectively jurors can appraise the credibility of human testimony. We look at the cues they use to detect truth and deception on the witness stand. Are these cues valid, in light of what we know about verbal and nonverbal communication, body language, and the physiological changes associated with lying? We then look at the extent to which extraneous factors enter into the decision-making equation. Are jurors hopelessly contaminated by pretrial publicity, inadmissible testimony, or the physical appearance of the litigants? And if so, do the courts' corrective measures provide a sufficient cure?

Information Processing

In order for a jury to dispense justice, it must first fulfill its role as an informa-tion-processing body. In concrete terms, that means that it must acquire, com-prehend, and retrieve from storage all relevant information presented at trial. When we speak of information, we are referring to the *facts*, as they are re-vealed from the witness stand, and the *law*, as described in the judge's instruc-tions.

The legal system defines the jury's mandate in narrow but clear terms. Simply put, doing justice consists first of establishing the facts in order to dis-cover what really happened and then matching those facts against abstract legal concepts such as purpose, obstruction, duress, and the like. Once a jury has completed that task, its verdict should be largely an actuarial matter. Thus, in many states, if the jury concludes that a defendant caused another person's death by committing an act in reckless disregard of its consequences, though without intent or malice, then unless there are extenuating circumstances, it is obliged to find that defendant guilty of involuntary manslaughter.

Two sets of questions are often raised about the jury's competence as an information-processing machine. The first is whether they can collectively achieve the necessary mastery of the facts, an especially troublesome question in complex civil cases that extend for weeks and sometimes months. The second is whether juries are able and, in some cases, willing to adhere to the law as provided in the judge's instructions. The information-processing demands placed on juries are often substantial. They are also quite necessary for informed decision making.

In the early 1980s there was an outbreak of toxic shock syndrome; hundreds of women were injured, some fatally, from having used Rely tampons. More than 400 lawsuits were filed against Procter and Gamble, the manufacturer. In one of these cases, 18-year-old Deletha Lampshire, of Denver, claimed that, as a result of using the tampons, she suffered a near-fatal bout with toxic shock syndrome, experiencing such symptoms as high fever, low blood pressure, swollen mucous membranes, peeling skin, and scarlet rash. Apparently, when moist, the cellulose chips appearing only in the Rely brand of tampon break down into simple sugars, causing the growth of the bacterium that scientists say is responsible for the illness. Lampshire requested an award of $5 million in compensatory damages and $20 million in punitive damages.

The trial was held in March 1982 and involved 11 days of technical testi-mony from scientists and medical experts. At one point, during their 3 days of deliberations, the jury requested from the judge a transcript of the testimony of a particular physician-witness. Apparently, they disagreed over what that witness had said about the plaintiff's medical condition. Since jurors are often not al-lowed to take notes or ask questions during the trial, one would imagine that the opportunity to review testimony in the privacy of the jury room is an effective way to compensate for the frailties of human memory. But in this instance, the judge denied their request—not, as we will see, an unusual decision. Instead, he said, the jury should rely on its own collective recall of the physician's testimony.

The jury's verdict in this case was rather startling. It found Procter and Gamble negligent for selling Rely tampons. But then it refused to award the plaintiff any damages—not even to compensate for the $4,000 in medical expenses she had already incurred. The unexpected outcome of this trial cannot be clearly attributed to the judge's denial of the jury's request for a rereading of testimony. Maybe they misunderstood or disagreed with his instructions on the law. Nevertheless, this case underscores an assumption about juries that is often taken as true—that through their collective memory, they can accurately recall the facts, arguments, and instructions that unfold throughout a trial. As we will see, other courts assume the worst of all possibilities—that juries are not competent as information processors *and* that little can be done to change that fact.

There is no ready mechanism for evaluating a jury's ability to retrieve information from the trial. It is as if the courts designed a procedure based on a cybernetic model of the jury and then left it to run itself. To make matters worse, even when the jury is aware that it lacks accurate information, judges are often unwilling to prescribe the necessary remediation. The Rely tampon trial is an example of how one judge's assumptions about human behavior can result in questionable jury-management strategies, increasing the probability of an erroneous outcome. As we argue in Chapters 6 and 7, this story is not atypical. The courts erect various obstacles to effective information processing and then bemoan juries' failures to overcome them.

The Deliberation

What goes on behind the closed door of the jury room? In the ideal, jury deliberations are characterized by a vigorous exchange of information, providing an opportunity for all members to express their respective points of view. This model of how jurors interact as a group provides a foundation for the argument that 12 heads are better than one. It is possible, however, that the deliberative process is not that rational, that juries spend too much time discussing marginally relevant personal experiences, and that consensus is achieved, not because jurors are persuaded by rational argument, but because they succumb under the heavy weight of pressures to conform.

Because deliberations are held in complete secrecy, out of the view of judges, bailiffs, social scientists, and the media, it is difficult to know how effectively they work. Occasionally, however, the goings-on in the jury room are reconstructed through interviews with those who participated. One of these is described in Victor Villasenor's book, *Jury: The People vs. Juan Corona.* Corona had been charged with the murder of 25 derelicts and drifters who were savagely killed and buried in the hills of northern California.[16] Villasenor attended the trial, which lasted for over 5 months and included 117 witnesses and 980 exhibits. He then extensively interviewed each of the jurors in an attempt to reconstruct what statements were made, what questions were raised, and how jurors privately felt during their 18 days in the jury room.

Assuming the factual accuracy of Villasenor's information, his book leaves its reader with a sense of respect and admiration for how the Juan Corona jury performed in this very challenging case. Still, its drive toward unanimity illustrates an important question about the ideals of deliberation. After spending a full day deciding whether to treat the 25 murder charges together, the jury took its first vote, in a secret ballot, the next morning. It was 7 to 5, apparently in favor of acquittal. We say "apparently" because we now know that two of the seven in the majority voted not guilty in order to prevent the jury from returning a premature conviction. To quote one juror: "I voted innocent, too. But not because I have any doubts that Corona isn't guilty. I was just afraid we might've convicted him on the first ballot and I don't think that's right. I think we should do all kinds of talking and explaining before we convict a man of murder." This first ballot was followed by 14 more, an erratic pattern of votes, and eventually an 11 to 1 standoff before the jury finally reached its unanimous guilty verdict. The story of how the final holdout juror came around raises the question suggested earlier. At one point, she said, "Please, I'll change my vote. Just don't hate me. I'll change my vote so you can go home to your wife." By the next day, however, she reported to the jury that "I think I've changed my mind. Yesterday you gave me a day's rest and I relaxed and I saw things differently." What happened here? Was this lone, unsupported holdout actually persuaded by her peers or did she simply capitulate under their pressure? Did she, in the end, still have a reasonable doubt about Corona's guilt? Normally, we do not know. But in this case she told a reporter after the trial that she was under great pressure to vote with the majority, that "although there was no physical coercion, there had been 'shouting.' "[17] What do you think—was this jury's unanimity more apparent than real?

In Chapter 8 we take a close look at how juries deliberate. Who says what to whom? What do they talk about? And how do they manage so often to achieve a consensus? Then in Chapter 9 we discuss how the quality of deliberations can be affected markedly by matters of judicial policy—the courts' instructions, the size of the jury, their voting requirements, and the like.

PEERING THROUGH THE KEYHOLE: THE METHODS OF JURY RESEARCH

Suppose you were offered substantial funds and told to find out as much as you could about how juries reach their decisions. How would you proceed? In 1952 the Ford Foundation offered that very opportunity and gave a $400,000 grant to finance what was to become known as the University of Chicago Jury Project.

Its director, Law Professor Harry Kalven, Jr., predicted it would be "the most comprehensive study of the workings of the American jury ever undertaken."[18] He was right. Accompanying Kalven was a team of social scientists that included Hans Zeisel, Fred Strodtbeck, Dale Broeder, and Rita James Simon.

With the purpose of their research clearly defined, the Chicago group proceeded as most of us would have. They sought to spy on the deliberations of real juries—the most direct approach, the clearest window through which to view the decision-making process in action. In the fall of 1953 they asked a federal judge in Wichita, Kansas, if he would assist in their study by allowing them to bug the jury room in his court. The judge said he was willing, so long as the chief judge of his circuit court of appeals sanctioned the project. In response to that request, the chief judge established a set of rules that were to be followed. It was his opinion that recordings should be allowed only in civil trials and, even then, only with the approval of the trial judge and counsel for all parties. Nobody should eavesdrop on the deliberations while they were taking place, the tapes should be kept under lock and key until the case is ultimately decided, and measures should be taken to protect the identities of participating jurors. Finally, the chief judge felt that, although juries should generally be informed, that was not a necessary safeguard. These precautions were taken and in the spring of 1954, with microphones hidden behind the heating system of the jury room, Harry Kalven and Fred Strodtbeck recorded five civil juries in Wichita. It was the first time in history—and it would be the last.

That summer the solicitor general, a U.S. Supreme Court justice, and about 200 other lawyers met at a conference in Colorado, where one of the jury tape recordings was played. What happened next could not have been fully anticipated. It was as if the Chicago group had hit a raw nerve. In October of that year a story about the recordings appeared in the *Los Angeles Times*. Within days, more articles and editorials appeared, nationwide, all critical of this invasion into the jury room. Leading figures in the legislative and judicial branches of government spoke out. It could have been the only time that civil libertarians and conservatives ever agreed. Then on October 5, in response to the uproar, Attorney General Brownell announced that the "Department of Justice will present for the Congress at the first opportunity a proposed bill to prevent such intrusions upon the privacy of the deliberations of both grand and petit juries of the Court of the United States by any persons whomsoever and by any means whatsoever." In defense of the Chicago group, 27 distinguished judges and lawyers announced their support for the research but to no avail.

On October 12 and 13 the Subcommittee on Internal Security of the Senate Judiciary Committee held an investigation into the matter. Several witnesses were called, including Kalven, Strodtbeck, and the judges and attorneys who had consented to the recordings. Passions ran high at the hearings. At one point Senator James Eastland, chairman of the subcommittee, said to Kalven, "I'll guarantee that you'll not do any more 'bugging' after Congress has passed some legislation.'' He was right. Almost immediately a federal law was passed making it illegal for anyone to observe or eavesdrop on a federal jury. Many states followed suit. Today deliberations are to be conducted in privacy, behind a closed door that cannot be opened by judges, social scientists, the jurors themselves, or anyone else.

There are two explanations for the overwhelming outrage over the Wichita scandal. One is that there is a legitimate concern over the effects and possible abuses of any opening of the jury room door. With ordinary citizens empowered to determine the fate of their peers, rich and politically powerful individuals and corporations, and with juries serving as a citizen review board to control abusive government practices, it is easy to appreciate how the institution has become sanctified. There is good reason to be sensitive about invasions of the jury's privacy. Unfortunately, there was a second, less noble motive for the criticism. Amidst the hysteria of the McCarthy era, members of the Senate Judiciary Committee and their staff took the occasion to smear those ''liberal academic types.'' Indeed after Harry Kalven's death, several years later, Hans Zeisel wrote that the committee ''seemed anxious to show that the research effort . . . was a communist-inspired plot to subvert the American jury system.''

Despite this initial setback, the Chicago Jury Project fulfilled all expectations. The Ford Foundation donated an additional $1 million to support another 4 years of research. In the end it produced dozens of important articles as well as Kalven and Zeisel's unmatched classic book, *The American Jury*, published in 1966.[19] No longer able to observe the jury first-hand, they developed alternative, less direct strategies: analyses of court records, posttrial interviews with jurors and other trial participants, the use of experimental mock juries, and the like. With some modification and refinement, these are the techniques we use today.

As we said earlier, this book is guided by our commitment to systematic research. Single case studies, autobiographical accounts, anecdotes, and war stories may make for good reading. We use them for illustrative purposes ourselves. They may even open our eyes to previously unnoticed phenomena. But isolated, often sensational, reports about a jury here and there should not form the basis for an evaluation of the system as a whole or for policymaking. This is an important point because there is an ever-present danger that these reports illustrate exceptions rather than the rules of jury decision making. With that caveat in mind, the rest of this chapter describes the various methods of jury research that are used. As we will see, no single method is perfect. But together they offer an attractive multimethod alternative to jury bugging.

Rummaging Through the Archives

One rather indirect way to learn about juries is to analyze already existing court records, looking for statistical relationships between various trial factors and their verdicts. An interesting study by Martha Myers illustrates this approach at its best.[20] Myers sampled 980 defendants who were charged with felonies in Indianapolis, Indiana, between 1974 and 1976. Overall, 317 of them went to trial and, of these, 201 were tried by a jury. To obtain information about these cases, Myers consulted prosecutors' files, police arrest records, telephone interviews with the crime victims, and posttrial court records. When she was done, she knew—for each trial—whether there was an eyewitness identification, fingerprints, an alibi, a recovered weapon, or other evidence; she also knew whether the defendant was male or female, black or white, young or old, employed or unemployed, and so on. By correlating literally dozens of trial factors with verdicts, Myers was able to find that, as a general rule, juries' decisions seemed to based more on the integrity of the evidence than on prejudice, sympathy, or other irrelevant characteristics.

To be sure, this archival method offers some unique opportunities to learn about actual jury verdicts. Court records are always available. Volumes of data can thus be collected, sampling a long span of time and a diversity of geographical regions. But there is a drawback. This method yields data that are correlational; as such, it cannot be used to draw firm conclusions about causes and effects. To illustrate this limitation, take as an example Myers' finding that juries were less likely to convict defendants who were employed than those who were unemployed. Does this result necessarily imply that a defendant's employment status affects jury verdicts, that perhaps it reflects a sympathetic bias toward working men and women? It is tempting to draw that conclusion. But on the basis of Myers' results, we cannot be sure. It is possible, for example, that the jobless are indeed more likely to have committed the crimes charged and that the evidence is stronger against them than it is against those who are employed. Or it may be that more unemployed than employed defendants are black and that race is the relevant factor.

Through sophisticated statistical techniques it is possible to test these kinds of alternative explanations. Referring back to our example, it is possible to establish a purer measure of the link between employment status and verdicts by factoring out the strength of the evidence and the defendant's race. If the original relationship persists after having done so, we would know that the finding was not just an artifact of these two alternative variables. But what about other variables that are not measured? In the real world of human events, there is always the nagging possibility that the original relationship reflects the influence of "invisible" factors.

Interviewing Jurors

Another way to collect information about juries is to interview jurors after their trial service. Jurors can be asked about how they personally felt and about what transpired during their group's deliberations. Interviewing is the method of choice for journalists. As with the archival method, it has the advantage of being based on real trial experiences. If enough different jurors and enough different trials are sampled, one could be reasonably certain that the results reflect more than just the idiosyncrasies of a single case.

Intuitively, it makes sense to obtain information straight from the horse's mouth. Jurors can offer insights into the decision-making process that are unmatched by other types of information. Even if we could hear what individual jurors had to *say* during their deliberations, only they can tell us what they actually *thought*. As we saw in the Juan Corona trial, the final holdout juror eventually voted for conviction. But did she truly agree with her peers or did she still harbor a reasonable doubt? Only she could tell us what was on her mind. Unfortunately, this method suffers from two major drawbacks. First, like analyzing court records, posttrial interviews cannot be used to determine causal relationships. Second, this method rests entirely on people's *ability* and *willingness* to disclose truthful information. Can they? And if so, would they? Psychologists have long recognized that what people say about their own behavior can be very unreliable. There are too many human failings, like simply forgetting, and too many motives, like the need to present oneself favorably to others, that interfere with the accuracy of self-report data. Jurors probably do not know, for example, when a litigant's physical appearance affects their opinions. And even if they did, they would probably not admit it in an interview with a stranger. As in other aspects of life, people like to portray themselves as rationally motivated. And there is jurors' ability to reconstruct the events that transpired during their deliberations. Probably few people can accurately recall what arguments and counterarguments were raised, by whom, and what effect they had on the group. For the investigator interested in mapping the jury's drive toward unanimity, they would have to remember how often their jury voted and, on each occasion, what the outcome was.

Interviewing Other Trial Participants

As an alternative to relying on what jurors themselves have to say, information can be obtained by questioning the other participants of jury trials. This approach was first taken by Kalven and Zeisel in their classic, *The American Jury*.[21] They sent questionnaires to 550 judges who presided over 3,576 criminal jury trials nationwide. After each trial, the judge indicated on the questionnaire what he or she thought the verdict should be. The judges also described the case facts and speculated on how the juries reached their decisions. As it turned out, judges and juries agreed on a verdict 78 percent of the time. When they disagreed, it was usually because the jury was more lenient than the judge. By analyzing the cases themselves, Kalven and Zeisel were able to explore the statistical relationships between jury verdicts and various trial characteristics.

Compared to the archival method, based entirely on the analysis of dry court records, Kalven and Zeisel's technique offers an opportunity to learn about what really went on in the courtroom. When the defendant was attractive and well dressed or when a key witness appeared to be nervous, judges reported these observations in their questionnaires. In a study of juries in England, John Baldwin and Michael McConville administered questionnaires not only to the judges but also to prosecuting and defense counsel, involved police officers, and even, in some instances, the defendants themselves.[22]

As we said, no method is without its drawbacks. Like the other approaches already discussed, none of the relationships between trial characteristics and jury verdicts can be used to answer questions about cause and effect. Also, like the problems with self-report data, other participants' perceptions of the jury are limited by their inability to probe the individual jurors or observe their deliberations. To make matters worse, other participants' reports are likely to be biased by their own unique perspectives, opinions, and interests in the outcome of the case. The jury is bound to be perceived as fairer in victory than in defeat.

Constructing Simulations and Mock Juries

In contrast to the naturalistic approaches is one that is based on a laboratory model of science. Referred to as the mock jury paradigm, this method involves simulating trials and then recruiting subjects to act as jurors. This technique is based on the idea that, by having mock jurors watch trial-like events in a precisely controlled setting, we can observe juries in action.

Let us illustrate how this method can be used to answer a specific question. For years, the U.S. Supreme Court has struggled over whether television cameras should be permitted in the courtroom.[23] One argument against it (there are others) is that the presence of cameras would distract or otherwise affect the performance and behavior of trial participants, most notably the jury. Are juries distracted by the sight of television cameras? When the Florida State Supreme Court sought an answer to that question, it interviewed jurors, witnesses, and lawyers who had taken part in televised trials. The result was a perfect illustration of why methods based on self-report are flawed: Everybody claimed that the cameras affected other participants but not themselves.[24] Consider as an alternative the following experiment conducted by the first author.[25] Fifty-one residents of Williamstown, Massachusetts watched a videotape of a civil case that was reenacted by trial lawyers. They watched the tape in small groups either in the presence or absence of a video camera to record their participation. For approximately half the subjects in each condition, the tape was interrupted at various points so that their ability to recall the evidence as the trial progressed could be tracked. It was assumed, of course, that if subjects were distracted their recall scores would suffer. When the trial was over, the subjects reached a verdict and answered additional questions on what they thought of the case. The results were quite informative: The camera did impair performance during the trial's opening moments. Over time, however, subjects rapidly adapted to it; ultimately, they were unaffected by its presence. This study also revealed that some people, depending on their personality, were more affected by the camera than others. Clearly, this research question could not have been addressed as effectively with the methods described earlier.

A good deal of current research on juries is based on simulation. This method is popular for two reasons. First, it enables the researcher to secure full control over the events that take place in the "courtroom" and, as a result, to establish causal relationships between specific trial characteristics and jury verdicts. In its simplest form this method is perfect for testing theories about the effects of one variable on another. This goal is achieved by comparing people's thoughts, feelings, and behavior in two or more conditions that are identical except for one specific difference, called the *independent variable*. In the TV cameras study, all subjects watched the same trial. Since the only systematic difference between the groups was whether or not the camera was present, any statistically significant differences in their behavior can be attributed to this variable.

The other advantage of simulation is that it offers an incredible amount of flexibility. By flexibility we mean two things. First, it enables the researcher to manipulate variables that cannot be tampered with in real trials for legal, ethical, and pragmatic reasons. With mock juries one can vary the evidence, the arguments, the judge's instructions, or the composition of the jury. The list of independent variables, of course, is endless. Second, we can measure all sorts of behavioral reactions that are otherwise too intrusive. With mock jurors one can ask questions while the trial is in progress, measure their attention, their physiological arousal, or their ability to recall the proceedings. One can even videotape their deliberations and accomplish what the Chicago group could not. In short, through simulation, we can observe not only the outcome but also the process of jury decision making.[26]

As with all indirect methods of inquiry, this one is not perfect. In exchange for the highly controlled environment, this approach suffers from the problem of *external validity*; that is, the question, "Do the results generalize to real trials?" Can we safely assume, for example, that the presence of cameras has the same effect in a court of law as it did in the laboratory? On this issue we speculated that, amidst the gallery of onlookers, journalists, and lawyers ordinarily in attendance at real trials, the camera's impact as an "observer" would be diminished even further. Without belaboring the details of this particular question, we can say, as a general rule, that the more closely our research conditions approximate the real event, the better off we are trying to generalize from the former to the latter. Still, this problem looms over all research conducted with mock juries.[27]

Hiring Shadows and Ghosts

In 1986 a Connecticut lawyer represented a defendant who faced trial for a second time after a hung jury. To prepare for the case, this lawyer hired as a consultant a juror who had served in the defendant's first trial.[28] This practice is not common. But it does resemble the shadow-jury technique developed by Hans Zeisel and Shari Diamond.[29] Here the objective is to recruit subjects to sit in the audience at real trials and then, as if participating on the jury, to deliberate and return a verdict.

This hybrid creature, half audience and half jury, goes by many names; thus, they are called shadows, ghosts, surrogates, and parallel juries. When you think about it, this technique is quite ingenious. As with mock juries, one can manipulate independent variables by randomly assigning shadow jurors to certain conditions. For example, groups of subjects sitting in the same trial could be given different instructions to read. One can also gather intrusive information from shadow jurors both during and after the proceedings. Thus, their deliberations can be videotaped for subsequent analysis—like mock juries but better: Since subjects "participate" in real trials, the shadow jury goes a long way toward solving the external validity problem that haunts mock jury research. Indeed, the only difference between real juries and their shadows (a difference whose impact can be evaluated) is that the shadows, unlike their counterparts in the jury box, make decisions that are not really of consequence.

There are two drawbacks to the use of shadow juries. First, there are limits to how much control can be exerted over subjects' state of information. The trial itself obviously cannot be tampered with. And it is disruptive to interview shadow jurors while court is in session. The second problem is one of pragmatics. In order to discover general principles of jury behavior, one must either sample a large number of juries who watch the same trial, as in mock jury research, or else sample from a larger number of different trials, as in the more naturalistic methods. With shadow juries, one would have to opt for the latter approach, one that would be very time consuming and very expensive.

Because no single method is perfect, we take an eclectic approach. Sometimes we draw on naturalistic studies; other times we rely more heavily on laboratory research. Only by gathering converging lines of evidence, and bringing various methods to bear on the same empirical question, can we truly hope to understand juries. On one matter we are certain: More is to be learned through research than from storytelling.

NOTES

1. Quoted in P. W. Low, J. C. Jeffries, & R. J. Bonnie (1986), *The Trial of John W. Hinckley, Jr.: A Case Study in the Insanity Defense*. Mineola, NY: Foundation Press, p. 117.

2. L. Caplan (1984), Annals of law: The insanity defense. *The New Yorker*, July 2, pp. 45–78, at p. 69.

3. W. Isaacson (1982), Insane on all counts. *Nation*, July 5, pp. 22, 25–27, at p. 26.

4. Caplan, supra note 2, p. 70.

5. See S. J. Adler (1986), How to lose the bet-your-company case. *The American Lawyer*, January/February, pp. 27–30, 107–110; also see J. Riley (1985), Aberration—or lesson in contracts? *The National Law Journal*, December, p. 13.

6. Judge's misgivings reported (1986), *San Francisco Chronicle*, April 12, p. 51.

7. R. Evans, Jr. (1979), Reaching the hearts and minds of jurors. *Trial Diplomacy Journal*, Fall, pp. 25–29.

8. Quoted in O. Friedrich (1981), We the jury, find the . . . *Time*, September 8, pp. 44–48, 54–56.

9. *Williams v. Florida*, 399 U.S. 78; this ruling was subsequently extended to federal civil cases.

10. *Johnson v. Louisiana*, 406 U.S. 356.

11. *Ross v. Bernard*, 396 U.S. 531.

12. The first denial of an otherwise valid jury demand appeared in *In re Boise Cascade Securities Litigation*, 420 F. Supp. 99 (1976); the first appellate ruling on the matter appeared in *In re Japanese Electronic Products Antitrust Litigation*, 631 F.2d 1069 (1980).

13. *Batson v. Kentucky* (1986), 54 U.S.L.W. 4425.

14. *Lockhart v. McCree* (1986), 54 U.S.L.W. 4449.

15. For a first-hand account of this intervention, see J. Schulman, P. Shaver, R. Colman, B. Emrich, & R. Christie (1973), Recipe for a jury. *Psychology Today*, May, pp. 37–44, 77–84.

16. V. Villasenor (1977), *Jury: The people vs. Juan Corona*. Boston: Little, Brown.

17. *New York Times* (1973), January 20, Section 1, p. 18.

18. Quoted in G. Ferguson (1955), Legal research on trial. *Judicature*, Vol. 39, pp. 78–82, at p. 79.

19. H. Kalven & H. Zeisel (1966), *The American Jury*. Boston: Little, Brown.

20. Rule departures and making law: Juries and their verdicts. In *Law and Society Review*, 1979, Vol. 13, pp. 781–797.

21. Supra note 19.

22. J. Baldwin & M. McConville (1979), *Jury Trials*. Oxford: Clarendon Press.

23. Its most notable decisions on the matter are *Estes v. Texas*, 381 U.S. 532 (1965), and *Chandler v. Florida*, 101 S.CT. 802 (1981).

24. This study was reported in J. Whisenand (1978), Florida's experiment. *American Bar Association Journal*, Vol. 64, pp. 1860–1863.

25. S. M. Kassin (1984), TV cameras, public self consciousness, and mock juror performance. *Journal of Experimental Social Psychology*, Vol. 20, pp. 336–349.

26. A more extensive discussion of this technique can be found in R. Bray & N. Kerr (1982), Methodological considerations in the study of the psychology of the courtroom. Appearing in N. Kerr & R. Bray (Eds.), *The Psychology of the Courtroom*, New York, Academic Press. For a description of practical applications, see S. Kassin (1984), Mock jury trials, *Trial Diplomacy Journal*, Summer, pp. 26–30.

27. For more detailed critiques of this method of inquiry, see R. Dillehay & M. Nietzel (1980), Constructing a science of jury behavior, appearing in L. Wheeler's (Ed.) *Review of Personality and Social Psychology*, Beverly Hills, CA, Sage. Also see E. Ebbesen & V. Konecni (1980), On the external validity of decision-making research: What do we know about decisions in the real world?, appearing in T. Wallsten's (Ed.) *Cognitive processes in choice and decision behavior*, Hillsdale, NJ, Erlbaum.

28. G. Gombossy (1986), Ex-juror retained as trial consultant. *The National Law Journal*, January 6, pp. 3, 6.

29. H. Zeisel & S. Diamond (1978), The effect of peremptory challenges on jury and verdict: An experiment in a federal district court. *Stanford Law Review*, Vol. 30, pp. 491–531.

2

PRETRIAL BIAS:
THE THIRTEENTH JUROR

On November 3, 1979, amidst growing tension between local factions of right- and left-wing groups, a predominantly black neighborhood in Greensboro, North Carolina, set the stage for a bloody confrontation. The morning began with a gathering of demonstrators who were singing folk songs as they prepared for an anti–Ku Klux Klan rally scheduled by the communist-sponsored Workers Viewpoint Organization. At one point a caravan of slow-moving pickup trucks, cars, and a van filled with members of the Ku Klux Klan and American Nazi Party entered the scene. The demonstrators kicked and hit the cars. Then, with television news cameras recording the event, the vehicles stopped. Several of the Klan supporters jumped out, reached into the trunks of their cars, pulled out shotguns and rifles, and opened fire. Four demonstrators were killed instantly, a fifth died two days later, and seven others were injured. None of the Klan supporters was hit.

In 1980, five of the gunmen were tried for murder in a North Carolina state court.[1] Although 25 percent of the state's population is nonwhite, the defendants were acquitted of all charges by an all-white jury. Three years later nine Klansmen and Nazis were tried in federal court for a lesser offense: conspiring to violate the victims' civil rights.[2] The government introduced videotapes to support its claim that the defendants had attacked a peaceful, lawful demonstration. An FBI analysis of the videotape soundtrack indicated, contrary to the defendants' testimony, that the first 11 shots were fired by Klansmen. Leaning against the base of the judge's bench were a dozen shotguns and rifles, chains, brass knuckles, pick handles, and clubs inscribed with the letters KKK. Despite the defendants' appeal on grounds of self-defense, patriotism, and a hatred of communism, the case against them was strong.

Because the initial murder trial resulted in an acquittal by a nonrepresentative all-white jury, the North Carolina courts were pushed to reform their jury selection practices. Surely one would expect differently from the federal courts, right? Wrong. With national attention focused on the proceedings, the judge questioned prospective jurors *in camera*, that is, behind closed doors, in order to ensure that they respond with candor to his inquiries. Sixty-nine prospective jurors, including 11 blacks, were taken into the judge's chambers. In the end the panel consisted of 18 people: 12 jurors and 6 alternates. All of them were white. And again the defendants were acquitted of all charges.

This story challenges the most cherished ideal of our jury system: that cases be tried by an impartial jury, one that is not predisposed to favor a particular outcome. For all we know, the two North Carolina juries might very well have been impartial. But in a jurisdiction containing a sizeable minority population, how did the defense manage twice to achieve an all-white jury? Would the trials have resulted in different outcomes if the juries, demographically speaking, were more representative of the community? This chapter focuses on these critical questions. But first we describe, in theory and in practice, how laborers, business executives, students, homemakers, government employees, retirees, and all others make their way into the jury box.

THE SELECTION PROCESS: FROM CITIZEN TO JUROR

The Constitution guarantees the right to trial by an impartial tribunal in only general terms. However, a series of U.S. Supreme Court decisions has established from that principle a requirement that the jury must constitute a representative cross section of the community. This ideal appears to be based on the *statistical* assumption that representativeness, at least in our pluralistic society, results in a heterogeneous pool of jurors, on the *psychological* assumption that heterogeneity increases the quality of group decision making, and on the *political* assumption that all segments of the community must be included for the public to feel confident about the fairness of jury trials.[3]

The Three-Staged Process

The selection process can be broken down into three stages.[4] First, a list of eligible jurors within a jurisdiction is compiled. Until recently there was no uniform means of achieving this goal in either federal or state courts. Several courts employed the so-called key-man system, whereby prominent members of the community were asked to submit the names of good people to serve as jurors. It was an "old boys network" plain and simple. Other jurisdictions were even less formal, calling on pedestrians, retirees, the unemployed, and whomever else could be found near the courthouse. In 1961 the U.S. Department of

Justice reported that 92 federal district courts used 92 different methods. And they all had only one thing in common: none of them produced juries that adequately matched the local population.[5]

All that changed in 1968 when Congress passed the Jury Selection and Service Act.[6] This law was committed to the principle that all litigants have the right to juries "selected at random from a fair cross section of the community" and that no citizen should be excluded from service "on account of race, color, religion, sex, national origin, or economic status."[7] The Jury Selection and Service Act thus provided (a) that the jury pool consist, at least, of all eligible voters and (b) that names be selected as needed on a strictly random basis—like a lottery.

Once a pool of eligible people is drawn, each is sent a questionnaire to fill out. Those who respond are then retained on the list, disqualified, or excused. People are disqualified if, because of their status or ability, they are presumed to be biased or incompetent. Visual blindness, an inability to speak the language, employment in a law enforcement occupation, and possession of a criminal record are some the more common reasons for keeping an individual from serving on a jury. Sometimes people are not disqualified permanently, but are instead provided with temporary excuses. The elderly, those responsible for the care of young children, students, and certain occupational groups considered vital (e.g., doctors, teachers, nurses, and members of the clergy) are permitted to decline or postpone their service.

Of those who are still qualified, a certain number are drawn from the list periodically and summoned for duty. Per trial, this venire, or panel of prospective jurors, usually consists of between 30 and 60 people. Upon their arrival in the courtroom, these venirepersons are subjected to a voir dire, a pretrial interview designed to provide attorneys with information upon which to challenge, or eliminate, jurors suspected of bias. Procedurally, the ways in which the voir dire is conducted are about as varied as the number of judges who hold trials. It depends on the jurisdiction, the judge, and, to some extent, the particular trial. In federal courts the judge usually conducts the voir dire personally. Some allow attorneys to ask questions; others do not. Sometimes prospective jurors are questioned individually; other times they are addressed as a group. Some judges limit the inquiry to case-specific matters; others allow lawyers to ask a broad range of questions concerning jurors' families, backgrounds, and lifestyles. The examination can be carried out in open court or it can be held privately, in judge's chambers. Many voir dires are completed within minutes; others last for weeks.

As the questioning proceeds, lawyers can eliminate prospective jurors in two ways. If someone knows one of the litigants, has a financial interest in the outcome of the case, or, for some reason, has formed an opinion about guilt or liability, the lawyer can challenge that prospective juror for cause. If the judge grants that challenge, the juror is excused. Each side can submit for the judge's consideration an unlimited number of challenges for cause. In fact, if it could be

demonstrated that an entire venire was improperly selected or exposed to prejudicial information, it too could be stricken in favor of a new panel.

In addition to using the voir dire to elicit open signs of bias, lawyers are
given the opportunity to make a limited number of peremptory challenges, enabling them to remove prospective jurors ''without a reason stated, without inquiry, and without being subject to the court's control.''[8] Lawyers can thus
reject a certain number of people based on little more than suspicion, even if
they cannot prove that they are biased to the judge. In making their peremptory
challenges, lawyers rely on their instincts, experiences, and stereotypes about
particular individuals or categories of people. The number of peremptory challenges allotted to the competing parties varies according to the jurisdiction, the
size and magnitude of the case, the amount of publicity it has attracted, and the
number of parties involved.

To summarize, the three-staged process of jury selection can be viewed as a
funnel-shaped path completed by only a percentage of eligible citizens. The
problem is that those who ultimately serve on juries are not a random sampling
of the population. Instead, the process favors certain demographically identifiable groups of people while systematically underrepresenting others.

A Trilogy of Problems

Although many states adopted the federal model prescribed by the Jury Selection and Service Act of 1968, at times juries are still selected in rather casual
fashion. Recently, for example, a judge in Laporte, Indiana, ran out of prospective jurors for the obscenity trial of a local bookstore owner. He solved the
problem by sending sheriff's deputies into the streets to seize 10 unsuspecting
passersby for jury duty.[9]

Even among states that use the federal approach, a fair cross section of the
community is seldom achieved. In the many courts that rely exclusively on voter
registration lists, the poor, the young, and racial minorities are substantially
underrepresented.[10] It is often argued that voters' lists should be supplemented
by telephone directories and lists of licensed drivers, but this suggestion is
seldom followed. The civil rights case against the Ku Klux Klan gunmen is a
case in point. The Middle District of North Carolina, the site of that 1983 trial,
relied exclusively on voter registration lists, which captured only 74 percent of
the black population. Adding the drivers list would have increased that figure to
85 percent.[11]

Turning to the second stage of selection, we find that the goal of impaneling
a representative jury is compromised even further. To begin with, many courts
fail to pursue those on their source list who do not return their jury questionnaires. As a result, certain segments of the population are missed in the process.
And then there are the exclusion policies. In the federal courts, old age, child
care responsibilities, financial hardship, and certain occupational categories are
automatic grounds for exemption upon request. Although there are reasonable

arguments for and against granting these requests freely, this policy is often carried to extreme lengths, especially in the state courts. Until 1979, for example, Missouri automatically exempted all women, mothers and nonmothers alike. Even today, some courts extend these dispensations to veterinarians, pharmacists, and telephone operators.[12] The result: many courts receive more than their fair share of excuses, only some of which are based on valid need.[13]

Finally, what we usually think of as jury selection—that is, actually choosing jurors from those who are physically present in the courtroom—is subject to its own share of abuse. Nobody questions the need to challenge for cause those people who exhibit clear signs of partiality. These are not granted freely. Unless a prospective juror has a concrete, verifiable interest in the trial's outcome or openly admits an inability to be fair and open minded, a judge is unlikely to strike that person for cause.

Peremptory challenges, however, are another matter. On the one hand, it is widely believed that they are necessary to protect the right to an impartial jury. On the other hand, they often are used to eliminate certain segments of the community, eroding even further the ideal of a representative panel. This tension between representativeness and impartiality surfaced in the 1965 landmark case of *Swain v. Alabama*, wherein the Supreme Court affirmed the sanctity of the peremptory challenge.[14] In that trial, Robert Swain, a black defendant, was convicted of raping a white woman and sentenced to death by an all-white jury. Claiming that jury selection was discriminatory, he appealed the verdict. Swain had a pretty good argument. In his own case there were six blacks in the venire, all of whom had been stricken. In addition, not a single black person had served on an Alabama jury since 1950! Swain lost his appeal, and the Supreme Court upheld the death sentence. The Court concluded that there was no proof that blacks had been systematically excluded from the jury system. Further, the Court stood firmly behind a selection procedure that enables lawyers to make peremptory challenges without judicial scrutiny, that the system "provides justification for striking any group of otherwise qualified jurors in any given case, whether they be Negroes, Catholics, accountants, or those with blue eyes."[15] This decision paved the way for the unfettered, racially motivated use of peremptory challenges.

We are thus reminded of the 1983 acquittal of the Ku Klux Klansmen, where all 11 blacks in the venire were dismissed. And the worst part is that these kinds of cases never go away. In 1985, two black men were convicted of robbery and assault by an all-white Michigan jury. During the voir dire the prosecutor used up his peremptory challenges to eliminate all of the 22 prospective black jurors; the defense lawyers, in turn, used their peremptory challenges to strike 37 white jurors. Afterwards, the prosecutor openly admitted to making his selections along racial lines but, after all, he said, the defense had done it too.[16]

These abusive practices may soon become a thing of the past. In the Michigan case the U.S. Appeals Court for the Sixth Circuit reversed the defendants' convictions on the ground that their right to an impartial jury had been violated.

In fact, arguing that the public too has an interest in the integrity of jury decisions, it held—for the first time—that defense attorneys, not just prosecutors, should be barred from systematically excluding "cognizable groups" from the jury. Similar decisions were reached by the U.S. Appeals Court for the Second Circuit[17] and in a handful of state courts, led by California.[18] Finally, in *Batson v. Kentucky*, a 1986 ruling, the U.S. Supreme Court overturned its *Swain* position. Noting that "the harm from discriminatory jury selection extends beyond that inflicted on the defendant and the excluded juror to touch the entire community," the Court suggested that judges try to determine whether a particular challenge was racially or legitimately motivated.

How will judges resolve the tension between the purpose of peremptory challenges on the one hand and the requirement that lawyers justify their selection strategies on the other? And what constitutes a cognizable group within the scope of this ruling?[19] It remains to be seen how these difficult questions are to be resolved. Future cases will inevitably be needed to establish the contours of this long overdue decision. Lest the reader conclude, however, that this ruling elicited unanimous agreement, we should note that Chief Justice Rehnquist and former Chief Justice Burger dissented from the majority view. With all the trappings of a "two (or more) wrongs make a right" logic, they wrote "there is simply nothing unequal about the state using its peremptory challenges to strike blacks from the jury in cases involving black defendants, so long as such challenges are also used to exclude whites in cases involving white defendants, Hispanics in cases involving Hispanic defendants, Asians in cases involving Asian defendants, and so on."

Looking at the theory and mechanics of jury selection, it becomes apparent that the system is based on an ideal that, in turn, requires that at least one of the following conditions be fulfilled: (a) that jurors appear in court in tabula rasa form, neutral and untainted by previous experience; (b) that jurors can leave their pretrial biases at the courthouse door, making fair and objective judgments despite their predispositions; or (c) that those candidates for jury service who are irrevocably prejudiced will be detected and eliminated at some point during the selection process. It is equally apparent that each of these conditions can be evaluated for their validity through psychological theory and research.

It would be easy to achieve an ideal and impartial jury if citizens appeared at the courtroom without predispositions. It obviously does not take a psychologist to know that this tabula rasa creature does not exist. Inevitably, we all perceive the world through the lenses of our own personal experiences. For that very reason, the Supreme Court recognizes that the search for an "indifferent" juror is not a search for one who is devoid of bias. That would be impossible.[20] Instead, we are content to settle for jurors whose partiality falls within "minimum standards."[21]

With the courts conceding that this first condition is implausible, two questions remain. First, what kinds of people are biased? That is, what identifiable demographic, attitudinal, and personality characteristics predispose a juror to foreclose on objective decision making? Second, how effectively does the voir dire guard the jury box and deny entry to those people suspected of such bias? We consider these issues in turn.

PREJUDICE, SYMPATHY, AND THE BIASED JUROR

Ever since the turn of the twentieth century, clinical and experimental psychologists have tried to develop taxonomies to classify people, according to their abilities, aptitudes, and temperaments, the way biologists classify plants and animals. With the help of psychometricians, standardized intelligence tests like the Stanford-Binet and Wechsler were constructed. And with the support of the medical community, so was the Diagnostic and Statistical Manual of Mental Disorders.

At the same time, personality theorists tried to penetrate the unconscious, profile the human personality, and then use this information to predict behavior. Freud thus distinguished between oral, anal, and genital character types; Jung distinguished between introverts and extraverts; and Adler described differences between first borns, middle, and youngest children. Over the years, personality psychologists have introduced into Western culture an extensive language of traits: We now think of people as being high or low in their self-esteem, need for achievement, authoritarianism, or manifest anxiety. We may be masculine or feminine, normal or neurotic, Type A's or Type B's, internals or externals, repressors or sensitizers. Accompanying these characteristics are personality tests, theories of how they develop from childhood, and a body of experiments linking those traits to observable behavior. The science of individual difference is, and always has been, an important force in mainstream psychology.

Beginning about 20 years ago, the discipline began a period of transition. In 1968, psychologist Walter Mischel challenged the prevailing assumption that people's behavior is necessarily predictable from their personalities—that high achievers work harder than low achievers or that extraverts talk more than introverts.[22] Reviewing over 50 years of research, Mischel found that, although people are measurably different from one another, there is only a weak statistical relationship between what we are and how we act. The problem, according to Mischel, is that people do not behave in ways that are consistent across time and situations. Instead, because people are responsive to contextual forces, they alter their behavior according to the demands of the moment. Every parent whose child is talkative at home and shy at school can appreciate the degree to which behavior is determined by situations rather than personalities.

Mischel's critique generated controversy and research. As a result of the dialectical tension between his situationist position and the traditional personality approach, the two converged into what has become known as the interactionist model. Now accepted by both sides of the debate, this model asserts that human behavior is a function of the reciprocal influence or "interaction" of the person and setting. Several specific patterns of interaction have been observed. One common pattern, relevant to jury decision making, is that in psychologically strong, highly structured situations, where the behavioral demands are clear, individual differences are negligible. Most drivers, cautious and reckless alike, stop at red traffic lights at busy intersections. And most jurors, conservative and liberal alike, vote to convict a defendant who openly confesses to the crime. Conversely, in psychologically weak, relatively unstructured situations, where behavioral cues are novel or ambiguous, individuals vary considerably in their behavior. Some drivers stop and others speed through unmarked intersections. Likewise, some jurors vote guilty and others not guilty when the evidence against a defendant is mixed.[23]

In light of this brief overview, it should come as no surprise that those interested in the psychology of juries are attracted like magnets to the study of how an individual's demographic status, attitudes, and personality affect his or her decision making. However, it should also come as no surprise that, for the most part, attempts to identify consistent and predictable verdict differences between cognizable groups of jurors have met with limited success.

The Broad Strokes of Demography

Without knowing anything about a juror's genetic makeup, childhood, work experience, politics, or interpersonal style, the legal system defines its cognizable segments of the community in demographic terms. Thus, jurors are distinguished on the basic census categories—race, sex, age, religion, socioeconomic status, education, and the like. With these characteristics in mind, the courts prescribe that juries reflect the diversity existing in a population. This objective is based on the belief that demographic heterogeneity increases both the appearance and the reality of justice. The reason is straightforward—people, including judges and lawyers, believe that verdicts are predictable from the sociological composition of the jury. More specifically, they ascribe to what social psychologists call the similarity hypothesis: that when faced with a defendant on the one hand, and the plaintiff or victim on the other, jurors will favor their own kind. Is that true? Would the Greensboro Klansmen have been convicted by black jurors? Are women harsher than men in their judgments of male rape defendants? Are youthful jurors more sympathetic than their elders when the accused is young? And then, where do a juror's sympathies lie when the defendant is similar on some demographic dimensions but not others or when the defendant and victim are both similar?

Anecdotes cannot prove or disprove the similarity hypothesis. There are plenty of jury verdicts that appear to have been tainted by prejudice. But for every story that illustrates racially motivated bias there is one that does not. As a case in point, consider the following. In 1982, Vincent Chin, a 27-year-old Chinese-American was about to be married. One night he was with two friends at his own bachelor party at the Fancy Pants Lounge, a topless-bottomless bar in Detroit. Two men, Ronald Ebens and Michael Nitz, arrived and exchanged words with Chin and his party. A fight broke out, the two men were injured, and Chin left the bar. About 20 minutes later, Ebens spotted Chin in front of a nearby restaurant. He immediately retrieved a baseball bat (a Louisville Slugger, Jackie Robinson model) from Nitz's car, chased his victim through the streets, and—in full view of several witnesses, including two off-duty policemen—clubbed him repeatedly. Chin died of head injuries four days later.

From that point on, the story roughly follows the pattern of the Greensboro KKK affair. Ebens pleaded guilty in a Michigan state court to a reduced charge of manslaughter. For that, he was sentenced to 3 years' probation and a $3,780 fine. The sentence prompted angry demonstrations by Asian-Americans across the country and, in turn, drew international media coverage. The victim's mother eventually asked the U.S. Justice Department to investigate the case. It did, and Ebens was taken to federal court for violating Chin's civil rights. At the trial some witnesses to the barroom confrontation testified that Ebens, a Chrysler assembly worker, was resentful of Japanese car imports. One witness, a dancer at the lounge that night, said she heard somebody say, "Because of you motherfuckers, we're out of work." During closing arguments the prosecuting attorney called the murder "a lynching with a baseball bat instead of a rope." Others, however, testified that the two men were drunk and that Chin had instigated the fight. Thus arguing that the incident was not racially motivated, the defense attorney characterized the killing as simply the result of "a fight between angry and intoxicated men."

The jury consisted of 12 natives of the Detroit area, none of whom was Asian. The trial lasted for 6 days. After 12 hours of deliberation, the jury found Ebens guilty.[24] The moral of this story, as it contrasts to the Greensboro case, is that anecdotes, however interesting, cannot substantiate claims about the determinants of jury decision making.

Research has uncovered few, if any, clear relationships between individual juror characteristics and decision making. Reid Hastie and his colleagues recruited more than 800 people from jury pools in Massachusetts.[25] After a brief voir dire, those subjects who were law enforcement officials, those who had been victims of a violent crime, and those who had heard about the experiment from other jurors were excused. The study was based on 69 twelve-person mock juries, all of whom watched a 3-hour videotape of a reenacted murder trial. Looking at their jurors' age, sex, race, level of education, occupation, income, marital status, and political ideology, these investigators found that no single characteristic correlated with verdicts; even the statistical combination of factors left them unable to predict jurors' opinions.

True, that result is based on jurors' reactions to only one trial. But the same weak relationships have been obtained from mock jurors in burglary, murder, armed robbery, rape, conspiracy, and civil negligence trials.[26] That is not to say, of course, that juror demographics are *un*important. Sometimes researchers do find that they make a difference. The problem is that these differences are volatile. Whether men are more conviction prone than women, whether the poor are more lenient than the rich, and so on often depends in complicated ways on the details of a specific case. In one study, for example, Rita Simon had people listen to a recorded simulation of a criminal trial involving either a breaking-and-entering or incest charge.[27] In both cases the defendant pleaded not guilty by reason of insanity. She found that compared to their male counterparts, female jurors were more lenient toward the housebreaking defendant but harsher toward the accused in the incest case. That kind of interaction is more the rule than the exception in the relationship between juror demographics and verdicts.[28]

The experienced juror.

There is one possible exception to the rule that demographic categories do not predict juror decison-making tendencies. Folk wisdom suggests that judges, as veterans of the courtroom, are tougher on the criminal defendant than naive jurors. Kalven and Zeisel's classic study corroborates this hypothesis. But what about experienced jurors? It is often thought that they begin to view the trial more like their counterparts on the bench than those in the community.

Over the course of a lifetime some people are called for jury duty more than once. In some jurisdictions, even within a single term of service, a person might participate in more than one trial. Compared to the novice, one wonders whether experienced jurors are tainted in any way by their previous service. Trial lawyers believe that they favor the prosecution.[29] Judges, however, do not seem to agree. In 1963 the U.S. Court of Appeals for the Tenth Circuit affirmed the narcotics conviction of a defendant who claimed that his jury was biased because 43 of the 44 venirepersons had previously served in one or more of eight similar cases supported by the same prosecution witnesses. The Court concluded that "an inference of prejudice in such a situation is based on nothing more than suspicion, speculation, and conjecture."[30]

Psychologically speaking, there is reason to expect novice and experienced jurors to differ in their decision-making tendencies. Sitting in judgment of another person can be a difficult and upsetting experience, leading the newcomer to be cautious about voting for conviction. In contrast, the veteran juror, like the professional judge, comes to understand that the evidence against a defendant is never perfect but that decisions must nevertheless be made. Research tends to support the idea that jurors are in some way affected by their own experience on a jury. Several years ago, hundreds of jurors in Baton Rouge, Louisiana, were polled. Those who had previously served were more likely to vote guilty.[31] In another study, 175 criminal trials were analyzed in Fayette County, Kentucky, where jurors are typically called for a 30-day period.[32] The juries in this study contained an average of 6.8 experienced members. Fifty-eight percent of the trials resulted in conviction, 26 percent in acquittal, and 16 percent were hung. Most importantly, as the number of experienced jurors in a trial increased, so did the chances of a guilty verdict. Still other research has shown that among people participating in a mock jury those who had served previously in actual trials were older, more conservative, more authoritarian, and more likely to favor capital punishment than those who were without such experience.[33] Taken together, these results support lawyers' beliefs. Keep in mind, however, that as compelling as these correlations appear, they do not necessarily imply the causal hypothesis that experience on a jury *leads* people to become conviction prone. Other explanations must be considered. For example, perhaps the courts through their jury selection procedures unwittingly favor the selection and reselection of venirepersons who match that prosecution-minded profile.

Turning to controlled laboratory research, we find that the effects of jurors' experiences are not that simple or clearcut. Consider the following research reported by the first author in collaboration with Ralph Juhnke.[34] In order to test the hypothesis that experience per se produces a judgmental bias, we actually manipulated our jurors' level of experience in a simulation study. College students, none of whom had ever served on a real jury, participated in six-person groups for either an auto theft trial, a narcotics trial, or both—separated by one week. In other words, for each trial, some subjects were experienced and others were not. We found that subjects' verdicts were not affected by whether they had participated earlier in another mock jury.[35]

The empirical evidence is thus mixed. Archival research supports the belief that experience engenders a judgmental bias toward conviction; our own research does not. But there is more to the story. First, our results do not mean that jurors are unaffected by their previous experience. They mean only that the experience did not drive them all in the same direction. Maybe the impact of experience is more complicated than we thought.

Let us assume that jurors use their trial experiences as a standard against which to evaluate the merits of a new case. If so, then consistent with what is referred to as adaptation level theory, psychologists would predict that exposure to any stimulus, physical or social, sets a level of adaptation that serves as an *anchor* or reference point against which new stimuli are judged.[36] That is why, in one study, college men rated their potential dates as significantly less attractive after watching ''Charlie's Angels,'' a TV program starring three very beautiful women, than after watching a more neutral show![37]

This phenomenon is relevant to the jury. In one study, subjects read either two assault cases, two murder cases, or one of each. They were then asked to judge the seriousness of these offenses. As predicted by adaptation level theory, subjects viewed the assault case as *less* serious if they had first evaluated the more severe murder rather than another assault. Likewise, they viewed the murder case as *more* serious if they had earlier read about an assault rather than another murder.[38] Subsequent research has shown that this ''contrast effect'' has a significant effect on the decisions jurors ultimately reach in their second trial.[39]

The Not-So-Hidden Hand of Personality

Despite the interactionist view of personality described earlier, personality psychologists from traditional schools of thought believe that decision making, like all other behavior, is the product of underlying dispositional states. Conscious or not, people behave in ways that fulfill needs, reduce tension, and confirm expectations. Jury researchers have looked at three traits thought to be predictive of juror bias—locus of control, belief in a just world, and authoritarianism.

Internal and external locus of control.

Does getting ahead require hard work and persistence or is it simply a matter of being in the right place at the right time? Can individuals influence their government's policies or are we at the mercy of a powerful few leaders? In 1966, clinical psychologist Julian Rotter published a classic paper on how people differ in their generalized expectancies for personal control. Conceived within his social learning theory of personality, Rotter maintained that, to varying degrees and depending on life experiences, people develop either an *internal* locus of control—the belief that one's fate is determined by one's own behavior—or an *external* locus of control—the belief that what happens is determined not by one's own actions but by powerful others, luck, and other external forces.[40] As a measure of the degree to which people are internally versus externally oriented, Rotter constructed a questionnaire popularly known as the I-E Scale.

In the decade or so following Rotter's influential paper, literally thousands of psychological journal pages were filled with studies of the relationship between I-E scores and various aspects of human behavior. Among the differences identified are the following: Internals are more health conscious, they are more persistent in their work, they are more difficult to persuade, they play a more activist role in personal and social matters, and they are more stressed by failure.[41] Is it possible that people project their expectations for personal control onto others? If so, then it stands to reason that in the courtroom, internal jurors would hold defendants personally responsible for their own predicaments. External jurors, on the other hand, would attribute defendants' actions to forces beyond their control. At first, research provided some support for this predicted relationship. In two studies, students completed the I-E Scale and then read brief descriptions of automobile accident cases. In both instances, internals were harsher in their judgments of the defendants' actions than were externals.[42] But in our own more recent study of personality and juror bias, we found that locus of control was consistently *un*related to mock juror verdicts in assault, conspiracy, and auto theft trials.[43]

The reason for our failure to obtain an I-E difference is simple and, interestingly enough, consistent with Rotter's social learning theory. In the earlier research, subject jurors made decisions on the basis of brief one-page case descriptions. In our study they watched more detailed videotapes of mock trials. As predicted by Rotter and other interactionist models of personality, individual differences in behavior appear only when immediate situational cues are weak or ambiguous. In the face of extensive, legally relevant evidence, however, decisions are unlikely to be determined by individuals' more generalized predispositions. This analysis thus compels the conclusion that in actual trials, where jurors are confronted with an extensive array of factual material, their verdicts are unlikely to follow reliably from their locus of control beliefs.

Beliefs in a just and fair world.

In 1970, psychologist Melvin Lerner proposed that people characteristically differ in their tendencies to believe in a just world where one gets what one deserves and deserves what one gets.[44] To strong believers in a just world, there is an intimate link between actions and consequences: good people are rewarded and bad people are punished. According to Lerner, this belief system serves a defensive function, enabling people to feel assured that tragedy will not befall *them*. What happens, though, when an apparently innocent victim suffers, through crime, illness, or accident? In these instances, just-world believers, threatened with a sense of vulnerability, adopt one of two strategies for restoring their sense of justice.

One is to *justify* the event by blaming victims, assuming they had somehow invited or provoked their misfortunes, and concluding that they had deserved their fates after all. This reaction may sound cruel, but it is known to happen. People often react to rape victims by derogating them, finding fault with their appearance, their behavior, and their lifestyles. She "dressed too seductively," "frequented the wrong kinds of establishments," and was "too outgoing" to be blameless. In a strange way, by making others' misfortunes appear deserved rather than capricious, these attributions provide a sense of comfort to us all.

A second way to restore our sense of justice in the face of apparently innocent suffering is to *compensate* for the event by demanding a harsher, more punitive treatment of the perpetrator, if there is one. When a hospital patient dies, the just-world believer might search for blame in the attending physician. Likewise, when a crime is committed, he or she might be all too ready to presume a defendant guilty. On the other side of the coin, defense attorney Percy Foreman once remarked that "the best defense in a murder case . . . is that the deceased should have been killed, regardless of how it happened." In one case, Foreman was so effective in vilifying the victim that he felt "the jury was ready to dig up the deceased and shoot him all over again."[45]

People who believe in a just world tend to be religious, politically conservative, and traditional in their values.[46] Whether they are also biased in their decision making is another matter. Kalven and Zeisel reported that juries in general were likely to vote guilty in trials that involved young and helpless victims; in rape cases, however, juries closely scrutinized the female complainant and tended toward leniency in their verdicts. Turning to whether *individual* jurors' biases can be predicted by the strength of their beliefs in a just world, studies suggest a cautious "yes, but" answer. Consistent with Kalven and Zeisel's findings, those who score high rather than low on the just-world scale,[47] are lenient toward the defendant in simulated rape trials, because they view rape victims as partially responsible for their own fate. In other kinds of cases, however, these same people are tough on criminal defendants—presumably as a means of restoring justice through punishment.[48]

There is another reason to be cautious about applying this research to jury decision making. In our studies of personality and juror bias, we administered the just-world scale to mock jurors, who then participated in three separate trials. Not once was the relationship between subjects' scores and their verdicts statistically significant.[49] As with locus of control, we are thus left to conclude that, although individual jurors' decisions can be colored by their just-world beliefs, the strength of this relationship in the context of an actual trial is likely to be small.

The authoritarian personality.

World War II and the horrors of Nazi Germany led a group of social scientists from the University of California at Berkeley to initiate a massive program of research into the causes of antisemitism. Believing that prejudice is rooted in the very fabric of the human psyche, they studied what has become known as the authoritarian personality.[50] Assuming that everybody has some authoritarian characteristics, individual differences were thought to be a matter of degree. To measure these differences, the Berkeley group developed the F (Fascist) Scale.

In its extreme form, people who score high on the F Scale are rigid, ethnocentric, sexually inhibited, politically conservative, intolerant of dissent, and highly punitive. They are obsequious when they find themselves in a subordinate position, but they are hostile and aggressive when they find themselves in a position of dominance. One expert described authoritarians as having a bicyclist's personality: "above they bow, below they kick."[51]

Over the years an impressive array of research has confirmed that authoritarians are aggressive by nature. Thus, when offered an opportunity, in the context of an experiment, to punish a stranger with electric shocks of varying severity, high-authoritarians administered more severe levels of shock than did the lows.[52] And they show the same kind of punitive orientation when they sit on a jury. Social psychologists Robert Bray and Audrey Noble recruited 264 people to listen to a simulated murder trial and participate in 44 mock juries. Those who scored high rather than low on the F Scale were more likely to vote guilty before their groups deliberated. In fact, so impressive was the bias toward conviction that the differences persisted even after the groups deliberated.[53]

Our own research, while failing to affirm the importance of I-E or just-world beliefs, clearly supports this conclusion. As one team of jury selection experts put it: "It is obvious that no defense attorney would want a jury loaded with extreme authoritarians."[54] But is that always true? Should defense lawyers administer the F Scale during the voir dire and then automatically challenge all venirepersons whose scores indicate an authoritarian personality? The idea of using written questionnaires is an interesting one that we will discuss later. But independent of that consideration, the answer is, not necessarily. Think carefully about the trait itself. While highly authoritarian persons are hostile toward subordinates, they are also deferential toward powerful others. And while they are intolerant of those who break the law in violation of established norms, it is conceivable that they admire those who break the law in the enforcement of those same norms. Research confirms these expectations. When faced with a defendant who commits a "crime of obedience" (e.g., a young Marine who commits murder in response to a superior's order or a parent accused of child abuse in the course of disciplining a son or daughter), or when the defendant is an authority figure like a policeman, authoritarian jurors actually become *less* punitive in their judgments.[55] From lions to lambs—it depends on the case.

Beyond Stereotypes: Attitudes, Values, and the Law

To this point we have seen that, with the exception of authoritarianism, neither demographics nor personality variables reliably predict jurors' decision-making tendencies. Women, the young, and the poor may be lenient in some trials but tough in others. And even then the relationships are statistically too weak to be of practical value for jury selection. The same is true of personality determinants. That is not to say that belief in a just world and locus of control do not predispose an individual to interpret others' actions in a particular way. But when jurors are provided with an extensive amount of behavioral evidence and then instructed to adhere their decisions to that evidence, their own personalities become buried under the weight of that information. Even the authoritarian personality, the harshest juror of them all, might favor the defendant under the right circumstances.

In contrast to the broad strokes of juror demography and the not-so-hidden hand of personality, there is reason to believe that individual jurors' predispositions do follow reliably from their attitudes on specific issues of relevance to their trial. It is the "specific" part that is important. An individual who has had the experience of being entrapped or arrested for a crime he or she did not commit is likely to have developed a basic mistrust of the criminal justice establishment. Likewise, the individual who has had the misfortune of being wrongfully sued for damages is likely to feel a measure of sympathy for the civil defendant. On the other side of the coin, the juror who has been the unwary victim of a crime or a civil act of negligence is likely to identify with the plight of a complainant.

Motivated by the principle that specific attitudes are better predictors of behavior than global traits, we constructed a juror bias scale (JBS), a 17-item questionnaire designed as a measure of jurors' predispositions.[56] Respondents who agree with statements like "Too many innocent people are wrongfully imprisoned" and "The defendant is often a victim of his own bad reputation" thus score as defense-biased. In contrast, those who believe that "Too often jurors hesitate to convict someone who is guilty out of pure sympathy" and "In most cases where the accused presents a strong defense, it is only because of a good lawyer" become classified as prosecution-biased.

In a series of validation studies conducted at Purdue University and in the community of Lafayette, Indiana, JBS scores were a better predictor of mock juror verdicts than the I-E Scale, the just-world scale, and even the F Scale. In numerical terms, we found that in four trials the average rate of conviction was 81 percent among prosecution-biased jurors and 52 percent among their defense-biased counterparts.[57] However, for a fifth case—a rape trial—we found an unexpected reversal of the predicted pattern. Compared to those who ordinarily favor the prosecution, defense-oriented jurors, people who are relatively liberal in their political views, sympathize more with the *victims* of rape than with the accused.

Our research with the JBS demonstrates that to some extent people's verdicts are predictable from their legal attitudes. But a generalized bias toward the prosecution or defense is still limited, as it is with authoritarianism, by the idiosyncrasies of a particular case. Clearly, the best way to predict individual differences in decision making is to identify the *specific* issues most relevant to a particular trial and then assess jurors' attitudes on those issues. In the following pages we look at two powerful examples: attitudes about rape and capital punishment.

Attitudes and myths about rape.

Few crimes arouse as much passion, anger, and confusion as rape. Sometimes committed by an acquaintance, even the victim's spouse, the consequences of rape to the victim and her family can be devastating. Because it is both a sexual and a violent act, rape is not like other crimes of assault. It is distinctly personal in nature. Defined by one psychologist as "the ultimate violation of the self,"[58] many victims experience rape trauma syndrome—an acute stress reaction that produces a cluster of behavioral, somatic, and psychological symptoms. And out of fear of public humiliation, many women never report the crime to the authorities.[59]

From a legal standpoint, rape has always been a crime of controversy. As far back as the seventeenth century it was referred to as "an accusation easily made and hard to be proved, and harder to be defended by the party accused."[60] There has always been the fear of innocent men languishing in prison because of the accusations of their rejected lovers. For that reason, the courts have erected extensive safeguards for the defendant, shifting the focus of attention to the sexual history, character, and veracity of the victim. It is no wonder that so many victims of rape report feeling as if they are on trial. Case histories indicate that juries are generally reluctant to convict an apparently normal male for rape. Instead, they appear to operate on the just-world assumption that "nice girls don't get raped and bad girls shouldn't complain."[61] Recent reforms, specifically the rape shield laws adopted in many states, now protect the victim in court by limiting evidence of her sexual past. Thus, in one case a judge refused to allow the defendant to introduce the fact that his accuser was on birth control pills. He had argued that this information was relevant to the claim that she had consented—despite the fact that at the time he had physically beaten his young victim.[62]

Precisely because rape trials are so controversial, they are particularly sensitive to the effects of nonrational and nonevidentiary factors.[63] That naturally leads one to wonder what it is about jurors that predisposes them to favor one side or another in a rape case. In an extensive series of studies, Eugene Borgida and his colleagues recruited several hundred men and women from the twin cities of Minneapolis–St. Paul to participate in mock juries.[64] After filling out a battery of questionnaires, subjects watched a simulated rape trial. The victim claimed she was forcibly raped; the defendant maintained that she had freely consented to have sex. The results were clear and straightforward. Subjects' background characteristics—their age, sex, level of education, and income— had no effect on their decisions. Nor did it matter whether they had served previously on a jury or even whether they had personally known a rape victim. It mattered little whether subjects were internals or externals, whether they were high or low in authoritarianism or belief in a just world, or whether they were masculine or feminine in their sex-role identification.

What did make a difference were the kinds of stereotypic beliefs jurors held about women and rape. Measured by the Rape Myth Acceptance Scale, people who think that "many women have an unconscious wish to be raped" or that "when women go around braless or wearing short skirts and tight tops, they are just asking for trouble" are unlikely to vote guilty in an ordinary rape trial. It may seem as if nobody really believes these myths, but they elicit a surprisingly high level of acceptance.[65]

We should say that some background factors are important. One researcher found that parents of male-only children are less conviction prone and less punitive toward a rape defendant than are the parents of female-only children.[66] And another found that people who watch films depicting graphic, sexually-oriented violence toward women (movies like "Tool Box Murderer") are also unlikely to vote guilty.[67] Still, jurors' attitudes toward rape are the single best predictor of how they vote.

Qualifying the arbiters of life and death.

On February 14, 1978, a gift shop and service station in Camden, Arkansas, was robbed and its owner murdered. That afternoon, Ardia McCree was arrested after he was spotted driving a maroon and white Lincoln Continental—the getaway car described by an eyewitness. McCree admitted to police that he was at the shop at the time of the murder. But he claimed that a tall black stranger wearing an overcoat had asked him for a ride and then took his rifle from the back of the car and used it to kill the owner. McCree claimed further that the stranger then rode with him to a nearby dirt road, got out of the car, and walked away with the rifle. This story was contradicted by two eyewitnesses who saw McCree in his car *alone* right after the time of the murder. The police found McCree's rifle and a bank bag taken from the shop alongside the dirt road. Based on ballistics tests, an FBI official testified that the deceased had been shot by a bullet fired from that rifle. McCree was charged with first-degree murder, punishable by death.

In Arkansas, juries in capital cases not only decide on the initial question of guilt and innocence but also the punishment question. For that reason, during the voir dire the trial judge removed for cause those prospective jurors, eight in all, who stated that they could not under any circumstances vote to impose the death penalty. In the end the jury convicted McCree of murder and sentenced him to life imprisonment without parole. The defendant appealed his verdict; he argued that by excluding those venirepersons who would refuse to impose the death penalty, a procedure known as death qualification, the court had stacked the deck against him. In August 1983 a district court granted McCree's appeal. Reviewing a wealth of social scientific evidence, the court concluded that death-qualification produces juries that are (a) not a representative cross-section of the community and (b) tilted in their predispositions toward the prosecution.[68] Shortly thereafter, the U.S. Court of Appeals for the Eighth Circuit, finding "substantial evidentiary support" for that decision, affirmed McCree's appeal.[69]

Buttressed by a large body of research, this case ultimately made its way to the U.S. Supreme Court. On May 5, 1986, in *Lockhart v. McCree*, the Court reversed McCree's earlier victories.[70] Writing for the majority, Chief Justice William Rehnquist conceded that death-qualified juries consist of people with "shared attitudes" who are "somewhat more conviction-prone" than other juries. But then he went on to argue that these empirical facts do not violate a defendant's constitutional right to an impartial jury. Writing for the minority, Justice Marshall expressed his outrage: "With a glib nonchalance ill-suited to the gravity of the issue presented and the power of the respondent's claims, the Court upholds a practice that allows the state a special advantage in those prosecutions where the charges are the most serious and the possible punishments the most severe. . . . Because I believe that such a blatant disregard for the rights of a capital defendant offends logic, fairness, and the Constitution, I dissent." So do we.

Let us review the history of death qualification and the psychological evidence against it. It used to be the case that prospective jurors in capital trials were excluded if, during the voir dire, they expressed *any* reservations (or, in the prevalent term, "scruples") about the death penalty. Then in 1968, in *Witherspoon v. Illinois*, the Supreme Court ruled that this practice violated the Constitution by creating "a tribunal organized to return a verdict of death."[71] According to the Court, venirepersons could still be excluded from service but only if they made it unmistakably clear that because of their views they would not, under any circumstances, vote for the death sentence. These prospective jurors, as a group, have since become known as the Witherspoon excludables. They were the ones removed for cause from McCree's jury.

We turn now to the psychology of death qualification. The questions are twofold. First, by eliminating the *Witherspoon* excludables, are the courts compromising the jury's diversity? Second, does this selection practice produce a panel that is uniquely prone to convict? In the years since *Witherspoon* the academic community has been openly critical of the Court's presumption that jurors' attitudes toward capital punishment are unrelated either to their demographic status or to their predispositions to vote on guilt and innocence. To date, at least 15 studies have addressed these issues.[72] The most sophisticated are a recent series of experiments conducted by social psychologist Phoebe Ellsworth and her colleagues at Stanford University.

Like the data on attitudes toward rape, there is a remarkably strong and consistent relationship between people's opinions on capital punishment and their behavior on capital juries. To begin with, death qualification irrevocably excludes significant and identifiable segments of the population—roughly between 10 and 15 percent of prospective jurors. In particular, women, blacks, the poor, and members of certain religious groups fall into the class of *Witherspoon* excludables at a disproportionately high rate. Then it turns out that jurors who survive death qualification and those who are excluded have systematically different perspectives on a whole cluster of criminal justice issues. Compared to those who oppose it, people who favor capital punishment are more concerned about the crime rate; they are more favorable in their attitudes toward the police and other figures of authority; they are cynical about the insanity defense; they are mistrustful of defense lawyers; they are intolerant of procedures designed to protect the accused; and they are likely to believe that a defendant's failure to testify is a sure sign of guilt. When the two groups are actually compared in their approaches to a single trial, we find that death-qualified jurors evaluate evidence as more favorable to the prosecution and express a greater willingness to risk an erroneous conviction. In short, people's attitudes on the death penalty are just the tip of an iceberg.[73]

Turning to the relationship between death penalty attitudes and verdicts, the findings, without exception, converge on the same simple conclusion: Death-qualified juries are more likely to convict than normally selected juries. Over the years this result has surfaced across a wide variety of subject populations, methods, and trials. The result is the same whether the subjects are blacks, southern college students, northern industrial workers, eligible jurors in California, New York, or Illinois, or a nationwide random sample. And the result is the same whether the data are obtained through posttrial interviews with actual jurors, public opinion surveys, or highly controlled laboratory simulations. The results are persuasive. It is no wonder that Justice Marshall, commenting on the majority's flippant dismissal of the evidence, concluded that "Even the Court's haphazard jabs cannot obscure the power of the array."[74]

The Supreme Court's ruling in *Lockhart v. McCree* is an offense to the principles of fairness. For reasons no better than convenience (so that the state need not impanel separate juries to decide on guilt and punishment), it justified the wholesale exclusion from the jury box of citizens who would refuse to impose the death sentence but who could be impartial during the more fundamental guilt-determination phase of the trial. To make matters worse, death qualification is subject to even further abuse. For example, there is reason to believe that prosecutors freely request the death penalty before trial, only to waive it in the end, in order to benefit from the strategic advantages of jury selection. The district attorney in McCree's trial did just that. Although we cannot be certain of his motives, the district attorney withdrew his original request for the death penalty after the defendant was convicted. And there is reason to believe that judges often exclude jurors for cause who oppose capital punishment in principle but do not qualify for exclusion under the *Witherspoon* criterion (i.e., those who say they could consider a death sentence under the right circumstances).[75] Finally, there is reason to believe that from the information obtained through death qualification, prosecutors systematically use their peremptory challenges to eliminate those venirepersons who oppose capital punishment but were not excluded for cause.[76] What more can we say? In an editorial comment the *New York Times* suggested that "the silver lining is that decisions like this are illogical on their face. If the only way capital punishment can be administered is by rigged juries, sooner or later a more patient court will have to undo both."[77]

NOTES

1. *State v. Fowler*, 79 CRS 17591.

2. *U.S. v. Griffin*.

3. For a discussion of these assumptions, see V. P. Hans and N. Vidmar (1982), Jury selection. In N. Kerr and R. Bray (Eds.), *The Psychology of the Courtroom*. New York, Academic Press.

4. For a complete description, see J. Van Dyke (1977), *Jury Selection Procedures*. Cambridge, MA: Ballinger; also see National Institute of Law Enforcement and Criminal Justice (1975), *A Guide to Jury System Management*. Washington, D.C.: U.S. Government Printing Office.

5. H. M. Hyman and C. M. Tarrant (1975), Aspects of American jury history. In R. J. Simon (Ed.), *The Jury System in America: A Critical Overview*. Beverly Hills: Sage Publications.

6. *Jury Selection and Service Act of 1968*, 28 U.S. Code, pp. 1861–1869. Washington, D.C.: U.S. Government Printing Office.

7. Ibid., pp. 1861, 1962.

8. *Swain v. Alabama* (1965), 380 U.S. 202, p. 220.

9. Unplanned jury duty ensnares passersby (1985), *New York Times*, August 10, Sect. 1, p. 29.

10. See Van Dyke, supra note 4: also see D. Kairys, B. Kadane, and P. Lehoczky (1977), Jury representativeness: A mandate for multiple source lists. *California Law Review*, Vol. 65, pp. 776–827.

11. J. Riley (1984), Selecting a trial panel: Whose peers are they? *The National Law Journal*, Vol. 6, No. 24, pp. 1, 22–25.

12. Id.

13. See Van Dyke, supra note 4.

14. Supra note 8.

15. Ibid., p. 220.

16. *Booker v. Jabe* (1985), 83–1136, 6th Circuit.

17. *McCray v. Abrams* (1984), 750 F.2d 1113.

18. The first challenge to the Swain opinion was made by the California Supreme Court in *People v. Wheeler* (1978), 2 Cal. 3d 258.

19. In a recent California case, a defendant was convicted by a jury that included a black man. However, the defense attorney argued that the prosecutor had systematically excluded a more specific cognizable group—black women. On appeal, the state Supreme Court agreed; see M. A. Galante (1985), California voir dire rules broadened. *The National Law Journal*, Sept. 9, pp. 9, 21.

20. *Irvin v. Dowd* (1961), 366 U.S. 717, p. 723.

21. *Beck v. Washington* (1962), 369 U.S. 541, p. 557.

22. W. Mischel (1968), *Personality and Assessment*. New York: Wiley; also see W. Mischel (1969), Continuity and change in personality, *American Psychologist*, Vol. 24, pp. 1012–1018. The same point was made about the relationship between attitudes and behavior, see A. W. Wicker (1969), Attitudes versus actions: The relationship between verbal and overt behavioral responses to attitude objects. *Journal of Social Issues*, Vol. 25, pp. 41–78.

23. For a comprehensive account of the interactionist perspective, see D. Magnusson and N. S. Endler (1977, Eds.), *Personality at the Crossroads: Current Issues in Interactional Psychology*. Hillsdale, NJ: Erlbaum; also see M. Snyder and W. Ickes (1985), Personality and social behavior. In G. Lindzey and E. Aronson (Eds.), *The Handbook of Social Psychology*, Vol. 2. New York: Random House.

24. *U.S. v. Ebens*, reported by T. Kiska (1984), The baseball bat killing: Was it race or alcohol? *The National Law Journal*, July 9, p. 8.

25. R. Hastie, S. D. Penrod, & N. Pennington (1983), *Inside the Jury*. Cambridge, MA: Harvard University Press.

26. See S. D. Penrod (1979), Study of attorney and "scientific" jury selection models. Doctoral Dissertation, Harvard University; also see M. Saks (1977), *Jury Verdicts*. Lexington, MA: Heath, and S. M. Kassin and L. S. Wrightsman (1983), The construction and validation of a Juror Bias Scale. *Journal of Research in Personality*, Vol. 17, pp. 423–442.

27. R. J. Simon (1967). *The Jury and the Defense of Insanity*. Boston: Little, Brown.

28. For a more extensive review, see C. Stephan (1975), Selective characteristics of jurors and litigants: Their influences on juries' verdicts. In R. J. Simon (Ed.), *The Jury System in America: A Critical Overview*. Beverly Hills: Sage Publications.

29. See J. H. Skolnick (1966), *Justice Without Trial: Law Enforcement in Democratic Society*. New York: Wiley. F. Lee Bailey, for example, expressed the prevailing sentiment that, as a criminal defense lawyer, "All other things being equal, new jurors are desired over experienced ones"; see F. L. Bailey & H. B. Rothblatt (1971), *Successful Techniques for Criminal Trials*. Rochester, NY: The Lawyers Co-operative Publishing Company, p. 107. In England this belief is so widely held that it has become known as the "first-day syndrome." As graphically described by one juror: "Acquittals were more frequent while jurors were green. If you are an accused, you will do well to have your case first on the list. At that stage plenty of jurymen will believe that there is a reasonable doubt if no one has actually seen you with your hand in the till. If, after long argument and with several of them still doubtful, they find you guilty and then discover that you have seventeen previous convictions for similar offenses, scales tend to drop from their eyes; they become old soldiers overnight and the next accused is viewed much more circumspectly"; see J. Baldwin and M. McConville (1979), *Jury Trials*. Oxford, England: Clarendon Press.

30. *Casias v. United States* (1963), 315 F.2d 614, p. 617; for a complete review of the case

law, see R. C. Dillehay and M. T. Nietzel (1985), Juror experience and jury verdicts. *Law and Human Behavior*, Vol. 9, pp. 179–191.

31. J. P. Reed (1965), Jury deliberations, voting, and verdict trends. *Southwestern Social Science Quarterly*, Vol. 45, pp. 361–370.

32. R. C. Dillehay and M. T. Nietzel (1985), Juror experience and jury verdicts. *Law and Human Behavior*, Vol. 9, pp. 179–191.

33. G. Y. Jurow (1971), New data on the effect of a death qualified jury on the guilt determination process. *Harvard Law Review*, Vol. 841, pp. 567–611.

34. S. M. Kassin & R. Juhnke (1983), Juror experience and decision making. *Journal of Personality and Social Psychology*, Vol. 44, pp. 1182–1191.

35. See also N. L. Kerr, D. L. Harmon, & J. K. Graves (1982), Independence of multiple verdicts by jurors and juries. *Journal of Applied Social Psychology*, Vol. 12, pp. 12–29.

36. H. Helson (1964), *Adaptation-Level Theory: An Experimental and Systematic Approach to Behavior*. New York: Harper & Row.

37. D. T. Kenrick & S. E. Gutierres (1980), Contrast effects and judgments of physical attractiveness: When beauty becomes a social problem. *Journal of Personality and Social Psychology*, Vol. 38, pp. 131–140.

38. A. Pepitone & M. DeNubile (1976), Contrast effects in judgments of crime severity and the punishment of criminal violators. *Journal of Personality and Social Psychology*, Vol. 33, pp. 448–459.

39. D. H. Nagao & J. H. Davis (1980), The effects of prior experience on mock juror case judgments. *Social Psychology Quarterly*, Vol. 43, pp. 190–199.

40. J. B. Rotter (1966), Generalized expectancies for internal versus external control of reinforcement. *Psychological Monographs*, Vol. 80, No. 609.

41. For an excellent review of this literature, see E. J. Phares (1978), Locus of control. In H. London & J. Exner (Eds.), *Dimensions of Personality*. New York: Wiley.

42. For a review, see K. C. Gerbasi, M. Zuckerman, & H. T. Reis (1977), Justice needs a new blindfold: A review of mock jury research. *Psychological Bulletin*, Vol. 84, pp. 323–345.

43. See Kassin and Wrightsman (1983), supra note 26.

44. M. J. Lerner (1970), The desire for justice and reactions to victims. In J. Macauley and L. Berkowitz (Eds.), *Altruism and Helping Behavior*. New York: Academic Press.

45. See M. Smith (1966), Percy Foreman: Top trial lawyer. *Life*, April 1, p. 96.

46. For a review, see M. J. Lerner (1980), *The Belief in a Just World: A Fundamental Delusion*. New York: Plenum.

47. See Z. Rubin and A. Peplau (1973), Belief in a just world and reactions to another's lot: A study of participants in the national draft lottery. *Journal of Social Issues*, Vol. 29, pp. 73–93.

48. For a review, see Gerbasi et al. (1977), supra note 42.

49. Kassin and Wrightsman, supra note 26.

50. T. W. Adorno, E. Frenkel-Brunswik, D. Levinson, & R. N. Sanford (1950), *The Authoritarian Personality*. New York: Harper & Row.

51. T. W. Adorno, cited in F. Greenstein (1969), *Personality and Politics*. Chicago: Markham.

52. For a complete review of the literature, see R. C. Dillehay (1978), Authoritarianism. In H. London & J. Exner (Eds.), *Dimensions of Personality*. New York: Wiley.

53. R. M. Bray and A. M. Noble (1978), Authoritarianism and decisions of mock juries: Evidence of jury bias and group polarization. *Journal of Personality and Social Psychology*, Vol. 36, pp. 1424–1430.

54. J. B. McConahay, C. J. Mullin, & J. Frederick (1977), The uses of social science in trials with political and racial overtones: The trial of Joan Little. *Law and Contemporary Problems*, Vol. 41, pp. 205–229.

55. See V. L. Hamilton (1976), Individual differences in ascriptions of responsibility, guilt, and appropriate punishment. In G. Bermant, C. Nemeth, & N. Vidmar (Eds.), *Psychology and the*

Law. Lexington, MA: Heath; also see L. T. Garcia & W. Griffitt (1978), Authoritarianism-situation interactions in the determination of punitiveness: Engaging authoritarian ideology. *Journal of Research in Personality*, Vol. 12, pp. 469–478.

56. Kassin and Wrightsman, supra note 26.

57. In a subsequent study, JBS scores were significantly predictive of mock jurors' opinions in an insanity case; see E. Gallun (1983), *The effect of the insanity defense and its consequences on jury verdicts*. Unpublished honors thesis, Williams College.

58. E. Hilberman (1976), Rape: The ultimate violation of the self. *American Journal of Psychiatry*, Vol. 133, pp. 436–437.

59. A. Burgess & L. Holmstrom (1974), Rape trauma syndrome. *American Journal of Psychiatry*, Vol. 131, pp. 981–986.

60. Sir Matthew Hale, cited in N. Connell & C. Wilson (Eds.) (1974), *Rape: The First Sourcebook for Women*. New York: Plume Books.

61. Task Force on Rape (1973), *Report of the District of Columbia Task Force on Rape*. Washington, D.C.: U.S. Government Printing Office; see also Kalven and Zeisel, supra note 1.19.

62. *People v. Smith* (1977), 391 N.Y.S. 2d 734.

63. See, for example, B. Babcock, A. Freedman, E. Norton, & S. Ross (1975), *Discrimination and the Law*. Boston: Little, Brown.

64. For a review, see E. Borgida & N. Brekke (1984), Psychological research on rape trials. In A. Burgess (Ed.), *Research Handbook on Rape and Sexual Assault*. New York: Garland. H. S. Feild (1978), Juror background characteristics and attitudes toward rape. *Law and Human Behavior*, Vol. 2, pp. 73–93.

65. For a complete presentation of the Rape Myth Acceptance Scale, see M. R. Burt (1980), Cultural myths and supports for rape. *Journal of Personality and Social Psychology*, Vol. 38, pp. 217–230; for additional evidence of the importance of rape attitudes, see H. S. Feild (1978), Juror background characteristics and attitudes toward rape. *Law and Human Behavior*, Vol. 2, pp. 73–93.

66. M. F. Kaplan & L. E. Miller (1978), Effects of jurors' identification with the victim depend on likelihood of victimization. *Law and Human Behavior*, Vol. 2, pp. 353–361.

67. C. L. Krafka (1985), *Sexually explicit, sexually violent, and violent media: Effects of multiple naturalistic exposures and debriefing on female viewers*. Unpublished dissertation, University of Wisconsin.

68. *Grigsby v. Mabry*, 569 F. Supp. 1277.

69. *Grigsby v. Mabry* (1985), 758 F. 2d 229.

70. *Lockhart v. McCree*, 54 U.S.L.W. 4449.

71. 391 U.S. 510, p. 521.

72. It is not our purpose to review this literature in detail. For that, see C. L. Cowan, W. C. Thompson, & P. C. Ellsworth (1984), The effect of death qualification on jurors' predispositions to convict and on the quality of deliberation. *Law and Human Behavior*, Vol. 8, pp. 53–79.

73. See R. Fitzgerald & P. C. Ellsworth (1984), Due process vs. crime control: Death qualification and jury attitudes. *Law and Human Behavior*, Vol. 8, pp. 31–52; W. C. Thompson, C. L. Cowan, P. C. Ellsworth, & J. C. Harrington (1984), Death penalty attitudes and conviction proneness: The translation of attitudes into verdicts. *Law and Human Behavior*, Vol. 8, pp. 95–113; N. Vidmar & P. C. Ellsworth (1974), Public opinion and the death penalty. *Stanford Law Review*, Vol. 26, pp. 1245–1270.

74. Supra note 70.

75. See E. Schnapper (1984), Taking Witherspoon seriously: The search for death-qualified jurors. *Texas Law Review*, Vol. 62, pp. 977–1084.

76. See B. J. Winick (1982), Prosecutorial peremptory challenge practices in capital cases: An empirical study and a constitutional analysis. *Michigan Law Review*, Vol. 81, pp. 1–98.

77. Loading the argument for death (May 7, 1986).

3

VOIR DIRE: SCIENCE AND INTUITION

That jurors differ is a self-evident fact of life. Every time there is a hung jury, indeed every time a first-ballot vote is less than unanimous, it signals the importance of individual differences in the decision-making process. But recognizing that verdicts are affected by jurors' predispositions and being able to identify in advance those people who should be excluded for bias are two different matters. Our review of the literature thus far compels the following conclusions.

Time and again, efforts to corroborate the assumption that juries' verdicts are predictable from their demographic composition have produced modest, inconsistent, and highly qualified results. It is not that demographics are always uninformative. On a case-by-case basis there are times when they are of consequence. Whether an individual has previous jury experience, for example, could influence his or her trial expectations and decision-making tendencies in important ways. And then, of course, there are the racially charged crimes. Even if they are infrequent, these cases leave a permanent scar, not only on the parties victimized by an unjust verdict but also on the jury system as a whole.[1]

Personality variables fare little better in the predictive equation. These so-called hidden psychological characteristics, those that cannot be seen with the naked eye or readily obtained during a voir dire, have produced little in the way of useful jury-selection information. For all the behavioral differences that do reliably distinguish between internals and externals, or believers and nonbelievers in a just world, juror decisions are not among them. Authoritarianism is an exception, but as we will see, trial lawyers, on their own, are already sensitive to this characteristic. And as predicted by interactionist models of personality, it too is subject to qualification.

The best way to predict a juror's predisposition is to identify, on a case-specific basis, what concrete attitudes are relevant and then to figure out where the individual stands on those attitudes. The value of this approach is demonstrated in at least two areas. In rape cases, which are unique in so many ways, jurors signal their intentions through their beliefs about women and rape. Likewise, in capital cases, jurors unwittingly tip their hands when they disclose how they feel about the death penalty. In both types of trials, involving emotional topics over which public opinion is polarized, the relationships between specific attitudes and verdicts are dramatic and consistent. There is every reason to believe that this same kind of predictive relationship can be found in other value-driven topics. Euthanasia cases are a good example. So is the 1987 trial of Bernhard Goetz, the New York City subway vigilante. Fed up with street crime that goes unpunished, New Yorkers in general, and the Goetz jury in particular, bent over backwards to justify the defendant's actions.

Through the practice of death qualification, courts may obstruct the ideal of impaneling an impartial jury in capital trials. Also, people hold near and dear to their hearts other beliefs, attitudes, experiences, and values that can interfere with objective decision making. This is little more than a statement about the human condition. Personal factors, however, are only part of the overall problem. Pretrial bias is also a *situational* fact of life that sometimes is nearly impossible to avoid. Confronted with news stories, rumors, and public sentiment, even people who are not prejudiced may become so before their trial actually begins. Jurors may even be influenced by well publicized news events that do not pertain to their own particular trial.[2] The following story is as dramatic an illustration as any of this chronic problem.

PRETRIAL PUBLICITY: THE BIASED SITUATION

On October 18, 1954, an unforgettable murder trial opened in a Cleveland area courtroom. Months earlier, on the morning of July 4, Marilyn Sheppard, the pregnant wife of Dr. Sam Sheppard, was beaten to death in their suburban home. Although the evidence was ambiguous, the police immediately suspected the victim's husband, a well-known and respected physician. And so did the local media. Newspaper articles and editorials appeared, charging that somebody, notably Sam Sheppard, because he was wealthy and influential, was "getting away with murder." Eventually, he was charged with the crime and tried in an Ohio state court.

As the trial was about to begin, the Cleveland newspapers published the names and addresses of the prospective jurors, all of whom then received anonymous letters and telephone calls concerning the case. Inside the courtroom itself a special table was set up inside the bar to accommodate about 20 journalists. Behind the bar the first three rows of benches were reserved for representatives of TV and radio stations as well as reporters from out-of-town newspapers and magazines. Private telephone lines and telegraphic equipment were installed in nearby rooms so that reports from the trial could be made public almost instantaneously. To further accommodate the press, daily transcripts of the proceedings were made available along with photographs of Sheppard, the judge, counsel, witnesses, and the jury. In a case that would offer mystery, murder, sex, and high society, the public had an insatiable appetite for information.

It is clear from virtually all accounts, however, that the jurors were bombarded right from the start with inflammatory and prejudicial stories about the defendant. On the eve of trial, for example, WHK radio station aired a staged debate between representatives of two Cleveland newspapers to decide which paper deserved more credit for Sheppard's indictment.[3] Shortly thereafter, an article appeared with the headline "Sam called a 'Jekyll-Hyde' by Marilyn, Cousin to Testify." Although the article went on to claim that "the prosecution has a 'bombshell witness' on tap who will testify to Dr. Sam's display of fiery temper," no such testimony was ever introduced. And that was just the beginning. From the media alone, jurors were led to believe that Sheppard had deliberately impeded the murder investigation, that he had conceded his guilt by hiring a nationally prominent lawyer, that he was sexually involved with numerous women, and that he had fathered an illegitimate child. Almost every day, the papers summarized and interpreted the testimony, drawing inferences, and freely straying beyond the evidence entered into the trial record.

Through it all the presiding judge refused the defendant's motions for a mistrial, continuance, and change of venue. He failed to insulate witnesses from the press. He also failed to sequester the jury or warn them adequately not to read or listen to outside reports about the case. It was in this charged atmosphere, with the media serving as the invisible thirteenth juror, that Sheppard was found guilty of murder. It was not until 12 years later that U.S. Supreme Court Justice Thomas Clark described the trial, in disgust, as a "Roman holiday."[4] In an 8 to 1 decision, the Court reversed the conviction, released Sheppard from prison, and granted him a new trial. Shortly thereafter, Sheppard was acquitted.[5]

Although this case is unusual, it depicts an inevitable tension that exists between two rights in conflict: the defendant's right to a fair trial on the one hand and the freedom of the press on the other. The fear, of course, is that juries are irrevocably biased by media publicity that appears before or during their trial. Is that true? Does exposure to news stories lead jurors to form their opinions prematurely and close their minds to the evidence subsequently introduced in court? The system has always been plagued by this nagging question. Then, in the 1960s, right after the assassination of President Kennedy, the courts began to feel an acute need to take affirmative action. Would it have been possible, it was asked, for Lee Harvey Oswald to obtain a fair trial in an American courtroom? The answer, we think, is painfully obvious.[6]

In 1968 the American Bar Association formed a committee to investigate the matter of pretrial publicity.[7] The Committee analyzed the contents of more than 20 major metropolitan newspapers and found that information thought to be prejudicial was published in a significant number of criminal cases. Included were reports that prospective defendants had a prior record, had confessed, tried to plea bargain, or refused to take a polygraph test. In the vast majority of cases, the information emanated from official sources, either the police or the district attorney. More recent analyses show that little has changed. Today's news is filled with stories about serious crimes that are presented from the prosecutor's vantage point, especially in notorious cases.[8]

According to public opinion surveys, in highly publicized crimes, people tend to align themselves with the prosecution. When Patty Hearst was arrested in 1976, after having been abducted several months earlier, the public overwhelmingly believed she was guilty. The same was true when John DeLorean was arrested in 1982 on cocaine smuggling charges. These are not anomalous cases. The more knowledge people have about a case, the more likely they are to favor the prosecution.[9] In a recent series of interviews, judges, trial lawyers, journalists, and law professors further agreed that pretrial publicity is especially problematic in small towns, in cases involving well-known public figures, and for murders and sex crimes.[10] The ultimate question, of course, is whether this publicity affects the jury.

As usual, single case studies are not particularly informative. Patty Hearst was convicted; John DeLorean was not. We thus turn for answers to controlled mock jury research. In the most thorough attempt to simulate the conditions of a real trial, psychologist Alice Padawer-Singer and sociologist Allen Barton recruited as participants 120 men and women, randomly selected from a list of eligible jurors in Nassau County, New York. Subjects appeared in groups of 12 at a local courthouse, where they sat in the jury box and listened to a 3-hour audiotape of a staged murder trial. In that case a prominent woman in Washington, D.C., had been shot to death in a park. A man was found nearby and arrested. He was later identified by an eyewitness who claimed to have heard the victim scream and then seen the defendant, from over 100 feet away, crouched beside her. The murder weapon was never found.

Before hearing the trial, subjects were exposed to newspaper clippings about the case. For half of them, the articles were prejudicial, as they revealed that the defendant had a criminal background and had initially confessed to the murder. As it turned out, even though the judge had admonished jurors to base their decisions only on the evidence introduced in court, pretrial publicity had a dramatic effect on their verdicts. Although only 55 percent of those in the neutral-news condition voted that the defendant was guilty, that number increased to 78 percent in the prejudicial-news condition. In a subsequent study, involving

266 residents of Brooklyn, New York, the percentage of guilty votes increased from 35 to 69 percent.[11] Additional research has corroborated the finding that pretrial publicity can violate the ideal of a fair trial. In fact, this effect appears to persist even when mock jurors are permitted to deliberate, even when they are cautioned by the judge, and even when those who admit to having been prejudiced are eliminated during a voir dire.[12]

Pretrial publicity is dangerous for two reasons. First, as in Padawer-Singer and Barton's study, it often provides jurors with information that, because it is irrelevant, unreliable, or illegally obtained, does not otherwise make its way into the trial record. Sam Sheppard's jury is a case in point. From the media alone, it was led to believe that Sheppard had an explosive temper, that he had been unfaithful to his wife, that he had impeded the investigation of her murder, and so on. As it turned out, these allegations were never made under oath from the witness stand, so they were not subject to challenge under cross examination. Like rumor, though, their impact on the listener is virtually inevitable — even if they are subsequently denied.[13] But there is more. Pretrial publicity can affect the jury even when it discloses matters that are later introduced into evidence. Because many news stories precede the actual trial, jurors become informed about certain facts before they receive a more formal presentation of the case in the courtroom. From what psychologists know about the power of first impressions, the implications of this foreknowledge are clear. If jurors learn, early on, that the defendant has a scandalous background, that information could take on added importance by distorting how they interpret the rest of the case. Like the boxer who suffers the first punch, the defendant might become disabled and unable to recover.

THE VOIR DIRE: AN EFFECTIVE SAFEGUARD?

Twelve Angry Men is a classic film depicting the passions of jury decision making. But as one writer put it, "how on earth were hang-'em high characters like Ed Begley and Lee J. Cobb ever seated on a young Puerto Rican's murder jury in the first place?"[14]

With prospective jurors tainted by both personal and situational forces, it is incumbent upon lawyers to conduct a skillful voir dire and identify those who cannot suspend their pretrial biases in the interest of justice. Does it work? Indeed, *can* it work? Are venirepersons who are predisposed, one way or another, effectively identified and eliminated? Does the voir dire deny entry into the jury box of people who harbor a latent prejudice? Does it, in the end, produce an impartial jury? In order for these objectives to be achieved, two conditions must be met. First, lawyers must use their opportunity to question jurors for the purposes intended. Second, they must know what they are doing. We suspect that neither of these conditions is satisfied.

Legitimate and Illegitimate Uses of the Voir Dire

The voir dire is designed by law to serve only one purpose: to enable counsel to probe jurors for information about their state of mind that might provide grounds for their removal. All too often, however, trial lawyers conceive of their role differently. To begin with, it is no secret that they strive to obtain not an impartial panel, but a sympathetic one. Herald Price Fahringer, a prominent New York attorney, said, quite frankly, "There isn't a trial lawyer in the country who wouldn't tell you—if he were being honest—'I don't want an impartial jury. I want one that's going to find in my client's favor.' "[15] In the context of our adversary system, in which truth is expected to emerge from the rough-and-tumble battles of the courtroom, this attitude is understandable. In theory, if two zealous well-matched parties reject as jurors those who are unfavorably disposed, then as a result of their respective challenges, only those individuals who are relatively neutral and open-minded will survive the screening. So far so good. But take a look at any of the leading "How to" manuals of trial advocacy, and you will find that many lawyers approach the voir dire with ulterior motives.

Take, for example, Ann Fagan Ginger's popular book entitled *Jury Selection in Criminal Trials*.[16] In it she lists the following 12 purposes of the voir dire:

1. To move the jury as a group
2. To discover prejudice
3. To eliminate extreme positions
4. To discover "friendly" jurors
5. To exercise "educated" peremptories
6. To cause jurors to face their own prejudices
7. To teach jurors important facts in the case
8. To expose jurors to damaging facts in the case
9. To teach jurors the law of the case
10. To develop personal relationships between lawyer and juror
11. To expose opposing counsel
12. To prepare for summation

Nine of these have nothing to do with the legally sanctioned objectives of the examination (numbers 2, 3, and 5 are the legitimate exceptions). In fact, a good deal of this advice is designed not to detect bias but to *create* it. Few if any lawyers would deny the charge that they use the voir dire to educate, socialize, indoctrinate, and influence their prospective jurors before the trial formally begins. Some of them take the opportunity to establish a personal rapport with the panel. One way to do that is by using a ploy known as the grand gesture. As recommended by attorney Louis Nizer, the lawyer would get up and histrionically decline the opportunity to question any of the venirepersons, while emphasizing his or her faith in the jury to render a just verdict.[17] With the dramatic assertion that "I'll take the first 12 citizens who enter the courtroom," it is believed, the lawyer conveys an unwavering sense of confidence in his or her case and, at the same time, manages to flatter the jury for its fair mindedness. Not everyone agrees that "massaging" jurors through ingratiation works. In fact, it could easily backfire. Not only does it mean losing the opportunity to remove potentially biased venirepersons, but it could be interpreted by jurors as a sign of laziness or incompetence.[18]

Other more sophisticated strategies are used by the experienced practitioner.[19] One is to indoctrinate prospective jurors by asking loaded questions designed to covertly influence their way of thinking about the case. For example, consider the often-asked question: Do you agree that if you have a reasonable doubt, you have an obligation to acquit the defendant? Or the question: If you are to hear testimony from the witness stand but the fellow has long hair, would that fact affect your decision in the jury room?[20] Since the chances are slim that anyone would publicly disagree with the first statement or agree with the second, it is clear that neither is really intended as a means of detecting bias. Instead, they are used to inform jurors about the reasonable doubt standard, to put them on notice about a possible source of prejudice, and to elicit from them verbal commitments to take a particular course of action. Trial practice books are filled with advice of this sort on how to gain adversarial advantage during the voir dire. Some of this advice, appearing in law school textbooks, professional journals, and workshops, is quite psychologically minded. In one article, for example, lawyers are told how to communicate with prospective jurors through "transactional analysis," originally a form of psychotherapy developed by psychiatrist Eric Berne in his book, *Games People Play*.[21]

There is no way of knowing for sure the extent to which lawyers use the voir dire for purposes other than selection. But what little research there is suggests that such abuses are prevalent. In one study, Dale Broeder observed 23 voir dires and estimated that lawyers spent only 20 percent of their time trying to differentiate prejudiced and unprejudiced jurors. They spent the rest of their time commenting on points of law, forewarning the panel about weaknesses in their case, and generally ingratiating themselves with the jurors.[22] In a more systematic study, Robert Balch and his colleagues watched ten different voir dire sessions, and then conducted a sentence-by-sentence analysis of the transcripts.[23] These investigators were surprised by what they saw. Because the purpose of the voir dire is to encourage self disclosure and to elicit admissions of bias, they expected to find that lawyers ask open-ended questions and thus arrange for the venirepersons to do most of the talking. However, the transcripts revealed that only 41 percent of all statements during the voir dires were made by prospective jurors. Further analysis indicated the reason for this result. Most of the lawyers' questions were instructional, designed to convey rather than elicit information. In fact, fully 63 percent of their questions called for and received a one-word answer—yes or no. "Does the fact that this trial resulted in a hung jury before bother you?" "Can you resist the temptation of identifying with the defendant?" What is the ordinary person supposed to say? It is no wonder that out of over 2,000 questions, only twice did a prospective juror fail to give the desirable response. If this sample of observations is any indication, the voir dire is used, not only as a screening device but also as a means of achieving illegitimate ends.

The judiciary and the trial bar are currently eyeball-to-eyeball over whether the voir dire should be conducted by the judge or the lawyers. In the federal courts it is entirely within the judge's control. In the state courts the procedures vary. The issues on both sides are clear.[24] Lawyers argue that when the Supreme Court held in 1932 that "the guiding hand of counsel" should be present at every critical stage of a criminal trial, it essentially placed the voir dire squarely within their control.[25] Moreover, they argue that only they are familiar enough with their cases, skilled enough in the art of asking questions, and motivated enough by the demands of their role as advocates, to conduct an effective examination. The courts' arguments for judicial control of the voir dire are strictly pragmatic. Lawyers, left to their own devices, take too much time, ask intrusive questions, and abuse if not undermine the process by using it to present their cases. A Federal Judicial Center study documented the assertion that jury selection, on the average, takes longer in the hands of lawyers than judges. However, to date, nobody has evaluated the question of whether lawyers conduct the more effective voir dire.

The trial bar would have us assume that there is a simple tradeoff between length and effectiveness. If that were the case, we would reserve judgment on the issue pending systematic research on the latter question. But at this point one cannot help but be struck by the degree to which lawyers use the voir dire to subvert the impartial juror ideal. The most glaring instance of this abuse is offered by Los Angeles lawyer Stanley Jacobs.[26] Confronted with a venireperson who has already revealed hostility, Jacobs recommends that instead of striking that person immediately, the lawyer should exploit him or her as a vehicle for influencing the other panelists. Specifically, he suggests directing an essay in the form of leading questions uniquely designed to condition other prospective jurors who are within earshot. Ultimately, regardless of who actually conducts the examination, or how broad its scope, questions should be limited in form to those that elicit rather than convey trial-relevant information.

Trial Lawyers as Intuitive Psychologists

In contrast to indoctrination-like models of the voir dire, many attorneys take seriously their opportunity to *select* a favorable or impartial jury. When they do, it is reasonable to question whether they are successful at it, that is, how effective they are at sizing up prospective jurors. Before considering this issue, however, we need to know what insights or rules-of-thumb guide their use of peremptory challenges.

Head shapes, body language, and baseball

Rumor has it that during the 1950s New York City lawyers used to select their juries through baseball.[27] According to Bert Neuborne, legal director of the American Civil Liberties Union, attorneys needed only to ask one question: What baseball team do you root for? The defense then would proceed to reject Yankee fans, while the prosecution struck all Brooklyn Dodger fans. At a time when New York was a three-team city, that left a jury of people who rooted for the Giants, "the only reasonable people in town." As outrageous as this sounds, it is just one of the hundreds of strategies trial lawyers have been known to use.

In everyday life our impressions of others are based on *implicit personality theories*.[28] Briefly stated, an implicit personality theory is an organized network of preconceptions that people have about how certain attributes are related to each other and to overt behavior. People tend to assume, for example, that a person who is unpredictable is also dangerous or that a person who talks slowly is also slow-witted. Implicit personality theories thus enable us to make general predictions about others on the basis of limited information. Psychologists do not agree on how accurate these beliefs are. What we do know is that stereotypes are based on implicit personality theories consisting of the belief that all members of a distinguishable group share the same attributes. People even have theories about others on the basis of their physical appearance. In *Characterology: An Exact Science*, a book published in 1920, McCormick proposed that an individual's personality can be seen, literally, in his or her head shape, body type, coloring, and the like. The author concluded, for example, that small ears mean a poor memory while bushy eyebrows signal an inflexible mentality.

Under pressure to make immediate selection decisions and with only limited information available, trial lawyers frequently base their peremptory challenges on instinct. Sometimes their strategies are easy to articulate. Richard "Racehorse" Haynes, a successful Texas attorney, once defended two white Houston policemen charged with beating a black prisoner to death. Like all lawyers, Haynes had his ideas about the kind of juror he wanted for his clients. After the trial was over, he was quoted as saying, in general terms, "I knew we had the case won when we seated the last bigot on the jury."[29]

What stereotypes do lawyers hold about their prospective jurors? Trial practice handbooks offer a wealth of free advice, much of it written by attorneys of prominence. Clarence Darrow, for example, made the following suggestions:

I try to get a jury with little education but with much human emotion. The Irish are always the best jurymen for the defense. I don't want a Scotchman, for he has too little human feelings; I don't want a Scandinavian, for he has too strong a respect for law as law. In general, I don't want a religious person, for he believes in sin and punishment. The defense should avoid rich men who have

high regard for the law, as they make and use it. The smug and ultra-respect-
able think they are the guardians of society, and they believe the law is for
them.[30]

From other sources we learn that athletes lack sympathy for the fragile, injured plaintiff, that accountants and "engineering types" are insensitive to emotional factors, and that cabbies are good plaintiff jurors unless the injured party is a pedestrian.[31] We also learn that people with physical afflictions sympathize with the underdog and that old women who wear too much makeup, because they are unstable, are bad for the state.[32] Then, of course, there are nurses—"they may become too intolerant to pain and suffering even though when you question them about it they will indicate that they have great empathy for such people."[33]

Beyond these surface characteristics, there are rules of thumb about other more subtle behaviors observable during the voir dire. One attorney notes that "if you don't like a juror's face, chances are he doesn't like yours either."[34] Another maintains that the best technique is an analysis of handwriting, as it appears on the juror questionnaires. Thus, "if a person's handwriting is such that the stroke ending a word extends horizontally to a distinctive degree, then that is a powerful indication that the person is generous and giving. A good plaintiff's juror. If the terminal strokes are clipped short and the writing is pressed or couched together, that is a strong indication that the person is thrifty. A good defense juror in a personal injury case." [35] Others recommend keeping a close eye on a prospective juror's body language throughout the voir dire: "The juror whose response to a question is accompanied by hands hidden behind the back or in the pockets, or moved upward to cover the throat or mouth, who scratches, blinks, or swallows, and who repeatedly licks his lips, is uncomfortable with his answer, probably because it is not a true one."[36] Still others are attuned to the color of a juror's clothing, preferring gray for the prosecution and red for the defense.

In addition to their implicit theories of personality, some lawyers make assumptions about group structure and dynamics. They speculate over which jurors are likely to emerge as leaders, and which as followers, during deliberations. Who is likely to be voted foreperson? What cliques will form? How will the individuals interact? In *Trial Tactics and Methods*, Judge Robert Keeton noted that many lawyers maintain a simple "one-juror verdict" theory. That is, they assume that the final decision is usually determined by one strong-willed, verbal, and influential juror. Those who adopt this model of the jury process search during the voir dire for one juror who is likely to emerge not only as sympathetic but also as an active, dominant force. Having found that individual, the astute lawyer would then systematically challenge others of status who are likely to compete for the group's leadership. Referred to as the "alpha factor" (or the "authority quotient"), these key jurors are easily identified: "An individual's status and power within the jury group will mirror his status and power in the external world.''[37] As we will see in Chapter 8, research supports this popular notion.

Are lawyers' strategies effective?

What a body of intuitive psychology lawyers bring to bear in their craft! Many successful trial lawyers claim that their cases are won or lost at the voir dire. Is there any truth to that overtly cynical view of justice in a trial by jury? Some say yes, others no. On the affirmative side, a recent president of the Association of Trial Lawyers of America asserted that ''Trial attorneys are acutely attuned to the nuances of human behavior, which enables them to detect the minutest traces of bias or inability to reach an appropriate decision.''[38] Indeed after Joan Little was acquitted of the murder of her prison guard in 1975, her attorney boasted that he had ''bought'' the verdict with a large defense fund that was used, in part, to determine through research what kinds of jurors to select.

Do lawyers really enter the courtroom with the instinctive sensitivity of Geiger counters, equipped to detect even the ''minutest traces'' of bias? Clinical psychologists and psychiatrists used to make the same claim about their prognostic abilities—that is, until research clearly showed otherwise. Judge Learned Hand, in a psychologically minded appraisal of lawyers' jury selection potential, commented that:

> It is of course true that any examination on the voir dire is a clumsy and imperfect way of detecting suppressed emotional commitments to which all of us are to some extent subject, unconsciously or subconsciously. It is the nature of our deepest antipathies that often we do not admit them even to ourselves; but when that is so, nothing but an examination, utterly impracticable in a courtroom, will disclose them, an examination extending at times for months, and even then unsuccessful. No such examination is required. . . . If trial by jury is not to break down by its weight, it is not feasible to probe more than the upper levels of a juror's mind.[39]

Others have argued, more simply, that because jurors are often intimidated by high ceilings and the black robe, the courtroom is an environment that is more likely to conceal bias than to reveal it.[40]

Casting intuition aside, is there any empirical support, one way or another, for the effectiveness question? Earlier we described Dale Broeder's in-court study of 23 voir dires conducted in the midwest. From his own observations and interviews, Broeder concluded that the selection process was grossly ineffective.[41] He felt that attorneys did not ask the right questions and that jurors were often untruthful in their answers. But another study, focusing on lawyers' abilities to predict how jurors will react to a case, yielded a more favorable evaluation. For a simulated personal injury case, experienced civil-trial attorneys were asked to rank jurors according to the size of the award they would advocate during deliberations. Their rankings were then compared to the actual awards proposed by the jurors in question. Both plaintiff and defense lawyers were able to predict with some success the variations in awards.[42]

In the most innovative effort to address the effectiveness question, Hans Zeisel and Shari Diamond looked at how the venirepersons peremptorily challenged by lawyers *would have* voted. In 12 criminal cases in Chicago, these investigators arranged to have the challenged jurors watch their respective trials from the spectator section of the courtroom and then vote as if they were on the jury.[43] In this way they were able to compare the verdicts of *actual* juries, composed of only those individuals who had survived the voir dire, with those of *hypothetical* reconstructed juries, consisting of the first 12 venirepersons (thus including both real and challenged jurors). As it turned out, the lawyers' selections had no effect on the outcomes of seven trials and only a marginal effect in two trials. In three instances, however, the differences between actual and hypothetical juries were substantial enough to suggest that the voir dire might have affected the final verdict. Whether these results mean that lawyers are generally effective or ineffective probably depends on who you ask.[44] But one result appeared without ambiguity. After calculating for each lawyer an "attorney performance index," Zeisel and Diamond found that there was a considerable amount of variability in performance between the different lawyers. This fact is consistent with a survey of 420 federal judges, 80 percent of whom agreed that "There are great differences among lawyers in this skill. Some are very talented in the selection of jurors, and some are not."[45]

We opened this section by saying that in order for the voir dire to produce an impartial jury, lawyers would have to *try* to use that opportunity for selection purposes and *know* how to make those selections. The evidence suggests that neither of these conditions is satisfied. In fact, for two reasons the situation is worse than that. First, the voir dire is so often exploited as a means of influencing the jury before trial that one must question whether its ultimate contribution is to create bias rather than reduce it. It is often said that attorneys overestimate their capacity to win a case at the voir dire. Perhaps not. Perhaps they do have the impact they boast about, but because of their ability to exert influence, not the removal of biased jurors. Second, the theory behind voir dire is that when two well-matched parties eliminate as jurors those who are unfavorably disposed, then out of that process emerges a panel of conscientious and neutral citizens. It now appears that this assumption is, in psychologist Gordon Bermant's words, an "adversarial myth."[46] The two sides of a dispute are frequently not well matched in their selection skills. As such, the final jury is probably more skewed in a particular direction than was the full panel that preceded the voir dire. What, if anything, can be done to reroute the process of voir dire toward its pursuit of the impartial juror ideal? Before addressing this problem, let us take a look at an important and controversial development—the use of psychologists and other social scientists as expert consultants in the selection of juries.

PLAYING THE ODDS: THE SCIENCE OF JURY SELECTION

Successful investors, baseball managers, and gamblers play the odds whenever they can. Whether that involves charting economic trends, selecting players based on their "stats," or counting cards in a blackjack game, it is understood that these methods are an improvement over intuition. So why not trial lawyers?

Recent years have seen a movement toward transforming the "art" of jury selection into a science. It all began in the tense and politically charged atmosphere of the Vietnam era. In 1971, Father Philip Berrigan and seven other antiwar protestors were arrested and charged by the federal government with conspiracy. They were accused of plotting to destroy selective service records, kidnap Henry Kissinger, and blow up underground heating tunnels in Washington, D.C. The trial was to be held in Harrisburg, Pennsylvania, then a politically conservative town. The assigned judge was a Nixon appointee. Jay Schulman, a sociologist active in the antiwar movement, was deeply concerned about the defendants' ability to receive a fair trial. He recruited a group of social scientists and offered their services as consultants for the defense.[47]

As a first step, Schulman and his colleagues, with the aid of 10 graduate students and several other volunteers, conducted a survey of the Harrisburg area. They sampled 840 local residents over the phone and interviewed 252 of them in person. From the interviews they obtained information about demographic characteristics, backgrounds, knowledge of the impending case, and attitudes on potentially relevant topics such as trust in government and tolerance for dissent. Further assisted by computer technology, they then looked for statistically significant correlations between the various background attributes and favorable or unfavorable attitudes. Several unexpected relationships were revealed. For example, those who were more educated and those who had greater exposure to the news were unexpectedly more conservative and favorable toward the government. In the end these investigators came up with a profile of their ideal juror: "a female Democrat with no religious preference and a white-collar job or a skilled blue-collar job."[48] Guided by this survey and supplemented with in-court observations and the reports of community spies, the defense team selected its jury. The rest is history. Against all odds, with the government having spent an estimated $2 million on the case, the trial concluded in a hung jury, split 10–2 in favor of acquittal. Referred to as the Harrisburg Seven, this case marks the birth of an industry—scientific jury selection.

Today the nation is littered with so-called jury experts who claim an ability to select favorable juries through scientific techniques. After winning the Harrisburg case, Schulman and his colleagues assisted the defense in a host of other political dissent cases. Then in 1975 they founded the National Jury Project, an organization with offices in several cities. Others psychologists, sociologists, and marketing researchers did the same. It is almost unusual now to come across an important case, criminal or civil, in which the jury is selected *without* the help of an expert. Indeed, it is perhaps a sign of the times that the ideological motivations that gave rise to Schulman's initial efforts have since given way to the dollar. Jay Schulman, who spent so much time assisting the political activists of the antiwar movement, in 1984 worked *for* General Westmoreland in his unsuccessful suit against CBS. When asked about it, he said, simply, "I had begun to believe that jury work was not a political thing; it was something you did to earn a living."[49]

Scientific jury selection is a controversial enterprise. And well it should be. What is it, is it ethical, and is it effective? This trilogy of questions has been raised by academics, lawyers, judges, the media, and the ultimate consumers of the service—the public.

Distinguishing Science and Pseudo-Science

In theory the point of scientific jury selection is to extend beyond stereotypes toward the construction of case-specific profiles. Before describing what this science is, let us first describe what it is *not*. To begin with, it is not the use of "hypnoanalytic" methods of assessing prospective jurors' unconscious motives through their courtroom behavior. No serious psychoanalyst or assessment specialist would ever claim an ability to render this kind of instant diagnosis. And it is not the study of facial characteristics. In the 1978 murder trial of boxer Ron Lyle, a so-called jury expert made selection recommendations to the defense attorney based on people's eyes. Explaining his strategy, this consultant noted "I could tell by that juror's eyes he was no good; squinty, close-set eyes are bigot's eyes. What I was looking for were sensitive, open minded, analytical people. In other words, people with fine hair, wide-set eyes and a lack of eyelid."[50] That is not science, it is science fiction. Years of research has shown that physiognomic cues such as these are strictly in the eye of the beholder. And it is not the measurement of pupil dilation, despite one consultant's claim that "the expansion of the pupil indicates acceptance; constriction shows negative feelings."[51] Psychological experiments have repeatedly failed to support claims of a relationship between pupillary responses and specific attitudes toward a stimulus.

There are even aspects of the approach used in the Harrisburg Seven case that are not scientific. As part of their overall effort, Schulman and his colleagues had the lawyers rate prospective jurors in court on a five-point scale. There is nothing empirically grounded about that technique. It is simply a means of converting a collection of lawyers' instincts into quantitative terms. The same is true when social scientists rate the prospective jurors for signs of authoritarianism or any other characteristic based on their voir dire behavior. As far as we know, for example, nobody has ever demonstrated through controlled comparisons that jurors who respond with deference to the trial judge exhibit the more prejudicial attributes of an authoritarian personality. It also is not clear whether the clinical insights of a psychologist in court are any better than those of an experienced trial lawyer. In fact, they may be worse. Schulman and his colleagues also took the opportunity to gather information about the panelists from other well-networked members of the community. Doing background checks on prospective jurors is of questionable ethics. Not only does it invade their privacy, but it carries the potential for making them feel harassed and threatened. Attorney William Kunstler was alerted to these dangers in a murder trial, where one juror got up during the voir dire and said, "I don't like my boss and my minister being called up and asked questions about me."[52] Besides, there is nothing particularly novel about this practice. On an informal basis, lawyers for the government have been using informants for years.

When we talk about the science of jury selection, we are referring to the use of out-of-court research that is specific to a particular trial, at a particular time, and in a particular jurisdiction. By surveying a random sample of those eligible for jury duty (not the venirepersons themselves) and ascertaining information about their backgrounds and attitudes, an expert can produce a matrix of correlations that link observable characteristics on the one hand, with decision-making predispositions on the other. Thus, when jurors disclose their religion, occupation, marital status, or even what newspapers they read, the well-researched lawyer, unlike his or her naive opponent, can use that information to estimate the odds that they would vote in a particular way. It is a strictly actuarial matter guided by the theory that although many important facts about an individual cannot be measured directly, they can be inferred from other readily accessible facts.

Consider the following examples. In 1978, Larry Flynt, the publisher of *Hustler* magazine, was tried in Georgia for the violation of obscenity laws. It obviously does not take an expert with computer printouts in hand to know that deeply religious people would be prejudiced against the defense. But there are other factors, not knowable through common sense, that also predicted such tendencies. Herold Price Fahringer, Flynt's attorney in this case, hired jury-selection consultants who, with the help of a survey, found "that it would be very bad for us to use a woman who was married to a salesman. It turns out there's a high ratio of infidelity in these marriages, and a lot of these women attribute their marital troubles to magazines like the one we were defending."[53]

Then there was the 1980 case in which the Ford Motor Company was tried on criminal charges of reckless homicide for the deaths of three young women who were passengers in a Ford Pinto that had burst into flames in a rear-end collision. Ford was accused of being careless in the design of its car and for failing to warn consumers of the potential dangers. An unfavorable verdict would have instigated dozens of civil suits totaling millions of dollars by Pinto crash victims. It would also have been the first time ever that a corporation was held *criminally* responsible for the harm caused by a defective product.

Eager to leave no stone unturned, Ford hired Hans Zeisel to help in the selection of a jury. A staunch empiricist, Zeisel conducted a survey of areas surrounding the trial site in rural Indiana. As in the Harrisburg Seven case, he surveyed respondents about their demographics and about attitudes relevant to the case. From this information, Zeisel was able to construct a profile of the best and worst possible jurors. Although we can never know for sure, Zeisel's efforts appeared to have worked like a charm. Prevailing wisdom had it that men would favor the defendant, especially men who were old enough to "remember the Ford Motor Company put American industry on the map." Conversely, it was believed that women would be unfavorable, especially if, like the victims, they were young. But an exception to this rule was discovered by Zeisel and so known only to Ford's attorneys: women who drove trucks tended to think like men and were, therefore, good jurors for Ford.

This secret information paid off. During the voir dire, a 31-year-old woman disclosed under questioning that she and her husband owned a small trucking business and that she personally drove 40-foot 18-wheel trucks called semi's. Should she be rejected? Knowing only that women tended to favor the state, the prosecuting attorneys must have been surprised when Ford neglected to challenge her, but it proved to be a smart decision. By singlehandedly persuading a male holdout juror to vote with the majority, she emerged as an instrumental figure in the jury's not guilty verdict.[54]

Tipping the Scales of Justice?

Is scientific jury selection, as we have defined it, effective? Does it uncover hidden clues about prospective jurors and increase a party's chances of winning? Trial lawyers disagree on the matter. F. Lee Bailey believes that the generalities offered by demographic data are not that helpful because they lack the richness of more detailed information about individuals. As he put it, "If I had my druthers, I'd pick a jury not by means of social science research, but by living with them for thirty days."[55] In contrast, Alan Dershowitz, a Harvard law professor and trial lawyer, places little faith in attorneys' clinical instincts: "I myself, even when I trust my instincts, like to have them scientifically confirmed."[56]

Anecdotes and individual case histories can be misleading one way or another. The success rate in highly publicized cases, most notably the political conspiracy cases of the early 1970s, is impressive. But are these cases the rule or the exception? Because it is impossible to know how often jury-selection experts are consulted outside the public spotlight and, then, how often they lose, we really have no means of calculating their true winning percentage. Besides, even if we could, there would remain the lingering question of how much, if at all, the jury selection techniques per se contributed to that success. Maybe the trial outcomes would have been the same without intervention. It is possible, for example, that those lawyers who hire the so-called experts are, in many other respects, more thorough in their preparation and more zealous as advocates, than their opponents.

Just as anecdotes cannot affirm the effectiveness of scientific selection methods, neither can they affirm their ineffectiveness. For example, take author Joe McGinniss's *Fatal Vision* case in which Jeffrey MacDonald, a Green Beret doctor, was accused of brutally murdering his wife and two young daughters in their North Carolina home.[57] MacDonald's lawyer hired a local psychology professor to come up with a demographic profile of the favorable juror. More than 900 local residents were randomly sampled and interviewed over the phone. They were asked about their backgrounds and about attitudes thought to be relevant to the impending case (e.g., whether they believed that people in military service were more likely to commit violent crimes than civilians, and whether they felt doctors made too much money). After analyzing the data, the expert concluded that an ideal jury would consist mainly of conservative, religious whites over the age of 35—in most cases, just the kind of jury sought by the prosecution! With an uneasy feeling in the pit of his stomach, MacDonald shook his head and said, "I hope you're as good as your reputation, because everything you're saying goes against my gut feeling. . . . Frankly, this scares the hell out of me."[58]

After three days of voir dire, the final jury closely matched the sought-after profile. Among the seven men and five women were two accountants, a former Green Beret sergeant, a former state policeman, and a chemist. At one point during the selection process MacDonald said, "Every time Bernie [his lawyer] stands up to accept one of them, I feel another nail being hammered into my coffin."[59] He was right. When all the talk was over, this "ideal" jury convicted him of first degree murder. Some critics cite this case as proof of the ineffectiveness of scientific jury selection. That is an overstatement for two reasons. First, like everything else survey research can vary in quality. In the MacDonald case it seems likely that the attitudes measured (e.g., whether doctors are overpaid) might not have been the most relevant. Second, anyone who has read *Fatal Vision* can appreciate how persuasive the evidence was against the defendant. At least in this case one need not point a finger at the jury to explain its verdict.

To date, there has been little in the way of evaluating the actual effectiveness of scientific, compared to intuitive, jury selection. So long as lawyers rely on stereotypes and guesswork, a more systematic and case-specific approach is bound to improve the quality of their selection decisions.[60] But we see two very important limitations to this enterprise.

First, controlled studies of individual juror bias, as reviewed earlier, suggest that the vast majority of verdicts are determined by the evidence, not by who sits in the jury box. Although there are the notable exceptions, it is entirely possible that in most ordinary, run-of-the-mill trials, those that do not awaken deep seated values, jury verdicts are more readily predictable from the strength of the evidence than from the characteristics of individual jurors. In short, contrary to the worst of fears, scientific selection procedures cannot reliably tip the scales of justice.

Second, even in those cases where individual juror bias is a factor, surveys are based on a psychological assumption of questionable value. Think for a moment about the logic. The jury expert looks for correlations between background information that is readily available, and attitudes that are not accessible but thought to be predictive of verdicts. In other words, the model assumes, generally speaking, that since A (demographics) predicts B (attitudes) which, in turn, predicts C (verdicts), then A must predict C. The logic is sound, as is the statistically derived relationship between A and B. But what about the untested assumption that there is a link between B and C, that is, between attitudes and verdicts? Without having established this pivotal link in the chain, surveys could prove dangerously misleading. Let us return, for an example, to the *Fatal Vision* case. Having found that conservative men (A) are unlikely to exhibit a prejudice toward the military (B), MacDonald's lawyer selected for the former on the assumption that favorable attitudes toward the military would correlate with a predisposition to acquit MacDonald. Was that assumption warranted? Not scientifically. It was based, apparently, on the intuitive notion that jurors would react primarily to MacDonald's uniform. In this instance, and likely in many others as well, the survey method of jury selection is only quasi scientific in nature.

There does exist the potential for a powerful, fully empirical approach in which the direct relationship between A and C can be statistically established without having to guess about the intervening link between B and C. Described elsewhere by the first author, it involves the use of mock jury trials. By recruiting subjects to watch or read about a miniversion of the impending case, the expert can measure how people from different walks of life actually vote when confronted with the details of the trial itself. To the extent that a mock trial resembles the real event, the predictive value of its findings can be substantial.[61]

NOTES

1. When an all-white, all-male jury acquitted four white police officers of the murder of a black insurance salesman in Miami, black neighborhoods erupted for several days in the worst riots that city had seen; see M. Gillespie (1980), What the Miami race riots mean to all of us. *Ms.*, April, p. 87. Also, consider Broeder's statement that "the case against the criminal jury as a protector of individual liberty extends further than to contests between government and citizens opposed to its policies. Minority groups have often suffered at the hands of jurymen. Wholesale acquittals of lynch-law violators, convictions of Negroes on the slightest evidence, and numerous other occurrences which have now almost become a part of the jury tradition might be instanced as examples"; see D. W. Broeder (1947), The functions of the jury—facts or fictions? *University of Chicago Law Review*, Vol. 21, p. 414.

2. In that study, mock jurors who had recently read a *Reader's Digest* story about the mistaken identification of an innocent man were more reluctant in their own cases to vote for a criminal conviction on the basis of eyewitness testimony; see E. Greene & E. F. Loftus (1984), What's new in the news?: The influence of well-publicized news events on psychological research and courtroom trials. *Basic and Applied Social Psychology*, Vol. 5, pp. 211–221.

3. See D. Gillmore & J. Barron (1974), *Mass Communication Law: Cases and Comment*, pp. 403–404.

4. *Sheppard v. Maxwell* (1966), 384 U.S. 333, at p. 356.

5. For an interesting description of the entire case, see F. Lee Bailey (1971), *The Defense Never Rests*. New York: Signet Books.

6. For an historical review of the case law surrounding the free press—fair trial controversy, see B. C. Schmidt (1977), Nebraska Press Association: An expansion of freedom and contraction of theory. *Stanford Law Review*, Vol. 29, pp. 431–476.

7. American Bar Association (1968), *Project on Standards for Criminal Justice, Standards Relating to Fair Trial and Free Press*. Chicago: American Bar Association.

8. See, for example, M. J. Shields (1981), The Atlanta story. *Columbia Journalism Review*, Vol. 20, pp. 29–35.

9. E. Constantini & J. King (1980/81), The partial juror: Correlates and causes of prejudgment. *Law and Society Review*, Vol. 15, pp. 9–40.

10. J. S. Carroll, N. L. Kerr, J. J. Alfini, F. M. Weaver, R. J. MacCoun, & V. Feldman (1986), Free press and fair trial: The role of behavioral research. *Law and Human Behavior*, Vol. 10, pp. 187–201.

11. A. Padawer-Singer & A. H. Barton (1975), Free press, fair trial. In R. Simon's (Ed.), *The Jury System: A Critical Analysis*. Beverly Hills: Sage Publications.

12. For a review of the empirical literature, see Carroll et al. (1986), supra note 10.

13. See D. M. Wegner, R. Wenzlaff, R. M. Kerker, & A. E. Beattie (1981), Incrimination through innuendo: Can media questions become public answers? *Journal of Personality and Social Psychology*, Vol. 40, pp. 822–832.

14. J. Riley (1984), Voir dire debate escalates over lawyers' participation. *The National Law Journal*, December 24, p. 1.

15. Quoted in M. Hunt (1982), Putting juries on the couch. *New York Times Magazine*, November 28, pp. 70–88.

16. Published in 1977 by LawPress in Tiburon, California.

17. See L. Nizer (1958), The art of the jury trial. In S. Gazan (Ed.), *Trial Tactics and Experiences*.

18. See, for example, M. Belli (1954), *Modern Trials*.

19. For an excellent review, see R. A. Blunk & B. D. Sales (1977), Persuasion during the voir dire. In B. Sales (Ed.), *Psychology in the Legal Process*. New York: Spectrum.

20. These voir dire questions were observed and reported by R. W. Balch, C. T. Griffiths, E. L. Hall, & L. T. Winfree (1976), The socialization of jurors: The voir dire as a rite of passage. *Journal of Criminal Justice*, Vol. 4, pp. 271–283.

21. See A. W. Estes (1976), *Jury selection: How principles of modern psychology can help you get the jury you want*. Paper presented at the annual meeting of the American Trial Lawyers Association, Atlanta, Georgia.

22. D. Broeder (1965), Voir dire examinations: An empirical study. *Southern California Law Review*, Vol. 38, pp. 503–528.

23. Supra note 20.

24. For an excellent, though not impartial review, see G. Bermant (1985), Conducting the voir dire examination. In S. Kassin & L. Wrightsman (Eds.), *The Psychology of Evidence and Trial Procedure*. Beverly Hills: Sage; Also see A. J. Stanley & R. C. Begam (1977), Who should conduct the voir dire? The judge vs. the attorneys. *Judicature*, Vol. 61, pp. 70–78.

25. *Powell v. Alabama*, 287 U.S. 45.

26. S. K. Jacobs (1983), Jury selection tips. *California Trial Lawyers Association Forum*, December issue, pp. 344–355.

27. This anecdote is reported in P. DiPerna's (1984) book, *Juries on Trial*. New York: Dembner Books.

28. See J. S. Bruner & R. Tagiuri (1954), The perception of people. In G. Lindzey (Ed.), *Handbook of Social Psychology*, Volume 2. Reading, MA: Addison-Wesley.

29. D. A. Phillips (1979), *The Great Texas Murder Trials*. New York: MacMillan, p. 77.

30. Quoted in E. H. Sutherland, & D. R. Cressey (1966), *Principles of Criminology* (7th ed.). Philadelphia: Lippincott.

31. See M. Blinder (1978), Picking juries. *Trial Diplomacy Journal*, Spring issue, pp. 8–13.

32. J. Sparling (1973), Jury selection in a criminal case. Reprinted in the *Texas Observer*, May 11.

33. See S. K. Jacobs, supra note 26.

34. S. Wishman (1986), *Anatomy of a Jury: The System on Trial*. New York: Times Books, pp. 72–73.

35. J. L. Sumpter (1979), Jury selection for the trial attorney. *ATLA Bar News*, March/April issue, pp. 6–7.

36. See Blinder, supra note 31, pp. 12–13.

37. R. Christie (1976), Probability v. precedence: The social psychology of jury selection. In G. Bermant, C. Nemeth, & N. Vidmar (Eds.), *Psychology and the Law*. Lexington, MA: D.C. Heath, p. 270.

38. R. Begam (1977). Voir dire: The attorney's job. *Trial*, Vol. 13, p. 3.

39. *United States v. Dennis* (1950), 183 F.2d 201, p. 221.

40. D. E. Vinson (1985), The biased juror. *The Brief*, Vol. 14, No. 2, pp. 22–29.

41. Supra note 22, p. 505.

42. F. Strodtbeck, reported in H. Zeisel and S. S. Diamond (1976), The jury selection in the Mitchell-Stans conspiracy trial. *American Bar Foundation Research Journal*, pp. 151–174.

43. H. Zeisel & S. Diamond (1978), The effect of peremptory challenges on jury and verdict: An experiment in a federal district court. *Stanford Law Review*, Vol. 30, pp. 491–531.

44. For an excellent critique of this study, see G. Bermant & J. Shapard (1981), Voir dire, juror challenges, and adversary advocacy. In B. Sales (Ed.), *The Trial Process*. New York: Plenum.

45. G. Bermant (1977), *Conduct of the voir dire examination: Practices and opinions of federal district judges*. Washington, D.C.: Federal Judicial Center.

46. Supra note 45.

47. For an extensive first-hand account of jury selection in the Harrisburg Seven trial, see J. Schulman, P. Shaver, R. Colman, B. Emrich, & R. Christie (1973), Recipe for a jury. *Psychology Today*, May, pp. 37–44, 77–84.

48. Supra note 47, p. 40.

49. Quoted in E. Hopkins (1985), Picking the right jury. *Newsday*, pp. 13–16.

50. See Hopkins, supra note 49.

51. Ibid.

52. Ibid.

53. Ibid.

54. See N. Totenberg (1982), The jury pickers. *Parade*, May 9, p. 12.

55. Quoted in Hunt, supra note 15, p. 83.

56. Ibid., p. 83.

57. J. McGinniss (1983), *Fatal Vision*. NY: Signet.

58. Ibid., p. 477.

59. Ibid., p. 488.

60. In an interesting but limited study, Irwin Horowitz trained law students in either the "art" or "science" of jury selection. One group was trained in the conventional, intuitive method and the other in the use of survey data. Students were then assigned to observe a voir dire in one of four mock trials and to then predict how each juror would vote after the evidence was presented. As it turned out, science outpredicted intuition in two cases, was as ineffective in a third case, and actually did more poorly in a fourth; see I. A. Horowitz (1980), Juror selection: A comparison of two methods in several criminal cases. *Journal of Applied Social Psychology*, Vol. 10, pp. 86–99.

61. See S. M. Kassin (1984), Mock jury trials. *Trial Diplomacy Journal*, Summer, pp. 26–30.

4

MAKING SENSE OF THE EVIDENCE

By law, juries are supposed to base their decisions only on the sworn testimony of witnesses, exhibits, facts agreed to by the opposing attorneys, and matters of common knowledge that are noted by the judge. To ensure that juries comply with this ideal, the legal system has developed over the years an elaborate set of rules designed to regulate the traffic of information in the courtroom. These rules determine who can testify as ordinary or expert witnesses, what they can say, what kinds of questions the lawyers can ask, and how they must phrase them. One legal scholar described the rituals of trial procedure as "the most careful attempt to control the processes of communication to be found outside a laboratory."[1]

In the ideal, juries are expected to accomplish two distinct feats. First, they have to appraise the quality of the evidence itself, to determine if witnesses are credible and if their testimony can be believed. Along the same lines, juries are called upon daily to evaluate questionable eyewitness identifications, confessions, polygraph results, business records, statistical data, blood tests, character testimony, medical records, certain types of hearsay, and so on. Although the courtroom acts as a filter, the proof of life is the proof of law.

The second prong of the ideal, to be addressed in the next chapter, is that the jury set aside and disregard all information that is not formally admitted into evidence. This includes lawyers' opening statements, closing arguments, the questions they ask, and all facts ruled inadmissible by the presiding judge. When you think about it, only a fraction of what juries do see and hear in the courtroom consists of evidence in a technical sense. As one can imagine, it takes quite a bit of vigilance for jurors to keep track of the distinction between admissible evidence and everything else. It takes even more vigilance for them to guard against being influenced by these latter, sometimes subtle sources of information. This is obviously not an easy task. And nobody expects juries to make these distinctions flawlessly. The real question, as we will see, is whether there are certain types of nonevidentiary influences that so consistently intrude on the decision-making process as to threaten the ideal of a verdict driven by the evidence.

THE JURY AS A HUMAN LIE DETECTOR

On July 12, 1979, Gary Dotson was sentenced to serve 25 to 50 years in prison after a jury had convicted him for the rape of a 16-year-old girl. Except for a few friends and relatives, nobody really noticed. Six years later, on March 21, 1985, the victim, Cathleen Crowell Webb, announced that her story of abduction and rape was a lie. She said she never knew Dotson, there had been no abduction, and there had been no rape. The torn clothes, the bruises, and the cuts were all self-inflicted. She panicked, she claims, out of fear that she was pregnant. Who are we to believe—Cathy Webb, the frightened teenager who single-handedly persuaded a jury to convict Dotson, or Cathy Webb, the contrite young woman who recanted the whole story 6 years later? The jury obviously believed her when she testified at Dotson's trial. Were they wrong? Could they have been so misled?

Judge Richard Samuels, who presided over Dotson's trial, does not think so. When Cathy Webb's recantation was first broadcast on television, he believed it, so he expedited the case, scheduled a hearing to vacate the conviction, and set a bond low enough to allow Dotson out on bail. But after seeing the "new" Cathy Webb under cross examination, and after hearing other witnesses retestify, Judge Samuels changed his mind. Referring to her recantation testimony as "combative and prone to selective memory," he explained that "I had a chance to hear her then and to hear her now. Demeanor is one of the factors that determines credibility. In 1979, at the trial, she was forthright, not a bit of evasiveness. Very candid. Her demeanor was that of a person actually telling a true story—and she was unshaken on rigorous cross examination. In April [1985] she was evasive throughout."[2] Based on these impressions and conflicts between Webb's testimony and the physical evidence, Judge Samuels reasserted his agreement with the jury, ruled against vindication, revoked Dotson's bond, and ordered him back to jail. In the end, Illinois Governor James Thompson agreed with the jury too, but "under the circumstances" he granted Dotson clemency.

This case is highly unusual, but it raises a fundamental question about how well juries perform in their role as a human lie detector. Most trials—criminal and civil—are, quite literally, tests of credibility. Confronted with two sides and inevitably conflicting testimony, jurors must accept what some witnesses say and reject others. According to Kalven and Zeisel, judges and juries tend to agree in their credibility judgments. But "A moment's introspection is sufficient to remind us how mysterious must be this process whereby we believe one person, suspect a second, and disbelieve a third."[3] Is it that mysterious? What cues lead people to make these decisions? It is often said that we can see through what others say by *how* they say it. Judges thus instruct juries to pay close attention to the *demeanor* of witnesses as they testify. As you would imagine, there is no way to assess how real juries actually perform at this aspect of their decision-making task. But there is an extensive body of research in psychology that addresses these kinds of issues.

It would be easy for the jury if witnesses were like Pinocchio, equipped with an observable, autonomic response to deception. They are not, of course. So judging the credibility of witnesses is often a matter of logic and common sense. In response to a series of specific questions, witnesses essentially tell a story. Jurors listen to that story and evaluate it according to five implicit standards. The first is *character*. Based on what they learn of the witness's background, jurors determine whether he or she is the kind of person who could be trusted, whether, for example, he or she has a reputation, in general, for honesty or dishonesty. We know from research on social influence that a communication is only as persuasive as its communicator. The second is the *ulterior motive* standard. Whenever an individual takes the time to appear on the witness stand, jurors naturally wonder what motivates his or her testimony. Whether the witness is a friend or enemy of one of the litigants, or stands to gain financially from a particular verdict, or is driven by prejudice are thus relevant considerations. Jurors cannot help but question the purity of a witness's motives and be generally wary when these motives appear self serving. Third, there is the standard of *plausibility*. The story itself should make sense. The event described by the witness should be physically and psychologically possible. As they do in other areas of life, jurors make these kinds of judgments on the basis of what they know from personal experience and culturally transmitted knowledge. Fourth, there is the question of *consistency*. Because trials contain more than one witness, an individual's testimony can be compared to other evidence, including what others have said about the same event. Obviously, if three out of four eyewitnesses to a crime fail to identify the defendant, the fourth's identification would be viewed with reasonable suspicion. Fifth, because witnesses are cross examined in an adversarial context, the *internal coherence* of their story is tested as well. The witness whose testimony is full of holes, who says different things at different times, or who changes his or her scenario in response to probing cross-examination questions, is unlikely to inspire much confidence in the jury.

Who witnesses are and what they say and the content and context of their testimony provide potentially the most valuable clues as to their credibility. Jurors may not articulate it in these terms, but character, ulterior motive, plausibility, consistency, and internal coherence are their standards of measurement. Indeed, psychological research has shown that people weigh these kinds of verbal cues heavily in their perceptions of truth and deception.[4] But there is more. If words alone were enough, then the courts might as well spare the expense of a live trial and have jurors make their decisions by reading a transcript of the proceedings. That suggestion, of course, would never and should never be implemented. The reason is that the courts realize that the judge and jury need to observe the demeanor of witnesses as they testify. John Henry Wigmore, one of the great scholars of legal evidence, stated flatly his belief that a witness's nonverbal behavior is often "a complete antidote to what he testifies."[5] What is one to conclude, after all, when two conflicting, similarly motivated witnesses tell equally plausible and coherent stories? Jurors are confronted with that dilemma all the time, as when the plaintiff and defendant paint different pictures of their automobile accident, or as when an accused rapist and his alleged victim disagree over whether she had consented to having sex. In these instances, what the witnesses say may be important, but they may not be enough. So how do jurors resolve the discrepancy? For better and for worse, they turn to the hidden language of nonverbal behavior.

Vocal Cues, Facial Expressions, and Body Language

Through the ages, men and women have always sought a means of knowing when others could be taken at their word. One document dating back to 900 B.C. provides early clues to the behavior of a person who is lying: "He does not answer questions, or gives evasive answers; he speaks nonsense, rubs the great toe along the ground, and shivers; he rubs the roots of his hair with his fingers." Turning to more obtrusive methods, the Bedouins of Arabia used to require that conflicting witnesses lick a hot iron—the one whose tongue burned was thought to be lying. Similarly, the Chinese used to force crime suspects to chew rice powder and then spit it out—if the powder was dry, the suspect was guilty.[6] Then there were Freud and his followers. As psychotherapists, they believed that the truth was revealed in dreams, word associations, slips of the tongue, and other difficult-to-control behaviors.

All these methods are based on the assumption that lying arouses a state of anxiety that, in turn, alters an individual's physiological and overt behavior in ways that cannot be faked or controlled. The hot iron and the sticky rice tests thus have in common the idea that the stress of lying causes a measurable dryness of the mouth. Today, of course, there is the *polygraph*—a mechanical instrument that records changes in respiration, perspiration, heart rate, and blood pressure. Better known as the lie detector test, it provides a more precise, multichannel means of observing physiological reactions that otherwise could not be seen with the naked eye.[7] Fidgeting, stammering, and slips of the tongue have in common Charles Darwin's observation that there are certain behavioral expressions of emotion that are not easily concealed or disguised.[8] Thus, regardless of what people say, they will inadvertently betray their true feelings by observable aspects of *how* they say it. In recent years psychologists have addressed two related questions. Are there behavioral cues that reliably signal truth and deception and, if there are, how adept are people at using these cues to make accurate assessments of credibility?

In 1969, psychologists Paul Ekman and Wallace Friesen proposed that when people lie, their anxiety "leaks out" in their demeanor. They suggested, in fact, that there is a *leakage hierarchy*: that some nonverbal behaviors are less controllable and, hence, more informative than others. According to Ekman and Friesen, the body is more revealing than the face. The reason is that people tend to monitor and control their own facial expressions but not their own bodily gestures, restless movements, and so on.[9] To test this hypothesis, Ekman and Friesen had 21 student nurses either tell the truth or lie about their feelings while viewing a series of brief films.[10] Some of the films showed disfigured burn victims; others depicted pleasant landscape scenes. While watching, the nurses were interviewed by someone who could not see the films. The nurses were instructed either to report honestly their impressions of the material or to conceal their true feelings from the interviewer. Suppose you were able to observe these sessions. How well do you think *you* could tell when the subject was being truthful or deceptive? Ekman and Friesen asked this very question. Through the use of hidden cameras, they videotaped the nurses as they watched the films and answered the interviewer's questions. They then showed the tapes to groups of observers and asked them to determine, for each one, whether the nurse was being honest or deceptive. But there was a hitch—some observers saw videotapes that showed only the nurses' faces as they spoke, while others saw tapes focused on their bodies, hands, and feet. The results were as predicted by the leakage hierarchy. Observers who watched the subjects' bodies were better as lie detectors than those who watched only their faces.

This research was just the beginning. Since then, social psychologists Robert Rosenthal, Miron Zuckerman, and Bella DePaulo, among others, have become interested in other aspects of truth and deception. From over 50 studies, we now know quite a bit about the subject.[11] To begin with, we know that lie detection is more difficult than most people think. Following Ekman and Friesen's research model, experiments have one group of subjects, or "witnesses," tell the truth or lie in response to a series of questions; a second group of subjects, or "jurors," then observe these interactions and make judgments about the witnesses' credibility. Observers make their judgments on the basis of transcripts, audiotapes, videotapes of the face or body, or some combination of these media. Overall, people are only moderately proficient at distinguishing truthful and deceptive communications. The problem seems to be that when people are left to their own devices, they focus on a speaker's face, a relatively uninformative cue. When people speak they are not only conscious of their own facial expressions but they are also often able to modify, suppress, and exaggerate them on command.[12]

Instead of concentrating on the face, we should pay attention to body language and paralinguistic cues. Ekman and Friesen's original finding that the body is more revealing than the face has been replicated several times.[13] Research has also shown that the raw *tone* of a speaker's voice, independent of what he or she actually says, leaks valuable information. When people lie, especially when they are highly motivated to conceal something, they hesitate more in their speech and the level of pitch in their voice rises.[14] Thus, when subjects listen to audiotapes, even when the speaker's words are filtered out of the sound track, they become relatively accurate judges of truth and deception. Apparently, our ears are better lie detectors than our eyes. The problem, as we said, is that people do not realize it. On our own, we are more sensitive to changes in facial expression than anything else. And that interferes with their ability to pick up on the more reliable cues.

The courts encourage jurors to pay close attention to witnesses' demeanor. The term "demeanor" very generally refers to an individual's manner or style. Knowing that people focus their attention on the face, and knowing that facial expressions are relatively uninformative, maybe jurors' attention should be redirected to better cues. Maybe judges should instruct their juries to listen closely to how witnesses sound when they testify. Is it possible to improve jurors' lie detection skills simply by providing them with the right kind of guidance? Consider the following experiment: Subjects watched videotapes of people making statements, some true, and others false. Before watching the tapes, subjects were instructed to pay particular attention to either what the speakers said, how they said it, or how they looked as they spoke. A fourth group of subjects received no special instruction. Those subjects whose attention was focused on the speakers' tone of voice were markedly more successful in their ability to discriminate truth and deception than were all the others.[15] On the question of whether judges can improve the effectiveness of their juries by redirecting their attention through instruction, at least when it comes to paralinguistic cues, this experiment suggests that it could work. And then, of course, there is Ekman and Friesen's finding that liars are also betrayed by their own bodies. Jurors could be instructed to consider these nonverbal cues as well. There is only one problem. In most courtrooms, the witness's lower body is hidden from view, ironically enough, by the witness stand itself—the very symbol of truth.

Deposition Testimony and the Surrogate Witness

Although it is believed that judges and juries are well informed by the demeanor of witnesses as they testify, they must often make judgments of credibility without ever seeing the actual witness. Every now and then, people who are scheduled to testify are unable to make an appearance in the courtroom. The death of a prospective witness, not an unusual occurrence in civil cases that drag on for several years, is an obvious problem. People who live beyond a certain distance from the courthouse, usually 100 miles, or who are sick, handicapped, out of the country, or in prison are also excused from attending the trial. In order to secure the substance of what these prospective witnesses have to say, the rules state that they may be required to provide a *deposition*, that is, testify under oath before the trial, answering questions on both direct and cross examination. In their absence these depositions are then entered into the trial record.

The use of deposition testimony in lieu of the live witness raises interesting procedural questions. What do we mean when we say that it is "entered into the trial record?" How is this information presented, and what effect does it all have on the jury's ability to detect truth and deception? By tradition, in most courts, deposition testimony is transcribed by a stenographer. Then during the trial the transcript is read aloud from the witness stand by a court clerk or by someone appointed by the witness's attorney. Sometimes this surrogate reads both the questions and answers; sometimes he or she reads the answers while the attorneys read the questions. There is an alternative. Even before the era of home video cassette recorders, Ohio Judge James McCrystal repeatedly urged the courts to use videotaped depositions. Jurors would then watch the pretrial examination of the absentee witness on a television monitor stationed in the courtroom.[16]

For several reasons, we think the jury is better off with videotaped depositions, or at least audiotaped depositions, than with readings of the transcript. To begin with, there is a limit to how attentive people can be when they have to listen to an individual droning on from a script that has already been played out. In some trials, juries have to endure full weeks of deposition reading. Without the drama accompanying the spontaneous exchange between lawyers and their witnesses, jurors' attention might just wander off in more interesting directions. This problem was documented in a mock jury study. As part of the trial, subjects watched a videotape of expert medical testimony. Half of them saw a physician testify for himself, and half watched an attorney read the same material presented as the physician's deposition. Overall, the testimony was remembered better and was viewed as more significant when it emanated from the source than when it was delivered through a messenger.[17] And then, of course, there is the question of how effectively jurors can evaluate the credibility of a witness from the bare bones of a deposition transcript. People are better at lie detection when they can hear a speaker's voice than when they have access only to his or her words.

There is yet another reason for videotaping depositions rather than having them read to the jury. The practice of using surrogate witnesses is subject to shocking kinds of abuse in an adversarial context. Consider the following true story. In 1981 the first author worked as a consultant for a group of Chicago lawyers who were representing some 40,000 customers in a class action suit against General Motors. The case was referred to in the media as the "Chevy-mobile" engine-switch case. Apparently, GM had installed Chevrolet engines rather than the usual Oldsmobile "Rocket" engine in 1977 models of Delta 88s, Custom Cruisers, and Omegas. Lawyers for the Olds' buyers contended that in making the switch without informing the consumer, GM had violated written and implied warranties. They requested in total between $56 and $131 million in damages. General Motors argued, essentially, that the Chevy engine it had installed in the Oldsmobile cars was a comparable product, and that interchanging parts between divisions within a corporation is a long standing and accepted practice in the automobile industry. About 6 weeks before the trial was scheduled to begin, lawyers for the plaintiff enlisted the first author's aid in conducting mock jury research as a way of preparing for the trial. What kinds of arguments are most influential? Which witnesses were the most convincing? To answer these kinds of questions, 18 people were recruited to serve concurrently in three mock juries. The mini trial lasted a full day and was staged in a real courtroom by four of the plaintiffs' attorneys, two of whom represented the defense. Several of the actual witnesses appeared. For others, their deposition testimony was read aloud from the stand. Afterwards, the three juries were escorted to separate rooms where they filled out questionnaires, deliberated, and returned a verdict.[18]

After analyzing the data it was apparent that those witnesses who had testified in person were more impactful than those whose testimony had been read from a transcript. Maybe that pattern was a coincidence, but probably it was not. During the proceedings, jurors looked conspicuously more attentive when they watched the actual witnesses. Among the first author's recommendations to the lawyers was that if they needed to resort to deposition testimony, they should use as readers people who have an engaging style. About 2 weeks later, more than 30 professional actors and actresses from the Chicago area were auditioned to play the roles of various witnesses who would be absent from the trial. They all read the transcripts flawlessly. What distinguished those who were hired from those who were not was their ability to project particular impressions of the witnesses they were called to represent. According to the rules, it should not be possible to use surrogates in this manner. Deposition readers should not unduly emphasize any words and should refrain from suggestive conduct. Nevertheless, many lawyers appreciate the potential for scoring points in this procedure. One manual written for trial lawyers advises that "whoever is playing the part of the witness on the stand will, most assuredly, be identified with that witness. True, he is nothing more than an actor, but human beings tend to associate a voice with a person; so be certain that the 'actor' projects a favorable image."[19] It is even suggested that when faced with a witness who will not come across well, the "imaginative" lawyer should consider taking a deposition and then replacing that witness with an attractive surrogate.[20]

Is it truly possible to alter the impact of a deposition and mislead the jury by manipulating the *surrogate's* demeanor? To test this hypothesis, the first author conducted the following experiment. Eighty-eight subjects read a summary of a civil case in which the plaintiff, Dennis Ottway, filed suit against a security company because he had been harassed and then shot by one of its guards. The defense maintained that Ottway was drunk and that he inadvertently shot himself during a scuffle with a guard. There were no eyewitnesses to the shooting and the physical evidence was ambiguous. For all practical purposes, then, a jury's verdict would hinge on whether it believed the plaintiff or the guard. After reading about the case, subjects watched a carefully staged videotape of Ottway's testimony. An actor was hired to play the witness in two contrasting roles. In one tape, he was attentive, polite, cooperative, and unhesitating in his response to questions; in the other, he read the same testimony, but was impolite, often annoyed, cautious and fumbling in his style. The actor read the same transcript in both conditions, varying only his tone of voice, facial expressions, and body language. Since a witness's demeanor is considered relevant, one would expect that even though all subjects heard the same testimony read by the same actor, the positive-demeanor witness would be viewed more favorably than the negative-demeanor witness. That expectation was confirmed. But what if subjects were told, both before and after watching the tape, that they were not seeing the actual witness, who could not appear in court, but an individual assigned to read from the witness's deposition? Since the demeanor of a surrogate is not relevant to judging the credibility of a witness, and since the two tapes were identical in their verbal content, jurors should not be affected by what they saw. But they were. Even though subjects were aware that they were merely watching a clerk reading from a transcript, those who watched the positive-rather than negative-demeanor tape rated the testimony itself as more believable, more accurate, and more persuasive. They were also more likely to return a favorable verdict.[21]

This study suggests that jurors may be unable to separate a witness and his or her testimony from the messenger who delivers it. As such, it uncovers another problem with the way most courts handle deposition testimony. Not only does transcript reading lead jurors to tune out, and not only does it deny them the opportunity to observe the demeanor of the real witness, but it can mislead them unnecessarily in their search for truth and deception. As we said, deposition readers are not supposed to embellish their performances. But can judges be counted on to detect the subtle nuances and manipulations of a professional actor? People are often not conscious of the nonverbal cues that guide their impressions. Besides, what about *nonbehavioral* sources of bias? A jury's evaluation of deposition testimony might very well be affected by whether the surrogate is tall, dark, and handsome. We will see later that people's perceptions of others are affected by their physical attractiveness. What, then, are judges to do, screen deposition readers on the basis of their appearance? What we are saying is that the opportunity for abuse is inherent in the simple substitution of one individual for another. For that reason, videotape should be used to preserve the witness's demeanor for the record without introducing yet another piece of extraneous information. The jury's task as a human lie detector is difficult enough as it is.

The Paradox of Cross Examination

When witnesses testify, they do not just tell their story as most of us do under ordinary circumstances. They must operate, instead, within boundaries defined by the case itself, the attorneys, and the laws of evidence.[22] When witnesses are called to the stand, they are examined first by the lawyer who called them. The main purpose of this *direct examination* is to elicit the witness's story through a succession of questions. On direct, lawyers generally ask open-ended questions; the kinds of questions that enable witnesses to do most of the talking. After directing an eyewitness to the scene of a crime, for example, the lawyer might just ask, "What, then, did you see and hear?" Although direct examination calls for narrative, sometimes rambling answers, the questions are not totally unstructured. Lawyers are discouraged from putting a witness on the stand and then asking him or her to just "tell all." The problem with this approach is that witnesses are likely to stray onto topics that are inadmissible. The eyewitness, for example, might go on to describe what other bystanders to a crime said they had seen. That information may seem perfectly relevant, but it is excluded because what others say is considered hearsay. If those other witnesses have a story to tell, they should tell it under oath and in front of the jury.

Lawyers must follow one cardinal rule in their direct examinations: they cannot ask leading questions. A *leading question* is one that suggests to the witness what answer the examiner wants to receive. There is no precise or objective measure of when a question is considered leading. The determination depends not only on how it is phrased, but on its content and context. Still, there is a "you will know it when you hear it" quality to many leading questions. Thus, while the question, "Was the culprit tall or short?" is acceptable, the question, "The culprit was tall, wasn't he?" is not. Lawyers are prohibited from asking these kinds of questions on direct examination to prevent them from putting words into their witnesses' mouths and shaping the testimony to suit their clients' needs. After all, whose testimony would it be—the lawyer's or the witness's—if lawyers could ask questions such as "Was the getaway car a red 1978 Firebird with whitewalls and a pair of dice hanging from the rearview mirror?"[23]

The rules of *cross examination* are completely different. Following direct, lawyers for the opposition get an opportunity to question the witness. The main purpose of cross examination is to discredit the witness's testimony by probing for signs of prejudice, incompetence, or a poor reputation for honesty. At this stage, lawyers are permitted and, in fact, encouraged to ask leading questions. Because they are interviewing witnesses who are not their own, and who have taken a position against their clients, there is little concern that lawyers could handily manipulate these witnesses through leading questions. Anybody who has watched an actual trial can appreciate how different direct and cross examinations sound. On direct, the witness does most of the talking; on cross, the examiner usually confines the witness to narrow, yes or no answers. The reason for this practice is strategic: it prevents the witness from disclosing unanticipated, potentially damaging information. Although attorneys are free to phrase their questions in leading terms, they are often restricted in the scope of their cross examination. In the federal courts and in most states, they can only ask questions on matters that were raised on direct examination. If they want to broach additional topics, they would have to call that witness as their own for direct examination.

The opportunity to confront opposing witnesses through cross examination is an essential device for safeguarding the accuracy and completeness of testimonial evidence. Described as ''an engine for discovering truth,''[24] cross examination is not a privilege but a right. Many notable lawyers believe that cases are won and lost on cross examination.[25] The question we raise is, what impact does an effective cross examination have on the jury's ability to reconstruct the truth about an event? Are there any dangers and, if so, what are they? In the ideal, cross examination would increase the credibility of witnesses who are telling the truth, and decrease the credibility of those who are lying. If so, then juries would be generally more accurate in their role as factfinders. Although there is no way of knowing for sure how effective cross examination is and the extent to which juries benefit from it, on balance it is an indispensable device. Many a deceptive witness has no doubt fallen from the stand, exposed, scarred, and discredited, from the battle of cross examination.

As psychologists, we suspect that cross examination can also be used to exert an influence over the jury that extends beyond, and maybe even subverts, the quest for truth. As in the way many lawyers use the voir dire, asking questions provides more than just a means of eliciting answers. It can be used to impart information to a listener through imagery, implication, and conjecture.[26] Many trial lawyers know what writers, actors, advertisers, and politicians know about the persuasiveness of vivid language. Carefully chosen words obscure and alter people's impressions, as when tax increases are called revenue enhancements or the strategic defense initiative (SDI) is referred to as Star Wars. Consider the following brief exchange between an attorney and a defendant charged with manslaughter for having performed an illegal abortion.

Q: You didn't tell us, doctor, whether you determined that the *baby* was alive or dead, did you doctor?
A: The *fetus* had no signs of life.[27]

In this example the defendant resisted the lawyer's imagery. In subtle ways, however, a person's answers can be shaped by how the questions are worded.

Consider the following experiment on eyewitness testimony. Subjects watched films of an automobile accident. Although everybody saw the same film, they were asked slightly different questions about it. Sure enough, subjects' reports were shaped by how the questions were worded. Those who were asked, "About how fast were the cars going when they *smashed* into each other?" estimated an average speed of 41 mph; those who were asked "About how fast were the cars going when they *hit* each other?" estimated an average of only 34 mph.[28] In fact, the wording of this critical question had a lasting effect on subjects' actual memories for the event. When asked one week later whether they could recall broken glass at the scene of the accident (there was none), only 14 percent of those previously asked the *hit* question said they did, compared to 32 percent of those who had been asked the *smash* question. Once the seed of misinformation is planted, it takes on a life of its own.

Even when a question does not mislead its respondent, it might still mislead the jury. What happens, for example, when a question implies something that is never explicitly stated? Does the listener process what is *said* or what is *implied*? Research on *pragmatic implications* reveals that people often confuse the two. In one study, mock jurors listened to an excerpt of a witness's testimony and then indicated whether certain statements were true or false. What would you assume about the behavior of a witness who says, "I ran up to the burglar alarm?" Would you interpret that statement to mean, "I *rang* the burglar alarm?" Most subjects did. It did not matter whether they heard the first statement or the second. Either way, subjects processed the information between the lines and assumed they had heard what was only implied.[29]

The real mischief of cross examination is the nearly unrestricted use of leading questions. Because lawyers can ask questions that suggest their own answers, jurors can be influenced by the information contained in the questions themselves, even if that information is not true. Imagine what the jury must have thought after hearing the following exchange:

Q: Have you been ill within the last eight or nine years?
A: Ill?
Q: Yes.
A: No.
Q: Are you certain about that?
A: Positive.
Q: Never in your life, up to today?
A: That's right.
Q: You have never spent any time in any hospital or institution of any kind whatever?
A: No, sir.
Q: And no illness of any kind?
A: No.

Q: Are you sure about that?
A: Yes.

This testimony is taken from the transcript of a real trial.[30] It seems as if the cross examiner knew something; that he was privy to information about the witness's past that impaired her credibility. The questioning was obviously calculated to leave in the jury's mind the impression that the witness had suffered from some kind of mental disorder. In this particular example, subsequent events revealed that the examiner had no hard proof, only unsubstantiated rumor, to support his insinuations. But did it matter or had the damage already been done?

Psychologist William Swann and his colleagues addressed this question in an interesting experiment.[31] What happens, they inquired, when people hear an interview in which the questioner implies that the respondent has certain personal characteristics? They had subjects listen to question-and-answer sessions in which the interviewer probed for evidence of either extraverted behavior (e.g., "What do you do when you want to liven things up at a party?") or introverted behavior (e.g., "Have you ever felt left out of some social group?"). A third of the subjects heard only the questions, a third heard only the answers, and a third heard both sides of the interview. Afterwards, they indicated what they thought of the respondent. When subjects heard only the questions, they inferred that the recipient of those questions had the traits being sought by the interviewer. They assumed, in other words, that the interviewer must have known enough to ask extraverts about livening up parties and introverts about difficult social situations. Suggestive questions thus serve as proof by conjecture. Even though leading questions are not evidence, juries might unwittingly treat them as though they were.[32]

In the context of a full-blown trial, of course, jurors hear not only the questions asked but the answers they elicit. It stands to reason that under these circumstances, conjectural evidence is buried under the weight of the witness's testimony. That is not necessarily the case. In the above excerpt the witness's repeated denials of having been hospitalized might not have been enough to erase the questions themselves, leaving the jury with lingering doubts about her credibility. As we said, Swann and his colleagues had a third of their subjects listen, as jurors would, to both sides of the interview. The result was the same; they too were mislead. How did that happen? In actuality, the respondents in this study did not possess the implied traits, so it is odd that their answers did not override the effects of the interviewers' questions. But think about it for a moment. Imagine yourself on the receiving end of an interview. Asked about what you do to liven up parties, you would probably talk about organizing group games, playing dance music, telling jokes, and the like. In other words, you would answer the question and, in doing so, your reply would make you sound like an extravert. Likewise, asked about difficult social situations, you might talk about how it feels to be new in town or how much anxiety you experience before making oral presentations. After answering enough of these kinds of questions, you would begin to sound like an introvert. That is what happened in the experiment. Respondents, limited in their testimony to answering specific questions, provided the behavioral evidence needed to confirm the interviewers' conjecture. Subjects who heard the full interview were thus left with false impressions of the respondents. As Swann and his colleagues put it, "once the answers 'let the cat out of the bag,' observers saw no reason to concern themselves with how the bag was opened."[33]

This research shows that suggestive questioning can mislead a jury in two ways. First, questions themselves can misinform through the power of conjecture. Jurors might thus assume that the attorney who asked about the witness's psychiatric history must have known something about her past, something she was unwilling to admit. Second, by constraining the witness's testimony, suggestive questions can actually produce support for that conjecture. If a lawyer wants to portray a witness as introverted, extraverted, greedy, lazy, or neurotic, he or she can do so simply by asking the right questions. Since witnesses can only tell their story in response to specific inquiries, it is not too difficult to get a witness to provide the necessary evidence. There is, of course, a safety valve in the system. After cross examination, an attorney has an opportunity to undo the damage and rehabilitate his or her witness by coming back with a redirect examination. Does it work? Can an effective redirect examination set the record straight? To some extent, it must. But it could be an uphill battle. We will argue in Chapter 6 that first impressions tend to stick. Once people form them, they often become insensitive to subsequent, contradictory information.

Robert E. Keeton, in his leading text entitled *Trial Tactics and Methods*, said of cross examination, that "it affords the opportunity for the most successful employment of an aptitude for quick thinking, sharp repartee, and dramatics."[34] It sounds like great theater. But there is good reason to challenge whether a method of examination that relies on leading questions advances or detracts from the cause of justice. On balance, it could make it more difficult for juries to discern the truth about a witness's testimony.

Leading questions can have a "do you still beat your wife?" quality to them. After all, what is a jury to think of the rape victim who is asked, "Isn't it true that you have accused men of rape before?" And what is the jury to think of the expert witness whose competence is challenged with questions like, "Isn't it true that your work is poorly regarded by your professional colleagues?" Witnesses can deny false assertions, of course; and their lawyers can try to restore their credibility on redirect examination; but these denials might fall on deaf ears. In fact, people are particularly suspicious of others who are forced to protest their innocence too vociferously.[35]

Because leading questions convey information, jurors must also try to separate in their memory the questions asked from the answers they elicit. That is not as easy as it seems. Social and cognitive psychologists find that people often remember the contents of a message but forget its source.[36] In the context of courtroom testimony, it is thus possible that the questions are as lasting in their effects as the answers.

Judges are reluctant to impose any restrictions on cross examination.[37] Only when lawyers insinuate that a witness has a criminal record are they required to substantiate their claim. Otherwise, they need not have proof, only a "good faith" belief that their accusations are true. In part, this hands-off policy is driven by the courts' profound respect for this aspect of the trial. But it is also based on the misguided assumption that false assertions, after all, can be denied. They can, but the potential for subverting the jury's quest for the truth is still substantial. Judges should be aware of the dangers and make a serious effort to control abusive practices. Unless they do, the great engine of truth can have a truly paradoxical effect.

THE PSYCHOLOGY OF EVIDENCE

Making judgments of witnesses' credibility is only part of what it takes to figure out the reality of some past event. Depending on the trial, juries must evaluate statistical or experimental data, physical evidence, hearsay admitted as an exception to the rule that prohibits it, confessions that were possibly coerced, testimony about people's character and reputation, polygraph tests, the authenticity of business records, and so on. There is enough research on how juries deal with these kinds of information to fill another book.[38] For now, we focus on two important types of evidence that regularly appear in America's criminal courtrooms: eyewitness identifications and confessions.

Vagaries of Eyewitness Testimony

Well-meaning witnesses often tell what they believe to be true, but are simply in error. People make innocent mistakes. Nowhere is this more evident than when eyewitnesses identify others from memory. In a 1982 case that drew an investigative report by "60 Minutes," Lenell Geter, a 26-year-old black engineer, was convicted and sentenced to life in prison for the armed robbery of $615 from a Kentucky Fried Chicken outlet in Greenville, Texas. Nine of his co-workers insisted that he was at work, 50 miles from the restaurant, during the time the robbery was supposed to have occurred. Geter, a college-educated man, had no criminal record. And there was no physical evidence linking him to the holdup. In fact, the culprit was initially described by the restaurant workers as about 5 feet, 6 inches, while Geter is 6 feet tall. And yet he was convicted. Apparently, the jury (and his court-appointed lawyer who spent more time trying to convince him to plea bargain than he did working on a defense) was persuaded by the testimony of five restaurant employees, all white, who mistakenly identified

Geter by picking his picture out of police photos. Although many of his co-workers pressed for a reopening of the case, and although pressure mounted as a result of extensive media coverage, local authorities did not drop the charges against Geter until four of the original eyewitnesses changed their minds and identified another suspect. In the end, Geter had lost more than a year of his life in prison.

Critics have cited this incident as an illustration of various problems with the system. To some, the all-white jury's erroneous verdict reflected racial prejudice. To others, it was a story about an attorney's failure to provide an adequate defense. Giving these participants the benefit of the doubt, we view the Geter case primarily as a failure of eyewitness identification. As such, it is one in a long list of tragic failures. The problems with eyewitness testimony are twofold. First, people are often wrong in their recollections of events. As eyewitnesses, we misperceive, forget, and often are unable to communicate accurately our observations. These imperfections of the human organism are an inevitable fact of life that we just have to live with. But they are compounded by a second, equally disturbing problem: that juries tend to place greater trust in eyewitness testimony than they should. Also, they are often unable to figure out when eyewitnesses are accurate in their identifications and when they are not.

Erroneous identifications.

Over the years, psychologists interested in social perception, cognition, and memory have conducted literally hundreds of studies of eyewitness testimony. From that extensive body of research, two general conclusions can be drawn. First, as we suspected from the many Geter-like cases that have reached the courts, eyewitnesses make many mistakes in their reports about people, places, and things. Lineup identifications are particularly troublesome. In December 1974, psychologist Robert Buckhout staged and videotaped a 12-second purse-snatching episode that was shown on a nightly news program in New York City. Viewers were then presented with a six-man lineup, told that the assailant might or might not be in that lineup, and asked to phone in their identifications. Out of 2,145 viewers who called in, only 15.3 percent of them picked the right man. Since there were only seven alternative responses that could be made, viewers could have been expected to receive an accuracy rate of 14.3 percent simply by guessing. The others either identified an innocent person or mistakenly concluded that the assailant was not present.[39] This demonstration, and others like it, underscores the U.S. Supreme Court's 1967 conclusion, that "the annals of criminal law are rife with instances of misidentification."[40] The second general conclusion to be drawn from empirical research is that there is an identifiable list of factors that systematically affect the accuracy of eyewitness reports. Psychologists have found it helpful to view memory and forgetting as a three-staged process. An individual must *perceive* the event in question, *store* it in long-term memory, and then later *retrieve* it on command. What this model has shown is that the process is relatively complicated and that error can result from failures at each of the stages.[41]

Erroneous eyewitness reports are a serious problem. Prosecutors often file charges when all they have is a positive identification, even in the absence of other incriminating evidence. That is bad enough when the identification is in error, and the machinery of the criminal justice apparatus is brought to bear on an innocent individual. But the problem is exacerbated when the judge or jury cannot distinguish between accurate and inaccurate reports during the trial. The inability to make these distinctions can mean convicting the innocent and acquitting the guilty. The question, then, is to what extent can juries make the right decisions? In the Geter case they obviously could not. On the other hand, consider the following remarkable story. In 1979 and 1980, Bob Dillen, a 29-year-old freelance photographer, was arrested 13 times for armed robberies of Fotomat and Foto Hut booths in Pittsburgh, Pennsylvania. Five times he was brought to trial only because of eyewitness evidence, and five times he was acquitted by a jury. In the thirteenth case a cashier who had been kidnapped and held hostage led the police to a cabin where they made an arrest. It was then that local authorities realized that Dillen's only offense was that he looked too much like the real criminal.[42] Which story reflects the jury's ability better, Geter or Dillen?

As a general rule, people place too much faith in witnesses who proclaim that "I saw it with my own eyes." Research by Gary Wells, a leading eyewitness expert, illustrates the point. In one study, he and his colleagues staged the theft of a calculator in front of unsuspecting witnesses who made an identification from photographs and then testified in a cross examination that was observed by mock jurors. Although only 52 percent of the eyewitnesses made the right choice in their identifications, 68 percent of them were believed to be accurate by the jurors. Those of us who have staged crimes in college classrooms only to see how surprised students are about their own failures to reconstruct those events can vouch for the fact that being an eyewitness looks easier than it really is. And yet overestimating the eyewitness is only part of the problem. The other part is that people are unable to distinguish between those who are right from those who are wrong in their identifications. In Wells' research, subject jurors may as well have flipped a coin. They were as likely to believe the witnesses who were wrong in their identifications as they were those who were right.[43]

What seems to be the problem? Why are people such poor judges of the eyewitness? To begin with, there is a lot about the subject matter of human perception and memory that we do not know through intuition and common sense. Certain factors are obvious enough. We all know that it is easier to see faces under good lighting than in the dark, that the longer a person has to watch an event, the more information about it they will pick up, and that we tend to forget things over time. Several years ago, comedian Richard Pryor appeared in

a skit on the "Saturday Night Live" television program in which he was accused of a crime and placed in a police lineup. The other members of the lineup
were a nun, a refrigerator, and a duck. Lo and behold, the eyewitness, having
earlier described the criminal as a black man, picked Pryor as the criminal. It
obviously does not take a psychologist to figure out the inherent unfairness of
that lineup. But what about the more hidden phenomena known to exist only
through theory and research? Did you know, for example, that people cannot
discern the color of objects under monochromatic light? Or that people have
trouble identifying members of a racial group other than their own? Or that
people's perceptions can be shaped by their expectations and stereotypes, or that
their memories can be altered through suggestive questioning? And did you
know that people consistently overestimate how long it takes for an event to
unfold? Chances are, unless you have read up on the subject or taken the right
psychology course, you were only vaguely aware of these facts, if at all. Your
intuitions may even have been at odds with them.[44]

Research has shown, for example, that the common practice of having witnesses search through volumes of mugshots can interfere with their subsequent
ability to recognize the original culprit from a lineup. In one experiment, subjects witnessed a live staged crime, after which they looked through a series of
mugshots. Several days later, they were called to view a lineup. The results
were startling but understandable, in psychological terms. Subjects were just as
likely to select from the lineup an innocent person whose face had appeared in
the mugshots as they were to identify the real criminal. By recognizing a face
while forgetting the context they had seen it in, witnesses can thus make serious
identification errors.[45] These findings, together with other research,[46] make it
clear that people's recollections of an event do not end with the event itself.
Whatever information they acquire afterwards, whether it is from suggestive
police questions, mugshots, or the stories told by other observers, can become
part of their malleable and everchanging memory. By the time eyewitnesses
enter the courtroom, what they originally saw can be irrevocably confused with
other information. To add to that problem, the witness, the lawyers, and the jury
are unlikely to ever know it. When 60 people were asked for their opinions on
the use of mugshots, for example, only 24 percent acknowledged the possible
dangers. The numbers are even lower for other reliable eyewitness phenomena.[47]

Matters of common sense.

Not knowing the factors that enhance, impair, or moderate the quality of eyewitness testimony, jurors base their judgments on how confident witnesses claim to
be about their identifications. That makes sense, doesn't it? If you were conducting an investigation and your witness made an identification, wouldn't your
first question be, "Are you sure?" And then having asked the question,
wouldn't you feel better about proceeding with the witness who is certain than
with one who is more tentative? It is difficult to resist the inference that self

confidence signals accuracy. Unfortunately, and much to our own surprise, it often does not. Out of 31 experiments recently reviewed, identification accuracy and confidence were significantly correlated only 13 times. Thus, although there are exceptions, eyewitnesses who make accurate identifications and those who do not cannot be reliably distinguished by their reported levels of certainty.[48]

One reason for this finding is that self confidence is a matter of personal style. Some people are confident in all their judgments, regardless of the topic at hand. On and off the witness stand, they speak without hesitation or qualification. Other people characteristically project a more modest style regardless of whether they are right or wrong in their judgments. The juror's problem is that witnesses are strangers. Without the opportunity to observe them in settings outside the courtroom the juror is unable to know that their expressions of certainty and doubt reflect their style of communication rather than the quality of their performance. Jurors are not the only ones, by the way, whose intuitions serve them poorly. In the 1972 case of *Neil v. Biggers*, the U.S. Supreme Court proposed guidelines for evaluating eyewitness identification evidence. It cited the witness's reported level of confidence as one of the most important factors to be taken into account.[49]

With jurors not being critical enough or knowledgeable enough about the vagaries of human memory, something should be done to make them better at it. It could be argued that our adversarial system has cross examination as a built-in safety valve. Once jurors are persuaded by the report of an eyewitness, however, it can become difficult to undo the damage. Psychologist Elizabeth Loftus, a leading eyewitness expert, had mock jurors read about the robbery of a grocery store in which the owner and his granddaughter were killed. Among subjects who were provided with only circumstantial evidence against the defendant, 18 percent voted for his conviction. When they also read about the testimony of a store clerk who positively identified the defendant, 72 percent of the subjects voted for conviction, a substantial increase. How do jurors react when the eyewitness testimony is discredited on cross examination? In a third version of this trial, subjects read about the store clerk's testimony but then learned that he was very nearsighted, and that he was not wearing his glasses on the day of the crime. From where he stood, the defense lawyer maintained, the clerk could not have clearly seen the defendant's face. Despite this apparently convincing information, 68 percent of the subjects still found the defendant guilty, a far cry from the 18 percent who were never aware that there was an eyewitness.[50] Obviously, it is not impossible for a lawyer to discredit an eyewitness. Cross examination can be very effective. But it is not easy.[51]

Educating the jury.

There are three ways to assist juries in their efforts to evaluate eyewitness testimony. One is to exclude it altogether in cases where it stands alone, without corroboration. This alternative is plainly unacceptable. It would needlessly paralyze too many legitimate criminal prosecutions. We know that eyewitness testimony can be remarkably unreliable. But research has also shown that under certain conditions it can be quite accurate; as when the witness has ample opportunity to observe an event, is questioned shortly thereafter, and is subjected to fair and nonsuggestive memory retrieval procedures. A second alternative is to require judges to read cautionary instructions if requested by one of the parties. These instructions would inform the jury that identification evidence can be wrong and encourage them to scrutinize it carefully. They might even describe specific findings that are relevant to the case. A number of courts have opted for this practice.[52] A third approach, one that is more controversial, more prevalent, and potentially more effective, is to enable parties to call psychological experts to testify about perception, memory, and eyewitness testimony. Indeed the two of us have served in that capacity ourselves. It is no different than calling a physician to testify about a patient's medical condition, an auto mechanic to testify about the safety of an automobile, or an economist to testify on antitrust matters. Called by a particular party, psychological experts educate the jury on relevant theory and research findings. They might testify about people's ability to recognize voices, the use of hypnosis as a memory aid, the problems with cross racial identifications, the effects of stress on perception, the relationship between accuracy and confidence, biased identification procedures, children's competence to testify, and the like. As with other witnesses, experts are subject to cross examination. Opposing lawyers can challenge their credentials as experts, the soundness of their conclusions, and the relevance of their research to the case at hand.

Eyewitness experts appear to have an effect on the jury. Elizabeth Loftus, who has testified in numerous trials, tells the following rather remarkable story. In 1981, two Arizona ranchers, brothers named Thomas and Patrick Hanigan, were charged with beating and torturing three Mexicans. What was unique about the case was that both defendants were tried at the same time and in the same courtroom, but by two separate juries. Although the evidence against the two men was nearly identical, consisting primarily of the victim's eyewitness testimony, an expert witness was offered only by one defendant. So while the Thomas jury heard the expert, the Patrick jury waited in the jury room. In the end, the verdicts were mixed. In what was described by one side as "the weirdest goddam thing I have ever seen," Thomas Hanigan was acquitted, while his brother Patrick was convicted.[53] It is entirely possible that the difference in verdicts was due to the presence of an expert in one case but not the other.

Rather than speculate on the matter, researchers have systematically varied the presence or absence of an eyewitness expert in mock jury experiments. In trials that include an eyewitness, they have found that the testimony of an expert leads jurors to scrutinize the evidence more carefully, to spend more time discussing it during deliberations, and to be more skeptical, generally, about the accuracy of eyewitness reports. For cases that hinge entirely on a questionable eyewitness, the presence of an expert could very well influence the jury's verdict.[54] Based on how people naturally view eyewitness testimony, a dose of skepticism is a healthy result, but it is not enough. The more important question is, can experts increase the *accuracy* of people's judgments? That is, can they improve the juror's ability not only to discount the inaccurate witness but to credit the accurate one? To this point, there is not enough research to provide an unequivocal answer to this question. But it is possible. Gary Wells, for example, had some subject jurors but not others hear an expert who provided specific pieces of advice. He told them to pay attention to the circumstances surrounding the witness's view of the perpetrator, how much time was available, and so on. He then reviewed the research on identification accuracy and confidence, and cautioned them against basing their judgments on how certain or uncertain the witness claimed to be. Overall, the results showed that the expert testimony achieved its objectives. Without it, subjects believed 53 percent of the witnesses who were accurate in their identifications, and 55 percent of those who were inaccurate. With the aid of an expert, however, subjects were better able to make the discrimination, as they believed 60 percent of those who were accurate, and only 45 percent of those who were not.[55]

Today the use of eyewitness experts is both widespread and controversial.[56] Aware of the unavoidable weaknesses in eyewitness testimony, an increasing number of federal and state courts welcome experts with open arms. Federal Judges David Bazelon and Jack Weinstein, both eminent scholars in their own right, are particularly strong advocates of using eyewitness experts.[57] As the California Supreme Court put it, the "factors bearing on eyewitness identification may be known only to some jurors, or may be imperfectly understood by many, or may be contrary to the intuitive beliefs of most."[58] Yet other courts are adamantly opposed to eyewitness experts. The reason, they claim, is that in order to qualify as a proper subject for an expert, the testimony should inform the jury on matters that extend beyond what it already knows. On those grounds, it is said, the eyewitness psychologist does not qualify. As one court put it, "The problem of perception and memory can be adequately addressed in cross examination and [that] the jury can adequately weigh these problems through common-sense evaluation."[59] How, then, should we characterize current practice? It depends. As in the oddly uneven trial of Thomas and Patrick Hanigan, some litigants today can call on eyewitness experts, and others cannot. It all depends on who the judge is, where the trial is held, and the availability of resources.

It is by no means clear, we should add, that psychological experts are the best remedy for the ills of eyewitness testimony. What we do know for sure is that judges and jurors alike do not know enough about human memory to make accurate assessments on their own. From that, it is clear that some form of assistance is called for. But there are problems with the use of experts, as we know from psychiatry, medicine, engineering, and economics. The main problem, one with which we are all too familiar, is the proverbial "battle of the experts." That is not the name of a new TV show, but a situation that develops when both sides call their own credentialed experts who predictably assert contradictory opinions of the same phenomenon. Sometimes that battle reflects legitimate disagreement within a professional community. Eyewitness psychologists, for example, disagree over the value of using hypnosis as a memory aid. In these kinds of situations, it might actually be helpful for a jury to observe that there is controversy. Remember, jurors do not enter the trial with a blank slate. Sometimes they are wrong in their assumptions and would benefit from a well reasoned duel. The hypnosis example is a good one. Many people assume that it works. For them, it would help to learn that its effectiveness is not to be taken for granted. There are other times, however, where the courtroom battle reflects little more than experts' willingness to say almost anything for the right price. Hired guns can be found in all professions. When they confront each other in court, their duel sadly deteriorates into a popularity contest. As far as the jury is concerned, the net effect is confusion and misinformation.[60]

There are two possible solutions. First, the courts should set more stringent standards when it comes to qualifying an expert. According to the rules, an individual is qualified "by knowledge, skill, experience, training, or education."[61] In current practice, that standard is rather loosely applied. Just as not all physicians are qualified to perform surgery, not all psychologists are experts on the topic of eyewitness testimony. At the very least, the courts should demand that their experts be "actively engaged" through teaching, writing, or research. The second possible solution is to have judges inform juries about the vagaries of eyewitness evidence through carefully written instructions. A few courts take this approach. What gets included in this instruction and how it is written are open for debate. Also, it remains to be seen whether eyewitness instructions have any impact on the jury. In short, we do not have a specific solution. But we believe that juries should not be left to their own devices. Too many courts do not permit eyewitness experts *and* do not use cautionary instructions. Without some means of education, they are disabling juries in their efforts to cope with the complexities of this very important evidence.

True Confessions, False Confessions

On June 3, 1981, Clifton Lawson, an 18-year-old high school dropout from Brooklyn, New York, confessed to the brutal rape and murder of an elderly woman. Every word of his confession was recorded on videotape. "I stabbed her three times. I don't know what came over me that day. . . . She said, 'Stop, stop, stop,' but I wouldn't stop. . . . I was having sex with her. . . . I didn't want for it to happen, but something strange happened to me." What really impressed the district attorney about the 20-minute confession was that Lawson supplied many details about the crime that only the killer and the police could have known. So persuasive was Lawson's confession, that his lawyer urged him to plea bargain in earnest. When he refused, insisting he was innocent, his lawyer resigned from the case.[62]

One can well imagine what Lawson's attorney must have been thinking at the time. There could be nothing more impactful to a jury than the sight of a defendant waiving his *Miranda* rights and confessing to the crime, apparently of his or her own free will. John Henry Wigmore, in his classic treatise, *Evidence*, agreed. He ranked confessions as the highest in his scale of evidence.[63] There are two reasons for this appraisal. First, confessions make their way into criminal prosecutions with astonishing frequency. Kalven and Zeisel estimated that disputed confessions—those that are retracted, denied, or otherwise challenged before trial—arose in 20 percent of the trials they sampled nationwide.[64] Second, self-incriminating statements, whether they are made in court or revealed in the newspapers, have an enormous impact on the disposition of a case, more so than any other kind of evidence. As one scholar put it, "the introduction of a confession makes the other aspects of a trial in court superfluous."[65] This is especially true, apparently, when jurors can see the confession for themselves on a courtroom TV monitor. According to the late Mario M. Merola, the Bronx District Attorney who first introduced the idea of videotaping interrogations to New York prosecutors, "We get a conviction in virtually every case."[66]

Let us now resume the Lawson story. Despite offers for a plea bargain, Lawson maintained his innocence, accepted a court-appointed lawyer, and went to trial two years to the day since he made his taped confession. Not unexpectedly, it became the centerpiece of the trial. Right from the beginning of his opening statement, the prosecuting attorney told the jury, "You will see a videotape . . . and on that videotape you will see the defendant confessing to the murder of Mrs. Randolph." Moments later, the defense attorney aggressively countered the anticipated evidence: "Don't just sit there and look at this tape and say, 'Well, this kid said he did it, he must have done it'. . . . The physical evidence that does exist in this case will prove that Clifton Lawson did not and could not have committed this crime." The battle lines were clearly drawn. As the trial unfolded, lasting for two weeks, the jury learned that Clifton Lawson had an IQ of 70, the emotional maturity level of a five-year-old, and a "disturbed mental condition." According to Lawson's attorney, he told the police what he thought they wanted to hear so he could be released to attend choir practice at his church. Concerning Lawson's intimate knowledge of the facts surrounding the crime, it turned out that during the nine hours he was being questioned or left unguarded at the police station, he had overheard the detectives and medical examiner discussing the details of the case. The defense then introduced forensic tests showing that although there were blood and fingerprints found in the victim's apartment, they were not Lawson's. Finally, in the most dramatic turn of events, the defense uncovered another suspect. A man who lived in the victim's building had been arrested for burglary based on the victim's identification just a week before she was killed. That man had been released on bail the night before the murder. At the time of the trial, he was in prison, having been convicted of the burglary charges. The jury deliberated for two full days and then returned a verdict of not guilty. It had more than a reasonable doubt about the so-called confession.

Third-degree tactics.

To the uninformed, confession evidence seems straightforward and without controversy. History has shown, however, that nothing could be further from the truth. Is the alleged confession authentic? Often reported by paid informers, overzealous police officers, and angry victims, can it be trusted? If so, was the accused of sound mind, or could he or she have confessed to misdeeds never committed? Was the defendant's statement coerced through beatings, threats, or trickery? Was his or her constitutionally protected privilege against self incrimination violated? These questions illustrate, but do not exhaust, the complex network of issues surrounding the use of confession evidence in court.

Three hundred years ago, confessions were routinely accepted. It was almost like pleading guilty. Since then, the courts' use of confessions has progressed through a series of discrete stages. By the twentieth century, the courts had become skeptical of certain types of confessions and had begun to establish rules to exclude those that were found to be coerced rather than voluntary. There are two reasons for excluding confessions that do not pass a test of *voluntariness*. The first is that they are unreliable because of the danger that people might be forced or tricked into confessing to acts they did not commit. On the question of when a confession can be considered voluntary, the U.S. Supreme Court has said it can be determined only by analyzing the "totality of the relevant circumstances."[67] As such, judges consider whether the accused was young, mentally handicapped, illiterate, or intoxicated; whether he or she was isolated, denied access to counsel, subjected to lengthy periods of interrogation, physically abused, threatened, or deceived through promises and reassurances. Given the complexity of the task, it is not surprising that judges are inconsistent in their rulings. As Justice Felix Frankfurter said, "there is no simple litmus-paper test."[68]

It is easy to understand how innocent people might confess to an interrogator after being beaten or tortured into submission. The Salem witchcraft confessions of the seventeenth century were of this variety. So were the confessions made by many black defendants during the early part of the twentieth century. In the 1936 case of *Brown v. Mississippi,* the classic case of this genre, three black men confessed after having been threatened by a lynch mob and whipped with steel-studded belts. Afterwards, they claimed that they had falsely confessed only in order to escape the painful beatings and avoid further punishment. The defendants were convicted at trial, but the U.S. Supreme Court overturned the verdict.[69]

Notwithstanding these kinds of extreme circumstances, it is hard for most of us to believe that people would actually confess to crimes they did not commit. But it happens, with some indeterminate frequency. When Charles Lindbergh's baby was kidnapped and murdered in 1932, more than 200 people offered unsolicited confessions. In an effort to explain that kind of occurrence, clinical psychologists and psychiatrists have speculated that some people have a "morbid desire for notoriety," the unconscious need to punish themselves for previous transgressions, and the inability to distinguish between fantasy and reality.[70] Then there is a phenomenon that has been dubbed the "station house syndrome," the idea being that police interrogation techniques, "can produce a trance-like state of heightened suggestibility."[71] In *Criminal Interrogation and Confessions*, the most popular manual written for law enforcement personnel, Fred Inbau and John Reid provide some insight into this process. They recommend the use of a special room that is bare, isolated, and soundproofed. They further advise that the accused be denied access to friends, relatives, all sources of distraction, and all reliefs from tension. Having created an oppressive environment, the interrogator is then armed with 16 ways to elicit confessions from initially recalcitrant suspects. These include frightening the suspect by exaggerating the seriousness of the charges and pretending to have fingerprints, eyewitnesses, and other inculpatory evidence.[72] Under that kind of pressure some unknown number of suspects have confessed to crimes they did not commit. Lest the reader conclude that these tactics represent little more than the prescriptions of their authors, we should note that a study of actual police interrogations showed that one or more of Inbau and Reid's tactics were used in at least 65 percent of the sessions that were observed.[73]

There is a second reason for excluding confessions that are not voluntary. It is that regardless of whether they are true or false, coerced confessions should not be accepted into evidence because "third degree" tactics violate an individual's constitutional right to due process and because they are inherently repugnant to a civilized society's concept of procedural fairness. To enable prosecutors to benefit from coerced confessions, it is said, would only encourage and perpetuate offensive police conduct. As the ultimate safeguard, the Supreme Court ruled, in the landmark 1966 case of *Miranda v. Arizona*, that unless the accused is informed of his or her rights to remain silent and to have an attorney present, all self-incriminating statements made in an interrogation are inadmissible.[74]

The jury's attributional dilemma.

In practice, the decision on whether or not a confession is voluntary and, hence, admissible as evidence, is made by the judge at a pretrial hearing. Confessions that are found to have been coerced are entirely excluded, and those deemed voluntary are admitted with the rest of the case.[75] In some states, juries are instructed to take up the voluntariness issue themselves before allowing it to affect their verdicts. Over the years, an important procedural question has been raised: by what standard should judges decide the issue of voluntariness? That is, how certain should they be about it before allowing the jury to hear of the confession? In 1972 the Supreme Court resolved the issue in favor of a relatively low standard. The court based its decision on the assumption that, on their own, juries are capable of evaluating the voluntariness of confessions and discounting those they feel are coerced.[76] Is that a sound assumption? Are juries able and willing to disregard questionable confessions?

These questions cannot easily be addressed through controlled research. In the study of eyewitness testimony, crimes can be staged and observers can be recruited to make lineup identifications that are *known* to be correct or mistaken. Jurors' ability to make credibility judgments can thus be measured by the extent to which they believe accurate rather than mistaken witnesses. But there is no analog of that technique in the study of confession evidence. In the ideal this research would involve having mock jurors evaluate confessions that are made by ''suspects,'' some of whom are known to be guilty and others who are known to be innocent of some offense. The problem is getting suspects whose actual behavior can be known. For ethical reasons, it would be difficult to goad research subjects into committing dishonest acts. It would be even more difficult, in mock interrogations, to apply enough pressure to elicit confessions from those who are innocent. Because this kind of information has not been obtained, we can only speculate through anecdotes about juries' ability to distinguish true and false confessions. In the Lawson trial, for example, the jury appeared to have correctly rejected the defendant's videotaped confession. But would they have rejected it if another plausible suspect had not been identified? We can never know for sure.

There is a second, also important question concerning how juries treat confession evidence. Over the years, certain kinds of police tactics have been ruled inherently coercive. In addition to the obvious methods of physical abuse, *threats* of harm and punishment as well as *promises* of leniency or immunity from prosecution have been cited repeatedly. Do jurors agree with that assessment? That is, do they reject confessions that, according to the law, were coerced? We have reason to believe that jurors might not be sensitive enough to the constraints and pressures of interrogation. An extensive series of studies has shown that when people evaluate others on the basis of their behavior, they commit what is known as the ''fundamental attribution error.''[77] In a number of studies, social psychologist Edward E. Jones and his colleagues had subjects read an editorial essay presumably written by a college student. The topics varied. Some subjects, for example, read an essay in favor of legalizing marijuana; others read an essay expressing an opposing point of view. Half of the subjects in the study were told that the student had freely selected his position; others were told that he had been assigned by an instructor to take that position. Afterwards, subjects were asked for the impressions of the essay writer's true opinion. As one would expect, when subjects thought that the student had chosen his own position, they assumed that what he wrote accurately reflected how he felt. But students who believed that the writer was forced to take his position made the same inference. The student who argued in favor of legalizing marijuana was thus seen as an advocate even though subjects knew that he had no choice but to take that position. This experiment and others like it demonstrate that when people evaluate others, they often accept their behavior at face value without sufficiently accounting for the situational forces that gave rise to it. If the student writes in favor of a position, for whatever reason, he must believe it. Likewise, if a suspect confesses to a crime, he must be guilty.[78]

To complicate matters further, the law defines both the threat of punishment and the promise of leniency as equally unacceptable forms of coercion. But jurors do not. People view others as freer and more responsible for their actions when they are striving to gain something attractive than when they are trying to avoid an aversive outcome. Does this asymmetry mean that jurors are less likely to discount the confession that is lured through the promise of leniency, relief from detention, or immunity from prosecution, than the confession that is obtained by the threat of maltreatment, harsh punishment, or other unfavorable legal action? We addressed this question in a series of mock jury studies.[79]

In our research, subjects read a detailed transcript of a criminal trial. Two cases were used, one involving an automobile theft and the other an aggravated assault. Both included the testimony of a police officer who revealed that the defendant had confessed to the crime. Four versions of each trial were written. In one, the defendant was said to have confessed on his own initiative, as soon as he was arrested. In the second the defendant apparently confessed after having been promised that, if he did, he would be treated well and probably receive from the judge a lenient, maybe even suspended, sentence. In the third the defendant confessed after having been warned that if he did not, he would suffer the consequences of maltreatment and a tough sentence, maybe even the maximum, from the judge. In the fourth version of each trial, the police officer testified that, when confronted, the defendant had flatly denied having committed the crime. After reading the transcript, subjects were asked to decide if the defendant's confession was voluntary or involuntary. They then voted, guilty or not guilty, on a questionnaire. In one study, subjects also deliberated in six-person groups and returned a single verdict.

The results were clear and consistent. Whenever the defendant was threatened with harm and punishment, subjects fully rejected his confession. That is, they viewed it as involuntary and, as such, they exhibited a relatively low rate of conviction. But when the defendant confessed in response to an offer of leniency, subjects did not completely dismiss it. Under these circumstances, they conceded that the confession was involuntary, but then they used that evidence and voted guilty anyway. That happened even when subjects were told by the judge that confessions made in response to promises or threats were considered coercive and should be rejected. We have referred to this pattern of results as the "positive coercion bias."

This bias presents an evidentiary problem for the courts. Apparently, jurors are unwilling to ignore a suspect's confession when it was elicited by the desire to secure an attractive outcome. Actually, that is not particularly surprising. People assume that the promise of reward is a weaker form of behavioral inducement than the threat of punishment, even when the two are equivalent in their effects.[80] When the suspect confesses under what is considered a minimum amount of pressure, jurors assume that he or she must be truly guilty. And as we will suggest in the next chapter, jurors are motivated by the desire to return verdicts that are accurate, even when it means using information that they are supposed to disregard.[81]

The fact that people do not discount confessions that are elicited through promises of leniency, immunity, and other positive incentives, suggests that the courts should be particularly guarded about admitting them. Alternatively, it is possible that cautionary instructions would work if they explained to the jury the underlying reasons for the exclusion of coerced confessions. We wrote such an instruction and found it to be effective.[82]

Videotaped interrogations.

Finally, there are questions raised by the use of videotaped records of interrogation sessions, as in the Lawson case described earlier. They are being used with increasing frequency by law enforcement officials, but with what effect? It is not surprising that prosecutors find them to be persuasive and, hence, to their advantage. It is one thing for jurors to hear a police detective read a written confession signed by the defendant. It is quite another for them to see the defendant confessing first hand. As one district attorney put it, "Jurors work backward from the videotape. They accept it as gospel and see if the evidence supports it."[83] To the extent that the videotapes accurately represent the circumstances surrounding confessions, they should assist juries in their efforts to evaluate their voluntariness. After all, just as the tapes provide a record of the defendants' behavior, they should also provide a record of the interrogators' behavior. But that is not necessarily the case. Often the police conduct their initial interrogations off camera. If the suspect confesses, only then do they ask permission to videotape the rest of the interview which, if needed, would be available as evidence in a trial.[84] What the jury would see, in other words, is the defendant's confession without the circumstances that led up to it. If a suspect were to capitulate under heavy pressure, the jury would not know it from the tape.

There are even more sinister possibilities to be guarded against. The first author recently testified as an expert witness in a 1987 arson-murder trial that took place in San Francisco. Part of the evidence against the defendant was an audiotape of a confession he had made after more than an hour of interrogation. Through the entire session, he denied any wrongdoing. Then following a Watergate-like eight-minute gap in the tape, he confessed. Having been under the influence of alcohol and other drugs, and having not slept the previous night, the defendant was unable to remember what had happened during the eight-minute interlude. But he did retract his confession and plead not guilty.

There is a second more subtle aspect of confession tapes that should be scrutinized. When people watch a conversation between two or more individuals, they overestimate the influence on that interaction of the individual on whom their attention is focused. Thus if subjects are seated in such a way that they are facing one interactant, while looking over the shoulder of the other, they will perceive the former as having led the conversation.[85] This phenomenon was demonstrated in a recent study of how people view videotaped confessions. A mock interrogation resulting in a confession was staged and recorded from three different camera angles so that either the interrogator, the suspect, or both were visible. Groups of subjects were then asked to watch one of these versions of the episode and then rate how coercive they believed the interrogation to be. As predicted, even though all subjects heard the same session, those who watched the suspect viewed the situation as less coercive than those who were focused on the interrogator. When both were visible, ratings were in the moderate range.[86] The implications of this result are striking. It suggests that jurors' perceptions of voluntariness can be systematically manipulated by something as simple as their visual perspective. With the camera's eye directing their attention toward the accused, as is commonly the case, jurors are likely to underestimate the amount of pressure being exerted by the hidden interrogator.

NOTES

1. E. W. Cleary (1952), Evidence as a problem in communicating. *Vanderbilt Law Review*, Vol. 5, pp. 277–295, at p. 282.

2. E. Black (1985), Why Judge Samuels sent Gary Dotson back to prison. *American Bar Association Journal* (September), Vol. 71, pp. 56–59, at 59.

3. Supra note 1.19, p. 169.

4. R. E. Kraut (1978), Verbal and nonverbal cues in the perception of lying. *Journal of Personality and Social Psychology*, Vol. 36, pp. 380–391.

5. Cited in J. Frank (1949), *Courts on Trial: Myth and Reality in American Justice*. Princeton, NJ: Princeton University Press.

6. Cited in B. Kleinmuntz & J. J. Szucko (1984), Lie detection in ancient and modern times. *American Psychologist*, Vol. 39, pp. 766–776.

7. The use of the polygraph as a measure of lie detection is highly controversial on scientific and ethical grounds; for a recent and balanced review, see: Office of Technology Assessment (1983), *Scientific Validity of Polygraph Testing: A Research Review and Evaluation*. Washington, D.C.: U.S. Congress.

8. C. Darwin (1955), *The Expression of the Emotions in Man and Animals*. New York: Philosophical Library (originally published in 1872).

9. See P. Ekman & W. V. Friesen (1969), Nonverbal leakage and clues to deception. *Psychiatry*, Vol. 32, pp. 88–106.

10. P. Ekman & W. V. Friesen (1974), Detecting deception from the body or face. *Journal of Personality and Social Psychology*, Vol. 29, pp. 288–298.

11. For an excellent review, see M. Zuckerman, B. M. DePaulo, & R. Rosenthal (1981), Verbal and nonverbal communication of deception. A chapter appearing in L. Berkowitz (Ed.), *Advances in Experimental Social Psychology*, Vol. 14. New York: Academic Press.

12. M. Zuckerman, D. T. Larrance, N. H. Spiegel, & R. Klorman (1981), Controlling non-

94   THE AMERICAN JURY ON TRIAL

verbal displays: Facial expressions and tone of voice. *Journal of Experimental Social Psychology*, Vol. 17, pp. 506–524.

13. For a review, see Zuckerman et al., supra note 11.

14. For example, L. A. Streeter, R. M. Krauss, V. Geller, C. Olson, & W. Apple (1977), Pitch changes during attempted deception. *Journal of Personality and Social Psychology*, Vol. 35, pp. 345–350; also see B. M. DePaulo, K. Lanier, & T. Davis (1983), Detecting the deceit of the motivated liar. *Journal of Personality and Social Psychology*, Vol. 45, pp. 1096–1103.

15. B. M. DePaulo, G. D. Lassiter, & J. I. Stone (1982), Attentional determinants of success and detecting deception and truth. *Personality and Social Psychology Bulletin*, Vol. 8, pp. 273–279.

16. For example, J. L. McCrystal (1973), Videotape trials: Relief for our congested courts. *Denver Law Journal*, Vol. 49, pp. 463–488; also see G. O. Kornblum (1972), Videotape in civil cases. *Hastings Law Journal*, Vol. 24, pp. 9–36.

17. M. D. Jacoubovitch, G. Bermant, G. T. Crockett, W. McKinley, & A. Sanstad (1977), Juror responses to direct and mediated presentations of expert testimony. *Journal of Applied Social Psychology*, Vol. 1, pp. 227–238.

18. For a more extensive description of this mock jury research, see S. M. Kassin (1984), Mock jury trials. *Trial Diplomacy Journal*, Summer, pp. 26–30.

19. A. E. Morrill (1972), *Trial Diplomacy*. Chicago: Court Practice Institute, p. 52.

20. Ibid.

21. S. M. Kassin (1983), Deposition testimony and the surrogate witness: Evidence for a "messenger effect" in persuasion. *Personality and Social Psychology Bulletin*, Vol. 9, pp. 281–288.

22. For an excellent review of these rules, see E. W. Cleary, Ed. (1972), *McCormick on Evidence* (2nd ed.). Minneapolis, MN: West Publishing Co.

23. E. F. Loftus and J. Goodman (1985), Questioning witnesses. A chapter appearing in S. Kassin & L. Wrightsman (Eds.), *The Psychology of Evidence and Trial Procedure*. Beverly Hills: Sage Publications.

24. See Cleary, supra note 22, p. 63.

25. For example, R. E. Keeton (1973), *Trial Tactics and Methods* (2nd ed.). Boston: Little, Brown; also see F. L. Wellman (1936), *The Art of Cross Examination*. New York: Coller.

26. See J. M. Conley, W. M. O'Barr, & E. A. Lind (1978), The power of language: Presentational style in the courtroom. *Duke Law Journal*, Vol. 6, pp. 1375–1399.

27. Cited in B. Danet (1980), 'Baby' or 'fetus'?: Language and the construction of reality in a manslaughter trial. *Semiotica*, Vol. 32, pp. 187–219.

28. When other verbs were substituted for these, estimates varied considerably, e.g., "collided" yielded 39 mph and "contacted" yielded 32 mph. See E. F. Loftus & J. P. Palmer (1974), Reconstruction of automobile destruction: An example of the interaction between language and memory. *Journal of Verbal Learning and Verbal Behavior*, Vol. 13, pp. 585–589.

29. See R. J. Harris & G. E. Monaco (1978), Psychology of pragmatic implication: Information processing between the lines. *Journal of Experimental Psychology: General*, Vol. 107, pp. 1–22; also see M. K. Johnson, J. D. Bransford, & S. K. Solomon (1973), Memory for tacit implications of sentences. *Journal of Experimental Psychology*, Vol. 98, pp. 203–205.

30. *U.S. v. Pugliese* (1945), 153 F.2d 497, p. 499.

31. W. B. Swann, T. Giuliano, & D. M. Wegner (1982), Where leading questions can lead: The power of conjecture in social interaction. *Journal of Personality and Social Psychology*, Vol. 42, pp. 1025–1035.

32. In support of this explanation of the results, Swann and his colleagues found, in a second experiment, that when subjects are told that the questions they heard were selected at random from a fishbowl, they then ignored the conjecture and inferred nothing from the questions about the respondent.

33. Ibid., p. 1033. Parenthetically, it is interesting to note how powerful this effect really is. Another study showed that the respondents themselves fall prey to it. After being interviewed, they

took personality tests in which they described themselves in various ways. Sure enough, those who had answered questions about introverted or extraverted behaviors later rated themselves as relatively introverted or extraverted, respectively.

34. R. E. Keeton (1973), *Trial Tactics and Methods*. Boston: Little, Brown, p. 87.

35. B. Yandell (1979), Those who protest too much are seen as guilty. *Personality and Social Psychology Bulletin*, Vol. 5, pp. 44–47.

36. See H. C. Kelman and C. I. Hovland (1953), "Reinstatement" of the communicator in delayed measurement of opinion change. *Journal of Abnormal and Social Psychology*, Vol. 48, pp. 327–335; also see M. K. Johnson & C. L. Raye (1981), Reality monitoring. *Psychological Review*, Vol. 88, pp. 67–85.

37. *Alford v. United States* (1931), 282 U.S. 687.

38. See S. M. Kassin and L. S. Wrightsman, Eds. (1985), *The Psychology of Evidence and Trial Procedure*. Beverly Hills: Sage Publications.

39. For a review of similar research, see R. Buckhout (1974), Eyewitness testimony. *Scientific American*, Vol. 321, pp. 23–31.

40. *United States v. Wade* (1967), 388 U.S. 218, p. 229.

41. For an excellent description of this model, see E. F. Loftus (1979), *Eyewitness Testimony*. Cambridge, MA: Harvard University Press; for a comprehensive review of recent research, see G. L. Wells and E. F. Loftus, Eds. (1984). *Eyewitness Testimony: Psychological Perspectives*. New York: Cambridge University Press.

42. Cited by J. C. Brigham (1986), *Social Psychology*. Boston: Little, Brown, p. 465.

43. R. C. L. Lindsay, G. L. Wells, and C. Rumpel (1981), Can people detect eyewitness identification accuracy within and across situations? *Journal of Applied Psychology*, Vol. 66, pp. 79–89; also see G. L. Wells, R. C. L. Lindsay, & T. J. Ferguson (1979), Accuracy, confidence, and juror perceptions in eyewitness identification. *Journal of Applied Psychology*, Vol. 64, pp. 440–448.

44. Several psychologists have actually assessed people's intuitions about the factors that influence eyewitness testimony; e.g., see A. D. Yarmey and H. P. T. Jones (1983), Is the study of eyewitness identification a matter of common sense? A chapter appearing in S. Lloyd-Bostock & B. Clifford (Eds.), *Evaluating Witness Evidence*. New York: Wiley.

45. E. L. Brown, K. A. Deffenbacher, & W. Sturgill (1977), Memory for faces and the circumstances of encounter. *Journal of Applied Psychology*, Vol. 62, pp. 311–318.

46. For example, see E. F. Loftus, D. G. Miller, & H. J. Burns (1978), Semantic integration of verbal information into a visual memory. *Journal of Experimental Psychology: Human Learning and Memory*, Vol. 4, pp. 19–31.

47. See Yarmey and Jones, supra note 44.

48. For a review, see G. L. Wells and D. M. Murray (1984), Eyewitness confidence. A chapter appearing in G. Wells & E. Loftus (Eds.), *Eyewitness Testimony: Psychological Perspectives*. New York: Cambridge University Press.

49. 409 U.S. 188.

50. E. F. Loftus (1974), Reconstructing memory: The incredible eyewitness. *Psychology Today*, December, pp. 117–119.

51. See D. M. Saunders, N. Vidmar, and E. C. Hewitt (1983), Eyewitness testimony and the discrediting effect. A chapter appearing in S. Lloyd-Bostock & B. Clifford (Eds.), *Evaluating witness evidence*. New York: Wiley.

52. In Kansas, see *State v. Warren* (1981), 635 P.2d 1236; at the federal level, see *United States v. Telfaire (1972)*, 469 F.2d 552.

53. See E. F. Loftus (1984), Expert testimony on the eyewitness. A chapter appearing in G. Wells & E. Loftus (eds.), *Eyewitness Testimony: Psychological Perspectives*. New York: Cambridge, p. 280.

54. For a review, see G. L. Wells (1986), Expert psychological testimony: Empirical and conceptual analyses of effects. *Law and Human Behavior*, Vol. 10, pp. 83–95.

55. Ibid.

56. There is a lively debate on the subject within the psychological community; for an excellent account of both sides of the issue, see *Law and Human Behavior*, Special Issue, June 1986, Vol. 10.

57. D. L. Bazelon (1980), Eyewitness news. *Psychology Today*, March, pp. 101–106; J. Weinstein (1981), Review of eyewitness testimony. *Columbia Law Review*, Vol. 81, pp. 441–457.

58. *People v. McDonald* (1984), 37 Cal.3d 351, at pp. 367–368.

59. *United States v. Thevis* (1982), 665 F.2d 616, at p. 641.

60. We should mention that most experts do not wear either the black or white hat, as we have rather simplistically portrayed, but more of a gray hat. The vast majority is probably competent and well intended. But the reality is that experts are almost never appointed by the court, but hired by one of the parties. Accordingly, they are asked only questions that will yield favorable replies. In the context of an adversary system, that places a heavy burden on the cross examiner who must be well prepared to do battle with the expert. For an extensive debate of these issues, see *Law and Human Behavior*, supra note 56.

61. *Federal Rules of Evidence*, Rule 702.

62. The full story, including all the quotes, is reported by J. Capeci (1983), Beating the videotape. *The National Law Journal*, July 4, p. 6.

63. J. H. Wigmore (1970), *Evidence*, Vol. 3 (Revised by J. H. Chadbourn). Boston: Little, Brown.

64. Supra note 1.19.

65. See Cleary, supra note 22, p. 316; also see the ABA Advisory Committee on Fair Trial and Free Press (1968), *Fair trial and free press: The Reardon report*, and G. R. Miller & F. J. Boster (1977), Three images of the trial: Their implications for psychological research. In B. Sales (Ed.), *Psychology in the Legal Process*. New York: Halsted.

66. Quoted in Capeci, supra note 62.

67. *Culombe v. Connecticut* (1961) 367 U.S. 568.

68. Ibid., p. 601.

69. 297 U.S. 278.

70. See M. Guttmacher and H. Weihofen (1952), *Psychiatry and the Law*. New York: W. W. Norton.

71. See H. H. Foster (1969), Confessions and the station house syndrome. *DePaul Law Review*, Vol. 18, pp. 683–701, at p. 690.

72. F. E. Inbau and J. E. Reid (1986). *Criminal Interrogation and Confessions* (3d ed.). Baltimore: Williams and Wilkins.

73. See M. Wald, R. Ayres, D. W. Hess, M. Schantz, and C. H. Whitebread (1967), Interrogations in New Haven: The impact of Miranda. *The Yale Law Journal*, Vol. 76, pp. 1519–1648; also see W. S. White (1979), Police trickery in inducing confessions. *University of Pennsylvania Law Review*, Vol. 127, pp. 581–629.

74. 384 U.S. 436. Since that decision, the Burger court has limited the scope of the Miranda ruling considerably; e.g., see *New York v. Quarles* (1984), 467 U.S. 649.

75. In the Clifton Lawson case, the judge had ruled that the confession was admissible about a year before the trial. It was then, in fact, that Lawson's first lawyer abandoned the case.

76. *Lego v. Twomy* (1972), 404 U.S. 477.

77. L. Ross (1977), The intuitive psychologist and his shortcomings. A chapter appearing in L. Berkowitz (Ed.), *Advances in Experimental Social Psychology*, Vol. 10. New York: Academic Press.

78. For a review of this research, see E. E. Jones (1979), The rocky road from acts to dispositions. *American Psychologist*, Vol. 34, pp. 107–117.

79. For a review of our program of research, see S. M. Kassin & L. S. Wrightsman (1985), Confession evidence. *In* S. Kassin & L. Wrightsman (Eds.), *The Psychology of Evidence and Trial Procedure*. Beverly Hills: Sage Publications.

80. G. L. Wells (1980), Asymmetric attributions for compliance: reward vs. punishment. *Journal of Experimental Social Psychology*, Vol. 16, pp. 47–60.

81. This positive coercion bias can also explain why juries are traditionally very harsh in entrapment cases like ABSCAM; see S. M. Kassin (1984), *Juries and the doctrine of entrapment.* Paper presented at the Meeting of the American Psychological Association, Los Angeles.

82. See S. M. Kassin & L. S. Wrightsman (1981), Coerced confessions, judicial instruction, and mock juror verdicts. *Journal of Applied Social Psychology*, Vol. 11, pp. 489–506.

83. Quoted in S. F. Domash (1985), Videotaped confessions grow. *New York Times*, October 6, Section 21, pp. 1,8.

84. Ibid.

85. For a review of this phenomenon, see S. E. Taylor and S. T. Fiske (1978), Salience, attention, and attribution: Top of the head phenomena. A chapter appearing in L. Berkowitz (Ed.), *Advanced in Experimental Social Psychology*, Vol. 11. New York: Academic Press.

86. G. D. Lassiter and A. A. Irvine (1986), Videotaped confessions: The impact of camera point of view on judgments of coercion. *Journal of Applied Social Psychology*, Vol. 16, pp. 268–276.

5

NONEVIDENTIARY TEMPTATIONS

In Topeka, Kansas, lawyer Pedro Irigonegaray represented the defendant in an unusual murder trial. The facts surrounding the incident were clear. His client went to work and shot his boss seven times with an automatic pistol. Twenty-five people were in the office at the time. They all heard the shooting. Some of them even saw the defendant holding what was literally a smoking gun as the victim fell, dying from his wounds. The defendant immediately told the witnesses to call the police because "he had done what he had to do." At that point, he left the building, drove his car to the Kansas River, threw the pistol into the river, and drove to the police station where he willingly signed a full confession. He was arrested and charged with first-degree murder. At the trial, the defendant justified his premeditated actions by asserting that his victim deserved to die because he was a demon, not a man. After only 45 minutes, the jury returned its verdict—not guilty. When the trial was over, the foreperson, one of the 11 members who believed in demonic possession, told Irigonegaray that, in his opinion, the defendant had done society a favor.[1]

In a recent civil case, Judith Haimes, age 42, of Clearwater Florida, filed a lawsuit against Temple University hospital and her doctor for allegedly destroying her psychic powers. Apparently, Haimes made a living by reading people's auras and helping the police solve crimes. She had been undergoing diagnosis for brain tumors at the hospital and claimed that she suffered an allergic reaction from dye injected during a CAT scan. As a result, she experienced severe headaches whenever she tried to concentrate on her work. After

Haimes presented her case, the judge ordered the jury to disregard her allegations about lost psychic powers and to consider only testimony about her physical symptoms. The jury deliberated for about 45 minutes and then awarded Haimes more than $1 million in damages. A "shocked" lawyer for the defendants charged that the jury did not listen to the judge's instruction, did not understand it, or simply chose to disregard it.[2]

With juries basing their verdicts on demons and psychics, one wonders how faithful they could possibly be to the idea that they disregard matters that are not formally admitted into evidence. These cases are obviously not typical. Trials involving the supernatural are not a recurring problem for the courts. But they illustrate that juries sometimes stray from the hard facts. The second case further illustrates that they sometimes ignore judges' admonitions concerning evidence that is ruled legally inadmissible. But what about the intrusion on their decision making of lawyers' opening statements, closing arguments, the questions they ask, the physical appearance of the litigants, and other extraneous cues picked up in the courtroom?

Jurors are expected to ignore a wide range of nonevidentiary influences from within and outside the courtroom. Most of us know better. The system has always been plagued, for example, by prejudicial media publicity, a chronic contaminant. And there are others. Within the trial itself, jurors are regularly exposed to information that is not in evidence. At times they even generate their own proof. Can they, in the end, distinguish the evidence from the nonevidence? And if they can, will they? At least under certain circumstances, they apparently do not.

BEAUTY AND THE BEAST

> *"Gentlemen of the jury," said the defense attorney, now beginning to warm to his summation, "the real question here before you is, shall this beautiful, young woman be forced to languish away her loveliest years in a dark prison cell? Or shall she be set free to return to her cozy little apartment at 4134 Seaside Street—there to spend her lonely, loveless hours in her boudoir, lying beside her little Princess phone, 312-6642?"[3]*

In principle, we are told that "Beauty is only skin deep," that "You can't judge a book by its cover." But as a practical matter, it is clear that our perceptions of others—their character, ability, and personality—are often affected by their physical appearance. Over and over again, studies reveal that when subjects are asked for their impressions of others whom they do not know, those who are attractive are assumed also to be more happy, kind, talented, honest, warm, and intelligent than their less attractive counterparts.[4] Although few of us would admit this bias to ourselves, the results are very convincing and, in hindsight, not that surprising. The notion that inner human qualities are reflected in outward appearance is deeply rooted in our cultural heritage. In ancient Greek and Hebrew literatures, pestilence, which results in a scarred appearance, is a punishment for sinful behavior.[5] From fairy tales we learn that Cinderella is beautiful and also very kind, that her stepsisters, who are ugly, are also cruel and selfish. The same is true of witches who are portrayed as "old, lame, bleareeied, pale, fowle, and full of wrinkles."[6] It is no wonder that even preschool-age children stereotype others according to their looks.[7]

We have reason to believe that the unconscious effects of appearance carry into the courtroom. Several of Kalven and Zeisel's judges thought there were times when their juries were influenced by the physical appearance of a defendant or victim.[8] Also, mock jury experiments show that unless an individual has used his or her attractiveness to commit a crime (as when a beautiful woman swindles an unsuspecting male victim), unless the objective evidence is overwhelming, or unless the plaintiff or victim is also attractive, it pays for a defendant to look good in front of a jury.[9] We might add that it helps to be good looking in front of a judge, too. In a study conducted in Pennsylvania courts, researchers rated the physical attractiveness of 74 criminal male defendants on a seven-point scale. When they later tracked the dispositions of these cases, they found that the more attractive the defendant, the lighter the sentence. In fact, once convicted, the attractive defendants were twice as likely to avoid prison.[10]

It is hard to imagine a setting more vulnerable to the physical appearance bias than rape trials. Are handsome men more or less likely to commit a sexual assault? Are beautiful women more or less likely to consent or become victimized? Thus far, research shows that people find it difficult to believe attractive men can be rapists. They believe attractive women stand a greater chance of being raped, though it is unclear whether these victims are somehow held responsible for their misfortunes.[11] When it comes to juries, the result is all too familiar—if the evidence is ambiguous, people are more likely to vote guilty when the accused is unattractive and the victim is attractive than the other way around.[12]

Beauty notwithstanding, other aspects of physical appearance affect our perceptions of an individual's character. Height, weight, and other measures of physique are important. So is the face. Most psychologists today are skeptical of theories that link the mind and the body. But juries are not made up of psychologists. In a survey of college students, 90 percent thought the human face is revealing of inner qualities.[13] These students are in good company. Aristotle described in detail the facial signs of strength and weakness, genius and stupidity, courage and timidity. In describing the characters in his plays, so did Shakespeare. One can only wonder what the defendant must have looked like in a trial wherein the prosecuting attorney exclaimed in his closing argument, "he had the worst face for an armed robber any man could have."[14]

There are some interesting relationships between measurable characteristics of the face and people's perceptions of the individual behind that face. Diane Berry and Leslie McArthur constructed faces with the identi-kit that is often used by the police in lieu of artist sketches. Through the use of transparencies, they were able to alter subjects' impressions of a target person simply by inserting features of different shapes, sizes, and location. For example, faces with angular-shaped jaws are perceived as older, stronger, and more dominant than identical faces with more rounded jaws; when large round eyes are added, or when eyebrows are placed relatively high on the forehead, faces take on a more youthful, naive, submissive, and honest appearance.[15]

In ways most of us are unaware of, our first impressions of others are affected by the shapes of their heads, their eyes, ears, chins, and noses. Whether these biases have important decision-making consequences, however, is another matter. To find out, Berry and McArthur varied the defendant's appearance in two written versions of a hypothetical trial. In one version, the defendant was charged with negligence for allegedly having forgotten to warn a customer about the potential hazards of the product he was selling. In the other he was said to have deliberately misled the customer in order to make the sale. For half the subjects, the defendant had a babyish face consisting of large round eyes, high eyebrows, and a small round chin. For the other half, he had the more mature features—small eyes, low brows, and a rectangular chin. Consistent with the hypothesis that people are responsive in an important way to structural properties of the human face, Berry and McArthur found that subjects readily perceived the babyfaced defendant as guilty of negligence, a crime that matched his appearance. In contrast, they viewed the mature-looking individual as guilty when charged with a crime of deceit.[16]

There is little we can do to alter an individual's facial structure for the sake of a jury trial. Plastic surgery notwithstanding, the most litigants can do is make small cosmetic changes and present themselves in court well groomed and appropriately dressed. Clothing, of course, contributes to an individual's overall appearance. "Dress for success" and "clothes make the man" are truisms familiar to trial lawyers and their clients. But there are times when even that is beyond their control, as when criminal defendants are forced to appear handcuffed, in prison attire, or in the presence of armed guards.

It used to be the case that defendants who were already in custody, because they could not post bail, were often brought into the courtroom looking like prisoners. They were also more likely to be convicted and severely sentenced.[17] Then in the 1976 case of *Estelle v. Williams*, the U.S. Supreme Court ruled that because prison attire serves as a constant reminder of the defendant's condition, to compel an individual to appear as such before the jury violates his or her right to a fair trial.[18] "The garb of innocence," as one court put it,[19] is needed to protect the presumption of innocence—unless, of course, the defendant chooses to wear prison clothing in the hope of eliciting a sympathetic reaction.

On the presence of armed guards in court, however, the Court has taken a very different position. In a 1984 case in Rhode Island, Charles Flynn and five others were charged with the robbery of a safe deposit box. At their trial, four uniformed and armed state troopers escorted the defendants into the courtroom and sat conspicuously behind them. After being found guilty, Flynn argued that the troopers' presence created an armed camp that undermined his right to be presumed innocent. The U.S. Court of Appeals for the First Circuit agreed and reversed his conviction. But then, emphasizing judges' need to maintain security, the Supreme Court denied the prejudicial impact of armed guards and reinstated the jury's verdict.[20]

Does the appearance of a defendant in prison clothing or in the presence of armed security guards create in jurors the impression of guilt? Do these conditions lead jurors to perceive the accused as more like the beast than a beauty? Gary Fontaine and Rick Kiger had people watch a videotape reenactment of a murder trial. While the defendant and other witnesses testified, their photographs were shown on the screen. The defendant, a young white man, was depicted in one of four ways. He was dressed in either civilian or prison clothing, and he was seated either next to his attorney or with a uniformed guard. Except for these variations in appearance, all subjects observed the same trial. These variations proved important. When the defendant was dressed in prison clothes *or* when he was accompanied by a guard, subjects were more likely to view him as guilty and recommend that he be punished with a stiff sentence.[21]

LAWYER TALK: COURT-SANCTIONED NONEVIDENCE

Although the courts try to keep juries from basing their verdicts on nonevidentiary temptations, there are notable exceptions to that rule. Surrounding the evidence, both before and after its presentation, is an opportunity for lawyers to speak *directly* to the jury. It is persuasion in its rawest form.

Let us begin with opening statements. Before the first witness ever takes the stand, lawyers are permitted to preview (but not argue) their cases. Depending on the circumstances, they may be limited to a brief, very general outline, very much like the table of contents of a book or they may recite in chapter and verse a detailed prospectus of who will testify, what they will say, and how it all fits into the big picture. As with other aspects of trial practice, lawyers vary in their use of opening statements. Some decline the opportunity altogether, others believe that cases can be won at this stage of the game. In the first trial of Juan Corona, described in Chapter 1, the district attorney's opening statement lasted for a day and a half.

The closing argument, or summation, offers lawyers an opportunity to address the jury later but in a less restrained, more free-wheeling manner. With the evidence having been presented, they may interpret it, comment on the witnesses, raise doubt about the opponent's case, and develop a theory to account for the events in question. Many attorneys believe that the most effective way to use the summation is to "hammer away at your best points."[22] Others maintain that because juries have a natural tendency to organize fragments of evidence into meaningful stories, lawyers should offer them plausible, coherent scenarios around which they could structure their deliberations. As one advocate put it, "A trial is a patchwork of bits and pieces of evidence. A jury may not appreciate the significance of many of these scraps until they have been pieced together by an artful advocate."[23]

At some level it makes good psychological sense to allow attorneys to address the jury directly. From the witness stand alone, jurors will receive little more than a disjointed array of facts. In order to enhance their competence as processors of that information, lawyers can provide them with "schemas," unifying themes that serve as frameworks for organizing the input and facilitating its retrieval from memory later on. As a demonstration of this point, imagine trying to recall the sentences from the following brief passage:

> *The procedure is actually quite simple. First, you arrange things into different groups. Of course, one pile may be sufficient depending on how much there is to do. . . It is important not to overdo things. That is, it is better to do too few things at once than too many. In the short run this may not seem important, but complications can easily arise. A mistake can be expensive as well. At first the whole procedure will seem complicated. Soon, however, it will become just another facet of life.*

Now consider how much easier that task would have been had you known that this passage had the title "Washing Clothes."[24]

In addition to providing schemas that serve as a mnemonic device, lawyers can enhance jurors' information processing competence by getting them to keep an open mind throughout the proceedings. As we will see in Chapter 6, jurors are expected to suspend their judgment until they retire for deliberations. Left to their own devices, they do not meet that expectation; instead, they form opinions, sometimes tentative, sometimes firm, based on the early returns. It is possible, however, that through the strategic use of opening statements, lawyers can keep jurors from being too heavily persuaded by the incomplete picture and, in turn, from making their judgments prematurely. Research has shown that forewarning members of an audience to anticipate a speaker's attempt to change their attitude increases their resistance to that speaker's arguments.[25] Aware of an impending effort to influence their opinions, people anticipate the message and generate counterarguments to it. The more counterarguments they come up with, the greater is their resistance.[26] To be forewarned, then, is to be forearmed. In the courtroom, this means that if lawyers can prepare jurors for the opponent's case and arm them with counterarguments, they could minimize its initial persuasive impact. If both sides were to use this strategy, the net result would be a jury that is vigilant, critical of the evidence, and reluctant to commit itself prematurely to either side.

By constructing schemas and forewarning the jury, lawyers can use their opening statements and closing arguments in ways that facilitate the jury's task. There is, of course, another side to the story. Opening statements are valuable precisely because of their precocious entry, before the evidence, into the trial. The following incident illustrates the point all too humorously. Two young lawyers in a Miami trial, having completed only their opening statements, disagreed over a point of law. The judge asked the jury to leave the courtroom while the issue was resolved. When the jury was summoned back, just a few minutes later, the foreman announced, "We've arrived at a verdict, Your Honor."[27]

Opening statements are like a two-edged sword. Although they can facilitate jurors' ability to process information by providing schemas that *organize* input, they can also affect how jurors *interpret* that input. Research has shown that schemas lead people to make unconscious inferences of what "must" have happened in an incomplete story. Thus, when people read about a character who visits the doctor, a script that conjures up familiar images for most of us, they later "recall" that he had his blood pressure checked by the nurse and other details that make sense within the script but were not contained in the actual story.[28] Schemas can also *prime* jurors to construe ambiguous evidence in particular ways. Thus, when people are repeatedly exposed to words associated with traits such as kindness or hostility, they then interpret other people's actions according to the category previously activated.[29] One can well imagine how the skilled attorney might take advantage of these phenomena within an adversarial context.

The closing argument introduces its own share of problems. Judges can control when summations are to be made and how long they should last. When it comes to questions of their content and the style of their presentation, however, almost anything goes. There is no uniform standard.[30] In practice, lawyers are permitted to stray far and wide from the facts. "To be palatable," closing arguments "may require the lubrication not only of appealing organization and presentation, but of emotion as well."[31] Maybe, maybe not. Relying heavily on appeals to emotion does not necessarily work. Consider the 1986 antitrust case involving the USFL and the NFL, competing professional football leagues. In that trial, the USFL lawyer tried hard to influence the jury with theatrics. In the end his client was awarded an insulting $1 in damages.[32]

As an opportunity to reach jurors through the heart instead of the mind, lawyers are known to use their closing arguments to arouse passions and sentiments, anger and sympathy. There are limits, of course. But what are they? In one recent murder trial, the defendant appealed his conviction and death sentence because the prosecutors referred to him in their closing arguments as "an animal" who should be on "a leash"; at one point, in fact, they declared that someone should have "blown his head off." The U.S. Supreme Court condemned these statements as improper but ruled that they did not violate the defendant's right to a fair trial.[33] It is ironic, we think, that juries are told to base their verdicts on evidence to the exclusion of everything else, and yet they are bombarded by sanctioned appeals to nonevidentiary temptations.

Lawyers usually preface their opening and closing remarks by telling the jury that what they say is not evidence. Judges make the same cautionary statement in their formal instructions. Does it matter? That is, does this kind of warning help jurors to maintain separate files in their memory for evidence, lawyer talk, and their own thoughts on it all? Probably not. Imagine being asked, after having taken a semester-length course in college, to use on a final exam only those aspects of your knowledge that you had obtained from the lectures, while disregarding all information acquired from the readings, meetings with the professor, or conversations with classmates. It is the same kind of task.

In an extensive series of experiments on "reality monitoring," cognitive psychologist Marcia Johnson and her colleagues have found that people are often unable to recall the sources of their information.[34] Thus under certain circumstances people remember the *content* of a message (what is thought or said), while forgetting the *source* of that information (who, if anybody, said it; when, and where it was thought or said). People are especially vulnerable to this kind of confusion when the possible sources of information are equally plausible—as when jurors must figure out, after the trial presentation, whether their beliefs are based on what is said by the lawyers or the witnesses, or whether they are the product of their own self-generated inferences. In the end, it means jurors might erroneously attribute their own versions of reality, or a lawyer's version, to reality itself.

All this has important practical implications for the psychology of lawyer talk to the jury. The second author, in collaboration with Tom Pyszczynski and others, tested the effects of opening statements in a series of mock jury experiments. Consistently they found that a strong opening statement is persuasive when it precedes all the evidence;[35] it even can be effective when it is not subsequently borne out by the evidence! In one study, subjects read one of three versions of an auto theft trial. In one version, the defense attorney claimed that "we will provide evidence that will show conclusively that the defendant could not possibly have stolen the car. Specifically, we will present testimony proving that he was seen at the Sundown Motel in Murray, Kentucky, at the very time the crime was taking place . . . there is no way he could have stolen the car." That promise of an ironclad alibi was made as part of the opening statement. As is turned out, however, no evidence of the sort was ever presented. But it did not matter. Compared to subjects to whom that claim was never made, those who were promised the alibi that never materialized were more likely to vote for the defendant's acquittal. That unsubstantiated claim failed only in a third version of the trial, where the prosecuting attorney reminded the jury of the gross discrepancy between what was promised and what was proved.[36]

From a practical standpoint, attorneys should never pass up an opportunity to address the jury whenever they can. It is no wonder that one consultant advises trial lawyers that "since jurors don't seem to be able to distinguish between arguments and testimony . . . in a very real sense, the advocate 'testifies' during his opening and closing statements."[37] But these findings also leave us with the uneasy feeling that reality monitoring in trials is more difficult than the courts realize; that on their own, jurors might be relatively insensitive to the sources of their trial beliefs. It is as if evidence, opening statements, closing arguments, and inferences are all blurred within the juror's overall picture of the case.

The Forbidden Fruit of Inadmissible Testimony

Anyone who has seen *The Verdict*, a 1983 movie starring Paul Newman, will recall the jury's poignant defiance of the judge who had refused to allow critical evidence into the trial record. Newman, playing attorney Frank Galvin, a solo practitioner, represented the plaintiff in a medical malpractice suit against a prominent Catholic hospital in Boston. The victim was a pregnant young woman who is brain damaged, a living corpse, as a result of complications experienced in surgery. Early on, it is clear to the audience that members of the hospital staff were negligent in her treatment and, with the help of a major corporate law firm, were conspiring in an elaborate and malicious coverup. It is a classic David and Goliath script. Through most of the trial, the plaintiff's performance is dismal. Then Galvin manages to track down an admissions nurse who had disappeared from Boston shortly after the incident. After pleading with her to testify, she reluctantly agrees. While on the stand, she produces a document that literally proves the plaintiff's case. The judge, who is overtly partial to the defense, rules that the nurse's testimony, as well as the document she produces, are inadmissible and that jurors should disregard them. But they do not. To the relief and delight of the audience, they find for the plaintiff and award the victim's family several million dollars.

As a work of fiction, *The Verdict* is rather contrived. In fact, it contains at least 15 legally erroneous rulings.[38] However, it very effectively portrays a situation that is not uncommon in jury trials—the conflict created when a jury is tempted by the forbidden fruit of inadmissible testimony.

In order for information to be allowed into evidence, it must pass two tests. First, it must be *relevant*. That means it must "make the existence of any fact that is of consequence to the determination of the action more probable or less probable than it would be without the evidence."[39] Thus if an individual is sued for causing an automobile collision by driving negligently, that person's accident record is relevant because it sheds light on his or her predisposition for negligence. In contrast, that a defendant may have hired an expensive attorney is not relevant because it does not increase or decrease the likelihood of his or her negligence.

According to the rules, all admissible evidence must be relevant, but not all relevant evidence is necessarily admissible. Even if information has probative value, the judge can still exclude it on other grounds: "the danger of unfair prejudice, confusion of the issues, or misleading the jury, or by considerations of undue delay, waste of time, or needless presentation of cumulative evidence."[40] Some of these reasons were offered recently by a judge who refused to let an accused rapist display his penis, a photograph, or a wooden model of it, to the jury. The defendant, in this case, had claimed that the rape with which he was charged was impossible because his penis was nine inches long "in the flaccid state" and more than five inches in its circumference. The physician who examined the victim, and found no vaginal lacerations, agreed. The defendant's girlfriend, his common-law wife, and the photographer, all testified on the size of the defendant's penis. Noting that "The potential for confusion of issues and misleading the jury was substantial," an appeals court upheld the judge's ruling.[41] Other, more mundane examples are numerous. The judge may decide not to allow a jury to see photographs of an accident victim, or pictures of the victim's surviving children, because it might arouse too much sympathy. Or, the judge may refuse to admit the results of a lie detector test because the jury might not appreciate the fact that it is potentially unreliable. Evidence may also be rejected for reasons of judicial policy. An example are the so-called technicalities that prevent prosecutors from introducing the admissions of a defendant who was not properly informed of his or her *Miranda* rights.

The rules of evidence are not as simple in practice as they are in theory. Judges often rule on questions of evidence before the trial. But not all issues can be anticipated. Every now and then, a lawyer will ask a question and the witness will provide an answer that should not have become known to the jury. When that happens, the opposing attorney is faced with a difficult choice. He or she can either object and request that the testimony be stricken from the record or remain silent in the hope that the revelation will not prove to be too damaging. In response to an objection, the judge would then rule on the admissibility question. If the objection is sustained, that is, if the judge decides that the testimony was prejudicial, unreliable, or illegally obtained, then the judge has two alternatives. One is to declare a mistrial, a costly strategy reserved for only the most harmful contaminants. The other is to strike the testimony from the record. The judge would then turn to jurors and tell them to disregard the information. Can people really strike inadmissible testimony from their minds as the court reporter can strike it from the record? And if the information is relevant, *would* they ignore it even if they were capable?

The answer is *no*. In one experiment, mock jurors read about the trial of a defendant who was charged with armed robbery and murder. When there was only weak circumstantial evidence against him, not a single subject voted guilty.

But in a second version of the case, the prosecution introduced an illegally obtained tape recording of a phone conversation in which the defendant had said to a bookmaker, "I finally got the money to pay you off . . . when you read the papers tomorrow, you'll know what I mean." The defense argued vigorously that since the wiretapping operation was illegal, it should not be introduced into evidence. The judge disagreed and ruled that the tape was indeed admissible. In this version of the case, the conviction rate increased, as expected, to 26 percent. But what if the judge had excluded the tape from the trial record? In a third version of the case, like the second, the tape was revealed and the defense objected. In this instance, however, the judge ruled that the wiretapping was illegal, that the tape was inadmissible, and that jurors should disregard it. They did not. As many as 35 percent of them voted for conviction.[42] In fact, additional research has shown that when the judge embellishes his or her ruling by admonishing jurors at length, they become even *more* likely to use the forbidden information.[43] It is just like what happens when people are told *not* to think about a white bear. Try it. In a recent study on the "paradoxical effects of thought suppression," Daniel Wegner and his colleagues found that when people actively try to suppress a particular thought, not only do they fail to do so, but they become preoccupied—even obsessed—with that very thought![44]

Not all members of the legal community would be surprised by these results. Admonishing the jury to strike information from their minds is a ritual described by eminent judges as a "mental gymnastic,"[45] "an unmitigated fiction,"[46] and a "judicial placebo,"[47] "like exorcising phrases intended to drive out evil spirits."[48] To make matters worse, admonishing the jury can backfire. Think about the psychology of this paradoxical command. For starters, it is bound to draw an unusual amount of attention to the information in controversy, more than it would have otherwise. Sit up and take notice—it must be important. But there is more to it than that. Telling the jury that it must disregard evidence is, to them, a form of censorship. It means restricting their decision-making freedom, something that people react strongly against. When information is banned, people assume it is important and are persuaded by it. As with any scarce commodity, we want most what we cannot have.[49]

Practically speaking, inadmissible testimony poses a real dilemma. Trial lawyers are advised, as a matter of strategy, that they should sometimes decline the opportunity to object. That leaves them in the unfortunate position of having to cut their losses. Is there anything else the courts can do to prevent the leakage of evidence that should not be on the record? One solution is to replace live trials with videotaped trials. Before it is shown to the jury, it is said, judges can view the tape, rule on objections, and delete all inadmissible testimony. The jury would then ingest a carefully edited, purified product.[50] As interesting as this proposal seems, one would have to question whether it is too drastic a measure to take. Like using dynamite to kill a field mouse, it could create greater problems than it solves.

Although a certain degree of random imperfection is to be expected, there are times when the legal system actually opens its doors to the introduction of inadmissible evidence. According to the rules, if evidence is allowed for one purpose but not another, the judge shall admit it, restrict its proper scope, and instruct the jury accordingly. This situation can arise in a number of ways. For example, the prosecution is normally not permitted to reveal if the defendant has a criminal record. This rule is based on a legitimate fear that juries would be prejudiced by the defendant's background, presume guilt rather than innocence, and vote to convict on the idea that "if he did not commit the crime charged he probably has committed or will commit other crimes."[51] So far so good. But if the defendant takes the stand, the prosecuting attorney, on cross examination, is allowed to ask about past convictions in order to impeach the defendant's credibility as a witness. The judge then tells the jury (a) that it may consider the defendant's record as it bears on his or her credibility, but (b) that it must not allow that same information to influence their beliefs about the defendant's guilt or innocence. This provision is known as the limited admissibility rule.[52] It assumes, of course, that jurors are able and willing to compartmentalize important evidence, using it to prove one aspect of the case, but then pretending as if it does not exist for another.

Viewed by many as a lesson in futility, this rule is one of the unmitigated fictions of evidence law. One survey revealed that 98 percent of the lawyers and 43 percent of the judges questioned were convinced that jurors could not possibly comply with this instruction.[53] They are right. Research subjects who learn that a defendant has a record and are then limited in their use of that evidence are more likely to vote for conviction even though their judgments of the defendant's credibility are unaffected by that information.[54] Likewise, deliberating juries spend a good deal of time talking about prior records, not for what they imply about defendants' credibility as witnesses, but for what they suggest about their criminal predispositions.[55] Nothing demonstrates the fiction of this rule better than this: mock jurors who are told about the defendant's record view the rest of the evidence as stronger and more damaging than those who are uninformed, even though both groups read the same exact case.[56] Can a defendant who takes the stand receive a fair trial if his or her past is scarred by a criminal record? In light of the limited admissibility fiction, probably not.[57]

Part of the problem is that juries do not share the courts' views of what constitutes a fair trial. The law defines justice within a due process model. A verdict is just if it is reached in a manner that is consistent with the rules and procedures designed to regulate the fairness of the process. But due process is not the jury's main concern. Ask any juror what his or her objective is, and the answer will be to come up with the *right* decision. There are times, as we will discuss in chapter 7, when juries bend this objective in order to make decisions that are fair and equitable, though not necessarily consistent with the law. But as a general rule, the jury defines justice in terms of the accuracy of an outcome. It is not how you play the game, but whether you win or lose that really counts.

Ordinarily, the due process and accuracy objectives are perfectly compatible. It would not have made much sense, obviously, to develop a method of adjudication that did not, in the long run, achieve accurate results.[58] Based on their experience and on their assumptions about human behavior, the courts have determined that certain kinds of information are so inherently prejudicial, unreliable, or unfair that they should not be made available to the jury. Granted, that policy might result in occasional verdict errors but, in the long run, the objectives of accuracy are well served. It is the "in the long run" part that is unsatisfying to many people. Precisely because juries want to make correct decisions, they find it difficult to resist the temptation to use information that is not in the trial record. There are countless numbers of documented cases in which well-meaning but overzealous jurors overstepped their bounds by actively generating their own evidence. The problem with jurors becoming investigators is that the parties are unable to cross examine them or otherwise confront their findings.[59] Probably the clearest example is when jurors make unauthorized visits to the scene of a crime, or when they seek additional information by privately contacting defendants, their lawyers, prosecutors, police officers, witnesses, and bailiffs. Jurors have even been known to conduct their own experiments and demonstrations. In one case, for example, the defendant had an alibi that located him in Reno, Nevada at a certain time before the crime was to have been committed in Carson City. A juror went to the defendant's place of employment, timed the drive from there to the scene of the crime, concluded that it was possible, and reported his findings to the others. The trial judge did not declare a mistrial because, in his view, the travel time between locations was common knowledge. But the appeals court disagreed and overturned the jury's conviction.[60] It is so important that juries restrict their findings to the trial record that a verdict can be reversed even if the jury just happened to stumble upon additional material during its deliberations. That occurred in a case against a defendant who was charged with forging securities. His attache case was introduced into evidence. When the jurors opened it, they found freshly laundered shirts. Although neither the government nor defense knew it, there was $750 in cash in one of the pockets.[61]

Voices from an Empty Chair

Suppose a party involved in a traffic accident fails to call to the witness stand a friend who was his passenger during the collision. Or, suppose that a defendant charged with burglary claims to have been drinking in a bar at the time, but fails to call the bartender as an alibi witness. In cases such as these, do juries naturally expect the witnesses to appear and, if they do not materialize, do juries assume that their testimony would have been unfavorable? Should lawyers be permitted, in their closing arguments, to cite the *absence* of particular witnesses as proof of their adverse testimony? And how should judges instruct their juries on the matter?

These questions are not uncommon in trial practice. To handle the problem, the courts have developed what has come to be known as the missing witness rule, or the empty chair doctrine.[62] First articulated by the U.S. Supreme Court in 1893, the rule states that "If a party has it peculiarly within his power to produce witnesses whose testimony would elucidate the transaction, the fact that he does not do it creates the presumption that the testimony, if produced, would be unfavorable."[63] The reasons for this rule are straightforward. The courts believe that parties who fail to call knowledgeable witnesses are concealing evidence and should be pressured to come forward with it. Besides, they claim, since juries assume the worst about missing witnesses anyway, the rule simply allows them to draw a natural conclusion.[64] In practical terms, this rule has two effects. First, it allows lawyers, in their closing arguments, to comment on the absence of witnesses and speculate about the damaging testimony that they would have provided. Second, it permits judges, in their final instructions, to invite the jury to draw those same negative inferences. There is one major exception to this rule. In the 1965 case of *Griffin v. California*, the U.S. Supreme Court erected a protective barrier around the criminal defendant. Based on the constitutional right of the accused to remain silent, the Court ruled that neither the judge nor the prosecuting attorney is allowed to comment on the defendant's failure to testify. If the judge says anything, it must be to instruct the jury *not* to draw the negative inference.[65]

Opponents of the empty chair doctrine argue that the courts can never know for sure what a witness would have said on the stand, that there are many reasons for not calling particular witnesses, and that to invite juries to speculate about hypothetical testimony would result in confused deliberations and inaccurate verdicts. The main problem, it is said, is that litigants might keep potential witnesses off the stand for reasons other than the substance of their testimony. For example, the witness might not come across well because of a criminal record, an unattractive appearance, or awkward mannerisms. Or a lawyer might fear that a particular witness would not cope well with the stress of cross examination, would be subjected to humiliating questions, or would reveal irrelevant facts that could prove damaging. Ultimately, the critical question to be answered is, how does the empty chair doctrine affect the jury? Do people naturally make the missing witness inference, as the courts have suggested, or does the rule alter their decision-making process?

Unfortunately, the issue has not been the subject of much research, so our answers are tentative at best. What we do know, however, suggests the following conclusion. There are times when witnesses are so central to a case and so conspicuous in their absence, that juries cannot help but speculate, even without prompting, about their failure to testify.[66] Imagine for a moment that you were a juror in the trial of a defendant who was accused of beating his 2-year-old stepson to death. Testifying on his own behalf, the defendant claimed that while he, his wife, and the child were in the bathroom, the child had a seizure, fell to the floor unconscious, and died. According to the defendant's story, his wife witnessed the entire event. And yet, she did not testify.[67] Is it possible to ignore the absence of this critical witness, the defendant's own wife who, more than anyone else, could have proved his innocence? In this kind of case, jurors are likely to make their own inferences, unsolicited by the judge or the opposing lawyer.

This phenomenon is revealed by how people react to the failure of a criminal defendant to take the stand. In a series of experiments, David Shaffer and his colleagues found that mock jurors exhibited a significant bias, in their deliberations and in their verdicts, against defendants who did not testify. This bias was apparent even when they were specifically admonished not to draw negative inferences from this nonevidence.[68] In this kind of situation, the negative inference is all too natural, even for those well trained in the law. As expressed by congressman Richard Nixon, when he confronted a recalcitrant witness while serving on the House Committee on Un-American Activities nearly 40 years ago, "It is pretty clear, I think, that you are not using the defense of the Fifth Amendment because you are innocent."[69]

But now let us consider the more common situation, where the potential witness is not so obviously central to the case. In these instances the chances are that jurors, already faced with evaluating the affirmative evidence, do not concern themselves with their absence. Ordinarily people are not acutely sensitive to events that do *not occur*.[70] In the trial context a recent study showed that subject jurors were highly affected in their judgments by the testimony of an eyewitness who either identified or said that he could not identify the accused. But those same subjects were unaffected by a report about another eyewitness who was unable to make an identification but did not testify as such in court.[71] "Out of sight, out of mind," as they say. That being the case, we tentatively conclude that jurors are not, on their own, sensitive to missing witnesses. If the courts want their juries to draw those negative conclusions as a means of pushing litigants to produce evidence, fine. But they should not rationalize that policy by asserting the naturalness of the inference. Without intervention, it is not as natural as one might think. It is often the court, not the jury, that drags the empty chair into evidence.

There is an additional reason to be concerned about the wisdom of this rule. In every trial, jurors are told over and over again to base their judgments only on the evidence produced in court. What are they to think when they are then instructed just the opposite, that they may, in fact, speculate about witnesses who never appeared and were never subject to cross examination? Sending these kinds of mixed signals can only confuse the jury about its role. By opening that door, the courts are inadvertently inviting jurors to stray far and wide from the ideal of a verdict driven by the *evidence*. Once the restraint is lifted and jurors have begun to procure their own proof by speculating about missing witnesses, what is to prevent them from pursuing the implications of other matters not in the record? It makes little sense, we think, to warn jurors against obtaining information through experiments, demonstrations, and the like, but then encouraging them to create evidence from the absence of evidence.

NOTES

1. P. Irigonegaray (1986), personal communication.
2. Psychic wins damage award for CAT scan (1986), *San Francisco Chronicle*, March 29, p. 3.
3. *Playboy's Complete Book of Party Jokes* (1972), p. 148.
4. For a review of this literature, see G. R. Adams (1977), Physical attractiveness research: Toward a developmental social psychology of beauty. *Human Development*, Vol. 20, pp. 217–239.
5. R. Crawfurd (1914), *Plague and Pestilence in Literature and Art*. London: Oxford.
6. O. M. Hueffer (1973), *The Book of Witches*. Totowa, NJ: Rowman & Littlefield.
7. See J. H. Langlois & C. W. Stephan (1981), Beauty and the beast: The role of physical attractiveness in the development of peer relations and social behavior. A chapter appearing in S. Brehm, S. Kassin, & F. Gibbons (Eds.), *Developmental Social Psychology: Theory and Research*. NY: Oxford.
8. *Supra* note 1.19.
9. See R. F. Baumeister & J. M. Darley (1982), Reducing the biasing effect of perpetrator attractiveness in jury simulation. *Personality and Social Psychology Bulletin*, Vol. 8, pp. 286–292; also see H. Sigall & N. Ostrove (1974), Beautiful but dangerous: Effects of offender attractiveness and nature of crime on juridic judgment. *Journal of Personality and Social Psychology*, Vol. 31, pp. 410–414; also see R. A. Kulka & J. D. Kessler (1978), Is justice really blind? The influence of litigant physical attractiveness on juridical judgment. *Journal of Applied Social Psychology*, Vol. 8, pp. 366–381. A review of this literature is provided by F. C. Dane & L. S. Wrightsman (1982), Effects of defendants and victims' characteristics on jurors' verdicts. A chapter appearing in N. Kerr & R. Bray (Eds.), *The Psychology of the Courtroom*. NY: Academic Press.
10. The correlation between physical attractiveness and sentencing severity was statistically significant even after controlling for crime seriousness. J. E. Stewart II (1980), Defendant's attractiveness as a factor in the outcome of criminal trials: An observational study. *Journal of Applied Social Psychology*, Vol. 10, pp. 348–361.
11. See G. L. Patzer (1985), *The Physical Attractiveness Phenomena*. NY: Plenum.
12. M. B. Jacobson (1981), Effects of victim's and defendant's physical attractiveness on subjects' judgments in a rape case. *Sex Roles*, Vol. 7, pp. 247–255.
13. J. C. Liggett (1974), *The Human Face*. NY: Stein & Day.
14. *People v. Jefferson* (1966), 217 N.E.2d 564.
15. For a review of this research, see D. S. Berry and L. Z. McArthur (1986), Perceiving character in faces: The impact of age-related craniofacial changes in social perception. *Psychological Bulletin*, Vol. 100, pp. 3–18.
16. Ibid.
17. A. N. Doob (1976), Evidence, procedure, and psychological research. A chapter appearing in G. Bermant, C. Nemeth, & N. Vidmar (Eds.), *Psychology and the Law*. Lexington, MA: Lexington Books.
18. 425 U.S. 501.
19. *Eaddy v. People* 115 Colo. 488, at p. 492.
20. *Holbrook v. Flynn*, 84-1606.
21. It is interesting, however, that when the defendant suffered *both* indignities, jurors viewed him with sympathetic eyes and judged him with greater leniency. It remains to be seen just how reliable that result is; see G. Fontaine and R. Kiger (1978), The effects of defendant dress and

supervision on judgments of simulated jurors: An exploratory study. *Law and Human Behavior*, Vol. 2, pp. 63–71.

22. P. R. Connolly (1982), Persuasion in the closing argument: The defendant's approach. A chapter appearing in G. W. Holmes (Ed.), *Opening Statements and Closing Arguments*. Ann Arbor, MI: Institute for Continuing Legal Education, p. 160.

23. J. Kaplan & J. R. Waltz (1965), *The Trial of Jack Ruby*. NY: Macmillan, p. 310.

24. Taken from J. D. Bransford and M. K. Johnson (1972), Contextual prerequisites for understanding: Some investigations of comprehension and recall. *Journal of Verbal Learning and Verbal Behavior*, Vol. 11, pp. 717–726; for complete reviews of this and related research, see G. H. Bower (1978), Experiments on story comprehension and recall. *Discourse Processes*, Vol. 1, p. 211; and J. D. Bransford (1979), *Human Cognition: Learning, Understanding, and Remembering*. Belmont, CA: Wadsworth.

25. W. J. McGuire and D. Papageorgis (1962), Effectiveness of forewarning in developing resistance to persuasion. *Public Opinion Quarterly*, Vol. 26, pp. 24–34; the effects of forewarning are especially apparent when people take part in an important task; see R. E. Petty & J. T. Cacioppo (1979), Effects of forewarning of persuasive intent and involvement on cognitive responses and persuasion. *Personality and Social Psychology Bulletin*, Vol. 5, pp. 173–176.

26. See R. E. Petty and J. T. Cacioppo (1981), *Attitudes and Persuasion: Classic and Contemporary Approaches*. Dubuque, Iowa: W. C. Brown.

27. M. Sams, Jr. (1982), My approach to opening statements for the plaintiff. A chapter appearing in G. W. Holmes (Ed.), *Opening Statements and Closing Arguments*. Ann Arbor, MI: The Institute of Continuing Legal Education, p. 22.

28. G. H. Bower, J. B. Black, & T. J. Turner (1979), Scripts in memory for text. *Cognitive Psychology*, Vol. 11, pp. 177–220.

29. T. K. Srull & R. S. Wyer (1979), The role of category accessibility in the interpretation of information about persons: Some determinants and implications. *Journal of Personality and Social Psychology*, Vol. 37, pp. 1660–1672.

30. See H. B. Vess (1973), Walking a tightrope: A survey of limitations on the prosecutor's closing argument. *The Journal of Criminal Law and Crimonology*, Vol. 64, pp. 22–55.

31. J. Kaplan & J. Waltz, supra note 23, p. 310.

32. See D. Anderson (1986), One hundred pennies for a thought. *New York Times*, July 30, pp. 19, 21.

33. *Darden v. Wainwright* (1985), reported in *The New York Times*, June 23, 1985.

34. For example, M. K. Johnson, J. D. Bransford, & S. K. Solomon (1973), Memory for tacit implications of sentences. *Journal of Experimental Psychology*, Vol. 98, pp. 203–205; for a review, see M. K. Johnson & C. L. Raye (1981), Reality monitoring. *Psychological Review*, Vol. 88, pp. 67–85; also see M. K. Johnson (1987), Discriminating the origin of information, a chapter appearing in T. Oltmanns & B. Maher (Eds.), *Delusional Beliefs: Interdisciplinary Perspectives*. New York: Wiley.

35. T. Pyszczynski & L. S. Wrightsman (1981), Effects of opening statements on mock jurors. *Journal of Applied Social Psychology*, Vol. 11, pp. 301–313; G. L. Wells, L. S. Wrightsman, & P. K. Miene (1985), The timing of the defense opening statement: Don't wait until the evidence is in. *Journal of Applied Social Psychology*, Vol. 15, pp. 758–772.

36. T. Pyszczynski, J. Greenberg, D. Mack, & L. S. Wrightsman (1981), Opening statements in a jury trial: The effect of promising more than the evidence can show. *Journal of Applied Social Psychology*, Vol. 11, pp. 434–444.

37. R. J. Crawford (1982), The psychology of evidence. *Trial Diplomacy Journal*, Vol. 5, No. 3, pp. 31–33, at p. 32.

38. R. Ostroff (1983), Legal, ethical problems abound in film. *Kansas City Times*, February 3, p. B-3. Interestingly, in the book on which the screenplay was based, written by an attorney, the judge admits the nurse's testimony into evidence.

39. Federal Rules of Evidence, Rule 401.

40. Federal Rules of Evidence, Rule 403.

41. B. Dickerson (1985), Ban on body, model display upheld in rape case. *The National Law Journal*, August 26, p. 13.

42. S. Sue, R. E. Smith, and C. Caldwell (1973), Effects of inadmissible evidence on the decisions of simulated jurors: A moral dilemma. *Journal of Applied Social Psychology*, Vol. 3, pp. 345–353; for an excellent demonstration of how inadmissible evidence can affect jurors, see T. R. Carretta & R. L. Moreland (1983), The direct and indirect effects of inadmissible evidence. *Journal of Applied Social Psychology*, Vol. 13, pp. 291–309.

43. S. Wolf and D. A. Montgomery (1977), Effects of inadmissible evidence and level of judicial admonishment to disregard on the judgments of mock jurors. *Journal of Applied Social Psychology*, Vol. 7, pp. 205–219.

44. D. M. Wegner, D. J. Schneider, S. R. Carter, & T. L. White (1987), Paradoxical effects of thought suppression. *Journal of Personality and Social Psychology*, Vol. 53, pp. 5–13.

45. *Nash v. United States* (1932), 54 F.2d 1006, at p. 1007.

46. *Krulewitch v. United States* (1949), 336 U.S. 440, at p. 453.

47. *United States v. Grunewald* (1956), 233 F.2d 556, at p. 574

48. J. Frank (1930), *Law and the Modern Mind*. New York: Tudor, p. 184.

49. This notion is based on Jack Brehm's 1966 theory of psychological reactance; see S. S. Brehm and J. W. Brehm (1981), *Psychological Reactance*. NY: Academic Press. There are several studies of how people respond to censored information, e.g., S. Worchel, S. E. Arnold, & M. Baker (1975), The effect of censorship on attitude change: The influence of censor and communicator characteristics. *Journal of Applied Social Psychology*, Vol. 5, pp. 222–239.

50. For a review of this proposal, see G. R. Miller and N. E. Fontes (1979), *Videotape on Trial: A View From the Jury Box*. Beverly Hills: Sage Publications.

51. R. O. Lempert (1977), Modeling relevance. *Michigan Law Review*, Vol. 75, pp. 1021–1057.

52. *Federal Rules of Evidence*, Rule 404(a)(3).

53. Note (1968). To take the stand or not to take the stand: The dilemma of the defendant with a criminal record. *Columbia Journal of Law and Social Problems*, Vol. 4, pp. 215–223.

54. R. L. Wissler and M. J. Saks (1985), On the inefficacy of limiting instructions: When jurors use prior conviction evidence to decide on guilt. *Law and Human Behavior*, Vol. 9, pp. 37–48.

55. See D. R. Shaffer (1985), The defendant's testimony. In S. Kassin & L. Wrightsman (Eds.), *The Psychology of Evidence and Trial Procedure*. Beverly Hills: Sage Publications.

56. V. Hans and A. Doob (1975), Section 12 of the Canada Evidence Act and the deliberations of simulated juries. *Criminal Law Quarterly*, Vol. 18, pp. 235–253.

57. It is conceivable that because so many crimes are actually committed by repeat offenders, juries who know about defendants' past convictions will, in fact, be biased toward guilty verdicts that are often accurate; e.g., see J. B. Weinstein and M. A. Berger's (1976), *Weinstein's Evidence*. New York: Matthew Bender. As Law Professor Wallace Loh noted, the limited admissibility rule appears to represent a compromise by which jurors can obtain the relevant information, while having its purpose limited. The problem with this analysis is that they do not restrict their use of this quasi-admissible evidence; see W. D. Loh (1984), *Social Research in the Judicial Process*. New York: The Russell Sage Foundation.

58. For an introduction to these two conceptions of justice, see H. L. Packer (1964), Two models of the criminal process. *University of Pennsylvania Law Review*, Vol. 113, pp. 1–68.

59. For a review, see D. Edwards, Jr. (1984), Comment: A judge's review of juror misconduct. *Howard Law Journal*, Vol. 27, pp. 1519–1547.

60. *Russell v. State* (1983), 661 P.2d 1293.

61. *Farese v. United States* (1970), 428 F.2d 178.

62. See R. H. Stier, Jr. (1985), Revisiting the missing witness inference: Quieting the loud voice from the empty chair. *Maryland Law Review*, Vol. 44, pp. 137–176.

63. *Graves v. United States* (1893), 150 U.S. 118.

64. See Stier, supra note 62.

65. 380 U.S. 609.

66. Law professor Stephen A. Saltzburg, in fact, argues that when judges rule on admissibility, they should take into account what inferences jurors would make if evidence that they expect to hear does not materialize because it is excluded; see S. A. Saltzburg (1978), A special aspect of relevance: Countering negative inferences associated with the absence of evidence. *California Law Review*, Vol. 66, pp. 1011–1060.

67. *Seyle v. State* (1978), 584 P.2d 1081.

68. For example, see D. R. Shaffer and T. Case (1982), On the decision not to testify in one's own behalf: Effects of withheld evidence, defendant's sexual preferences, and juror dogmatism on juridic decisions. *Journal of Personality and Social Psychology*, Vol. 42, pp. 353–346.

69. Cited in Shaffer, supra note 55, p. 141.

70. See Ross, supra note 4.77.

71. M. R. Leippe (1985), The influence of eyewitness nonidentifications on mock jurors' judgments of a court case. *Journal of Applied Social Psychology*, Vol. 15, pp. 656–672.

6

PROCESSING THE INFORMATION

Long before the computer was invented, the jury's role was defined in information-processing terms. Confronted with a vast array of input from the bench, the bar, and the witness stand, the jury must acquire, comprehend, store, and retrieve all verdict-relevant information before it can dispense justice. It is no small feat to live the life of a flowchart.

In order to evaluate the extent to which juries succeed in traversing the information-processing requirements of their task, we consider the issue in two parts. First, we confront head on the debate over whether jurors are competent in their fact-finding abilities. On this question, we will see, only the harshest of critics believe that jurors fail under routine circumstances. But a respectable number of observers are concerned about their ability to endure the intricacies of long, complex civil cases. Today the nation's federal courts clash in their opinions on the issue. It is only a matter of time before the United States Supreme Court steps in to resolve it.

Next we consider a second aspect of the jury's computer-like role: its ability to suspend all judgmental processes until the necessary data have been received. With trials unfolding over an extended period of time, jurors should store all the information they obtain "as is" in long-term memory and evaluate it only after the trial presentation is over. Through it all they are supposed to maintain an open mind until the door to the jury room closes behind them. In a way this objective is an extension of the impartiality ideal; not only should jurors begin their service with an open mind, nondisposed to favor a particular outcome, but they should maintain that openness until they convene as a group. Judges thus instruct their juries not to express or even form an opinion until all the evidence is in. Are people capable of such detached information processing? Can they be as receptive to the last witness as they are to the first?

THE JURY AS A FACT-FINDING MACHINE

When we talk about a jury's competence, we are referring to its ability to achieve mastery over the information needed to make a rational decision. Whether jurors weigh that information poorly, ascribing too much credibility to some witnesses and not enough to others, whether they contaminate their decision making with factors extraneous to the trial, or whether they refuse to adhere their decisions to the letter of the law, are irrelevant to our evaluation of their information-processing performance. In short, we define a jury's competence strictly by its ability to place the necessary facts—evidence, arguments, and instructions—accurately and fully at its own disposal.

Do juries achieve this very basic ideal within the circumstances of ordinary criminal and civil trials? In more concrete terms, are people attentive when they sit on a jury? Do they understand the proceedings? And in the end do they remember what they observed when it comes time to deliberate? Not everyone thinks so. In 1945, historian Carl Becker said, in general terms, that "trial by jury, as a method of determining facts is antiquated . . . and inherently absurd —so much so that no lawyer, judge, scholar, prescription clerk, or mechanic in a garage would ever think for a moment of employing that method for determining the facts in any situation that concerned him."[1] In 1937, Osborn, a legal scholar, wrote:

> When a group of twelve men, on seats a little higher than the spectators but not quite so high as the judge, are casually observed it may appear from their attitude that they are thinking only about the case before them. The truth is that for much of the time, there are twelve wandering minds in that silent group, bodily present but mentally far away. Some of them are thinking of sadly neglected business affairs, others of happy or unhappy family matters, and, after the second or third day and especially after the second or third week, there is the garden, the house painting, the new automobile, the prospective vacation, the girl who is soon to be married and the hundred and one other things that come to the mind of one who is only partly interested in the tedious proceedings going on before them. There is probably more woolgathering in jury boxes than in any other place on earth.[2]

If this florid description of the jury were true, then the system could not survive. Obviously, juries cannot base their verdicts on information they never received in the first place. To make matters worse, when juries do not master the information presented at trial, they base their judgments instead on a host of irrelevant and unpredictable factors.[3]

There is no support for Osborn's cynical view that jurors routinely fail in the information-processing component of their task. Actually, there is no clear empirical support either way. Part of the reason is logistical: How would one evaluate a jury's fact-finding performance? Asking jurors to report on their own levels of comprehension and recall obviously would not provide accurate estimates of their actual knowledge. It would be more appropriate to test jurors during or immediately after their trials. This approach is feasible, especially through the use of mock juries. But how would we then interpret their scores? In the TV cameras study described in Chapter 1, individual subjects accurately recalled 67 percent of the case facts on which they were tested. Is that an acceptable level of performance? The answer, however evasive it may sound is, it depends. First, it depends on the difficulty level of the questions asked. Anybody can construct a test deliberately designed to elicit high or low accuracy rates. Second, it depends on whether the facts accurately recalled, forgotten, or misunderstood are central or peripheral, important or trivial, in the context of the case as a whole. Not all trial information is created equal. Some facts are necessary for decision making; others are not. Third, it depends on how successfully an alternative decision maker, like a judge, would have performed under the same circumstances. This is not a trivial point because it illustrates that the standard of excellence against which juries are evaluated should be stated in human terms, as something less than 100 percent. Fourth, there remains the ultimate question of how individual jurors' recollections combine to yield a composite group memory. Assuming that individuals accurately recall different facts, a jury's performance should reflect not the average but the sum of its individual members' contributions.[4]

As far as we can tell, at least in run-of-the-mill trials, the jury's ability to process information is not a problem. The judges in Kalven and Zeisel's study almost never attributed their disagreements with the jury to the jury's inability to grasp the case facts; in fact, this attribution was made only once in the 3,576 cases sampled! Kalven and Zeisel also found that the incidence of judge-jury disagreement was no higher for difficult than for easy cases. If the jury had a fact-finding problem, that problem would have surfaced in the more difficult cases leading, in turn, to an increase in the level of judge-jury disagreement. In short, Kalven and Zeisel's research is inconsistent with a portrait of the jury as an incompetent factfinder.[5]

The Nightmare of Complex Civil Litigation

Every now and then a trial comes along that distinguishes itself clearly from ordinary litigation and creates a unique set of problems for its adjudication. The following two cases are good examples.

1. The National Union Electric Corporation (NUE) was a major domestic television manufacturer until its demise in 1970. That year, it filed a complaint against its successful Japanese competitors, including Sony, Mitsubishi, To-

shiba, and several of their subsidiary companies, for alleged violations of antitrust and international trade laws. NUE charged that between 1966 and 1970, the defendants tried to drive American companies out of the market by selling their own TVs at artificially depressed prices through a series of complicated rebate schemes. NUE further charged that these underhanded practices were part of a worldwide conspiracy; that the defendants acted not only with each other, but in agreement with over 90 other companies; and that the Japanese government enabled the defendants to finance the scheme by fixing high prices for TVs sold in Japan.

Four years later the Zenith Radio Corporation, a well-known electronics manufacturer, filed a similar complaint against NUE's defendants, a few additional subsidiaries, and two American companies—Motorola and Sears, Roebuck. Zenith's complaint covered not only TVs but also radios, stereo equipment, and electronic components. A group of Zenith's Japanese defendants filed two counterclaims, charging Zenith and its distributors with their own antitrust violations.

In 1979 the NUE and Zenith suits were consolidated. Overall, the case involved two plaintiffs, 30 of their distributors, 24 defendants, 100 coconspirators, and the Japanese government. Both NUE and Zenith demanded a jury trial. Many of the Japanese defendants, however, tried to prevent it. The case, they said, would be far too complex for a jury. To support their argument, the defendants pointed out that there were millions of documents and over 100,000 pages of depositions already collected through nine years of pretrial investigation; the trial, they projected, would last a full year; and the issues involved were conceptually very difficult (issues such as predatory intent, relevant market products, relevant geographic markets, and the like). The plaintiffs, on the other hand, argued vehemently that the evidence could be clearly summarized for a jury on computer printouts, and that expert testimony in accounting, marketing, and electronics could simplify technical matters. Hearing both sides of the argument, a federal judge in Eastern Pennsylvania concluded that "the actual size of complexity of this litigation falls somewhere in between the two extremes portrayed by the parties." He then ruled that the plaintiffs were entitled by law to a trial by jury regardless of its complexity.[6] The U.S. Court of Appeals for the Third Circuit disagreed.[7]

2. When U.S. Financial (USF) was first incorporated in 1962, it was engaged primarily in the business of financing small accounts. Its total assets were in the $300,000 range. In 1964 it expanded into real estate financing and title insurance and made its first public stock offering. In 1966, R. H. Walter was appointed president. He brought two real estate development companies with him, formed U.S. Mortgage as a subsidiary, and led USF into a period of astronomical growth and expansion. Over the next four years, USF formed and acquired several companies and sold millions of shares of common stock. By 1971, USF was in the business of developing, constructing, operating, mar-

keting, financing, and insuring real estate projects, individually and in joint ventures. In keeping with this growth, its common stock was listed on the New York Stock Exchange. Through all this wheeling and dealing, USF's assets climbed to $310 million.

In 1972, after investigating USF's operations and accounting practices, the Securities and Exchange Commission suspended trading of its securities. USF soon filed for bankruptcy. Shortly thereafter, 18 lawsuits were filed by the SEC, various banks, and purchasers of USF stock offerings, against 100 defendants —USF, its companies, underwriters, attorneys, and accountants. The defendants, many of whom also filed suits against one another, were charged with fraud, negligence, malpractice, and violations of state and federal securities laws. The cases were consolidated for trial and assigned to a federal judge in Southern California.

Several of the parties on both sides requested a jury trial. To that point, three years of pretrial activity had produced 150,000 pages of deposition testimony and an estimated five million documents. The judge projected that the trial would last for two years, contain testimony from more than 240 witnesses, and involve the presentation of hundreds of thousands of pages of documentary evidence—enough to form a stack of paper as high as a three-story building. The subject matter: Everything you always wanted to know (and more) about real estate transactions, securities, and accounting practices. On June 24, 1977, the judge struck the demands for a jury trial. The case, he said, was factually and legally too complex for a jury. The alternative, of course, was a trial by judge.[8] The U.S. Court of Appeals for the Ninth Circuit disagreed.[9]

Are these cases too complex to be tried by jury? That question is a current and lively topic of controversy. The U.S. Court of Appeals for the Third Circuit concluded that the *Japanese Electronics Products* antitrust case described earlier might very well have exceeded a jury's information-processing abilities. In contrast, the U.S. Court of Appeals for the Ninth Circuit held that the *U.S. Financial Securities* case did not. What accounts for the discrepancy—was the antitrust case, in fact, more complex than the securities case? Are jurors in the Ninth Circuit smarter and more sophisticated than their counterparts in the Third Circuit? At what point does a jury's level of competence fail to meet a minimum threshold requirement? And when does a case cross that critical line from being just plain "complex" to "too complex"? These are not legal questions, but psychological ones.

Background: The Case Against Juries

A party's right to a trial by jury in federal civil cases is guaranteed by the Seventh Amendment to the Constitution. In a 1969 opinion, however, the U.S. Supreme Court suggested, albeit in a footnote, that "the practical abilities and limitations of juries" might provide grounds for a complexity exception to that right.[10] Since then, trial judges across the country have taken the unprecedented step of denying litigants' requests for a jury. The federal courts are now in conflict. In the *Japanese Electronics Products* case, the Third Circuit overruled the trial judge's ruling that plaintiffs were entitled to a trial by jury.[11] The Third Circuit based its decision on the argument that a case that is too complex compromises the jury's capacity to render a fair and rational verdict, as guaranteed by the Fifth Amendment. It thus justified its decision by reasoning that when the two values conflict, the right to a fair trial is more important than the right to a jury.

Opposition to this viewpoint is based on two arguments. In the *U.S. Financial Securities* case, the Ninth Circuit refused to recognize any legal justification for a complexity exception. However, it also refused to accept the assumptions about human behavior on which it is based. In the strongest of language the Ninth Circuit said: "this argument unnecessarily and improperly demeans the intelligence of the citizens of this nation. We do not accept such an assertion. Jurors, if properly instructed and treated with deserved respect, bring collective intelligence, wisdom, and a dedication to their tasks, which is rarely equalled in other areas of public service. . . . We do not believe any case is so overwhelmingly complex that it is beyond the abilities of a jury."[12]

The battle lines are clearly drawn. Although various emotional, political and judicial-administrative agendas contaminate the debate, the essential questions are empirical in nature. First, are there trials so complex that juries cannot make rational decisions and, if so, can these trials be identified in advance? Second, if such cases exist, are judges more competent than their counterparts in the jury box? And third, if such cases exist, is there any way to increase juries' information-processing performance?[13]

The case against juries in complex civil litigation is based entirely on speculation. Some trials are plainly overwhelming in their appearance. As such, they are assumed by many to exceed the jury's capacity. Imagine, for example, having to sit on a jury in what has become known as the "megatrial."

In downtown San Francisco, in the spring of 1985, a high school auditorium was converted into a courtroom equipped with cameras, microphones, speakers, 26 counsel tables, 1,000 spectator seats, and a light-signal system for regulating the exchange of information—all in order to accommodate the proceedings.[14] Five former asbestos manufacturers, having already been sued by 24,000 injured workers and their families, were now suing more than 75 insurance companies who denied that their policies had covered the claims. Literally billions of dollars were at stake. The volume of activity generated in this case was staggering. With attorneys from 96 law firms in attendance, one participant quipped, "that the lawyer population in court could outdraw the San Francisco Giants baseball team."[15] Another participant, commenting on the evidence, estimated "there are 60,000 trial exhibits, probably 2,000 deposition transcripts, and God knows how many deposition exhibits. After this, I'm not sure any case will ever seem big again."[16] In fact, the judge and several of the law firms used computers to keep track of the evidence, objections, and judge's rulings on admissibility.

Those who favor abandoning juries in cases that strain human capacity are fond of quoting the jury foreman in the *ILC Peripherals Leasing Corporation v. IBM* antitrust case who, after the 5-month trial and 19 days of deliberation resulting in a deadlocked jury, said "If you can find a jury that's both a computer technician, a lawyer, and an economist, knows all about that stuff, yes, I think you could have a qualified jury, but we don't know anything about that."[17] Likewise, they cite the jury foreman in the *MCI Communications Corp. v. AT&T* antitrust suit who, after listening to seven weeks of testimony about real versus operating cash flows, microwave interconnections into the phone system, and an economic study on the present value of future losses, said "I'm not a telecommunications expert, and I'm not an economist, but most of the testimony was by economists or telecommunications experts. It was tough to keep a handle on what they were saying."[18]

Nobody would seriously deny that claim that juries are sometimes overwhelmed by the intricacies of complex civil cases. But that is not reason enough to altogether abandon their use for an entire, ill-defined category of cases. It is clear, at this point, that the opposition is based on a set of assumptions about human behavior. First, it is assumed that there are certain trials, characterized by a large volume of information and difficult subject matter, that are obviously beyond the grasp of ordinary people. Moreover, it is assumed that cases are easy to identify. "You'll know it when you see it" is, essentially, the approach taken by the Third Circuit in the *Japanese Products Litigation* case.[19]

But there is more. According to former Chief Justice Warren Burger and others, juries in complex cases are composed of *less* than ordinary citizens.[20] Augmenting one assumption with another, they argue that for trials promising to endure for several weeks or months, the well educated professionals within the venire escape jury duty. Holding positions of responsibility and unable to afford the burden of protracted jury duty, they are readily excused. This "deselection" thus leaves a panel that consists of homemakers, retirees, and the unemployed. And then, as the argument continues, it is unfair to those who do serve for prolonged periods of time, leading them to feel resentful and compromising even further the quality of their decision making.

Finally, there is a hidden assumption upon which the entire argument is firmly rooted: that the individual trial judge is more competent to try complex cases than his or her counterparts in the jury box. It is interesting how opponents of the civil jury so conveniently neglect this comparative issue. Former Chief Justice Burger, in a speech about the problems associated with lengthy trials, quipped "We would have to move to incorporating the doctrine of primogeniture so that the eldest child of each juror would take the place of the parent as the

case dragged on.'' And what about judges' eldest children? Long and complicated trials will not disappear with the jury.[21]

These assumptions are without empirical support. Nobody has actually
tested the information-processing performance of jurors, real or experimental, in
complex civil cases. More importantly, the critical comparison between the
judge and jury has never been made. In 1981, however, an initial step was taken
to address these issues. The Federal Judicial Center interviewed 68 judges and
lawyers who had participated in 17 complex civil cases held during the years
1977, 1978, and 1979. Of these trials, the shortest lasted for two months; the
longest took 30 months to complete. Seven were jury trials; ten were bench
trials. The results failed to support the charge that juries in complex civil cases
are incompetent. First, judges and lawyers uniformly affirmed the diligence of
their juries and the validity of their deliberations. Second, the vast majority of
respondents who thought their trials were difficult also thought that the jury had
made the correct decision. In short, judges and lawyers—indeed, the courtroom
veterans themselves—gave their approval on both the process and outcome of
the jury's performance.[22] This study uncovered another interesting result: for
each of the 17 trials, the judge and lawyers involved indicated whether the case
itself was difficult. As it turned out, they exhibited surprisingly little agreement.
This finding calls into question the assumption that it is obvious when difficult
cases become too difficult. It is in the eyes of the beholder, as they say.

It is said that the problem of incompetent juries in complex cases is exacerbated by the deselection of well-educated members of the jury pool. Those who
make that argument cite the *SCM v. Xerox* antitrust suit in 1978 as proof. In that
case, several venirepersons with relevant backgrounds and experience were excused, leaving a jury that had an average tenth-grade level of education.[23] If this
case represented the rule rather than an exception, we would have cause for
alarm. But in an empirical test of this deselection hypothesis, Joe Cecil of the
Federal Judicial Center compared 209 jurors who served in ordinary civil trials
with 281 jurors who served in lengthy trials.[24] By and large, these groups were
similar in the demographic characteristics. The only dramatic difference between the two groups was that more women served in long trials than in short
trials (57 to 43 percent). Although other differences appeared, they were insub-
stantial. For example, compared to those who served in ordinary cases, long-
trial jurors were only somewhat less likely to be employed (70 to 78 percent) or
college educated (22 to 32 percent). These results provide only weak support for
the hypothesis that long trials attract jurors assumed to be incompetent.

Finally, there is the notion that those called into prolonged service develop
negative attitudes that impair their decision making. Another Federal Judicial
Center study, this one conducted by Allan Lind, challenges the validity of that
charge too.[25] Jurors who participated in 28 ordinary civil trials and 22 protracted
trials were questioned about their experiences. In both types of cases, the majority of jurors—more than 80 percent in all—said they would be willing to

serve again if they had it to do over. If jurors who serve in lengthy trials are embittered by the experience, it did not come through in these results.

ODDITIES OF TRIAL MANAGEMENT

The question, are juries competent in complex civil litigation, is bothersome. It is bothersome because it implies that competence is an intrinsic characteristic of juries per se, and that complexity is an intrinsic characteristic of trials per se. They are not. Competence and complexity depend on the interaction between a particular jury, a particular case, and the system within which the jury operates. The system is important. It refers to the set of information-processing rules that shape, guide, and constrain the jury's fact-finding task. In short, competence and complexity are not fixed but malleable characteristics. How competent a jury is, and how complex a trial is, depend on extraneous factors.

One of the most important of these factors is the lawyers themselves. Cast into the leading roles of the trial drama, the lawyers more than anyone else are responsible for the direction and flow of events. Thus, we ask: must antitrust and securities cases overextend the jury's reach, or can the skillful and motivated trial advocate present that material clearly? Gerry Spence, a prominent Wyoming lawyer, writes:

> What is a complex case? I tried one in Chicago a couple of years ago with hundreds of boxes of documents that filled a room as large as a cow barn and with enough paper to feed all the goats in Egypt. But it was not a complex case. I have tried cases with many exhibits, cases that took months in which scores of witnesses were called, cases with jury instructions as thick as the Monkey-Ward catalog and supposed issues as entangled as the Gordian knot. But I never have tried a complex case . . . all cases are reducible to the simplest of stories. . . The problem is that we, as lawyers, have forgotten how to speak to ordinary folks.[26]

Similarly, San Francisco attorney Alvin Goldstein Jr. believes that the lawyer's job is "to make them understand, and if he has not achieved that objective, he has failed, not the jury."[27] That sounds a bit harsh. After all, some cases, like the *Japanese Electronics Products* litigation, are inherently complicated. But there is an interesting footnote to that story, one that sheds light on the defendants' motives trying to avoid a trial by jury. It turns out that attorneys for two of the American companies had made prejudicial, ethnic remarks concerning their Asian adversaries. In fact, the defendants conducted a public opinion poll and found that many Americans harbored prejudice against the Japanese. Confronted with the prospect of facing an all-American jury, it now appears that the defendants were really concerned about the jury's bias, not its *competence.*[28]

Lawyers can certainly make cases appear more or less complex by their presentations. But judges, too, can exert a measure of influence over the jury's competence. How are juries expected to conduct their search for facts? Should they adopt an active or passive approach to their information processing? Looking at case law and at trial-management books written for judges, it is apparent that there is not only a lack of consensus about how juries should conduct themselves, but confusion as well. Warren Urbom, Chief Judge for the District of Nebraska, put it best when he said that "Jurors are rarely brilliant and rarely stupid, but they are treated as both at once."[29]

The Pencil-and-Paper Debate

In what is believed to be the longest-running trial in American jurisprudence, a jury in Belleville, Illinois, sat through 3½ years of testimony to determine whether 65 residents of a small Missouri town were injured when a tank car derailed, spilling 19,000 gallons of chemicals, including the highly toxic substance dioxin.[30] One of the lawyers involved likened the ordeal to the contest of a "great racehorse that ultimately is still running but not thinking." Under these circumstances, one wonders how much of the proceedings jurors can possibly recall with or without the aid of taking notes. It is a thought that borders on the absurd. Thankfully, the jurors in this trial were permitted to keep a written record, so they all did (one juror, in fact, had amassed 74 pages of notes within the first year). Others are usually not that fortunate.

   Should notetaking be permitted? Although the Supreme Court has never directly addressed the question, it has long been a source of controversy. The state courts vary considerably in their opinions and practices. In some states, jurors are allowed to take notes; in others they are not. In some states, jurors are permitted to take their notes into the jury room; in others they are not. In some states, jurors are carefully instructed on how to use their notes; in others they are left to their own devices. The federal courts let their judges decide for themselves, but a source at the Administrative Office of the U.S. Courts estimates that 90 percent of the federal judges do *not* permit jurors to take notes.

   Those of us who take extensive notes in the classroom, on the job, and in other settings, are stunned to find out that it is often prohibited in the courtroom. Three arguments are offered against allowing jurors to take notes. First, it is said that jurors would take notes that are inaccurate, incomplete, too focused on idiosyncratic details, and perhaps even biased. To make matters worse, it is said, because people attach such significance to the written word, jurors would rely too heavily on their faulty notes, making them prone to error in their recollections. Second, notetaking is a distraction. Jurors who are preoccupied with their pencils and paper, it is said, cannot attend carefully to the testimony. They can hear what the witnesses say all right, but unable to observe their nonverbal demeanor, notetakers would suffer in their ability to evaluate witnesses' credibility. Third, it is thought that the presence of written notes in the jury room would tilt the balance of power during deliberations. Through their access to "privileged" information, those who take notes will emerge as leaders and impose their will on the rest of the group.

There is an element of arrogance and hypocrisy to the notion that jurors would be so adversely affected by taking notes. As Judge Urbom noted, "if there are reasons for note-taking by lawyers and judges during a trial, there are at least the same reasons for note-taking by jurors."[31] The reasons, we think, are self evident to all of us who kept notebooks in school. First, the very act itself of taking notes would engage jurors, make them feel more involved, and heighten their attention to the proceedings. Second, if made available during deliberations, jurors' notes would refresh their memories and, in turn, provide them with a greater factual basis for their decisions. Third, in response to the charge that jurors with notes would exert undue influence over others in their groups, we would simply point out that leaders emerge regardless of whether or not notetaking is permitted. Indeed, "Why is it better, as a matter of law, for a jury to be dominated by good speakers than by good note-takers?"[32]

Despite all the armchair speculation, there is surprisingly little in the way of systematic research on notetaking. In 1984 the Committee on Juries of the Judicial Council of the Second Circuit released a report of its own study.[33] They had 6 judges in 32 trials furnish their juries with pencils and paper and allow them to take notes. Most did. Judges were favorably impressed with the procedure; the lawyers were evenly split in their opinions.

Steven Penrod conducted a more extensive study in the Wisconsin state courts.[34] Jurors in approximately half of 63 trials were permitted to take notes. Of these, 66 percent took advantage of that opportunity. Most of the judges and lawyers who took part in these trials disagreed with assertions that notetaking was disruptive or costly, or that it produced a bias in favor of a particular party. As far as jurors themselves were concerned, the vast majority felt that notetaking was helpful. Based on jurors' own reports, those who took notes were *not* more influential during the deliberations than those who did not.[35]

Are jurors better information processors with or without taking notes? To this point, we do not know. The notetaking question has generated more talk than action. It is safe to conclude from what little research has been done that notetaking does not offend judges and lawyers. There is thus not a hint of support for a strong opposition to notetaking. Even the eminent Judge Learned Hand, in 1950, referred to arguments against it as "far-fetched" and "imaginary."[36] So why is there so much resistance?

Does Anybody Have Any Questions?

One of the notable differences between how judges and juries conduct their affairs is that judges have the opportunity to influence the flow of information from the witness stand by asking questions. Although jurors are usually not prohibited by law from doing so, very few courts allow it.

The reasons for permitting jurors to ask questions are simple, particularly in cases that involve technical subjects and feature doctors, engineers, economists, and other experts. If jurors could ask questions of the witnesses, they could clarify complicated issues, explore relevant but previously unanswered questions, and become actively engaged in their own efforts to reconstruct events of the past.

Very few courts allow juries to ask questions. Opposition to the procedure is based generally on a fear of the anarchy that would result from enabling jurors to exert some measure of control over the trial proceedings. Specifically, the following concerns are expressed. First, repeated questions from the jury box would disrupt the orderly examination of witnesses. Second, jurors might ask prejudicial or irrelevant questions that would contaminate others on the jury, place objecting counsel in an awkward position, and increase the risk of mistrial. Third, lawyers would begin to direct their appeals to those jurors who signal their leadership status by asking questions.

These fears are ill founded. The practice need not be implemented loosely. Although a small number of judges permit their jurors to ask questions in open court, a less controversial procedure is to instruct jurors to submit their questions to the court in writing. Before each witness is excused, the judge would review the questions with the attorneys and ask those that are not objectionable. Conducted in this manner, the natural flow of testimony is uninterrupted, leading jurors are not identified, and prejudicial questions are not introduced. In fact, we would argue that the latter problem could be converted into a benefit. After all, it is better for tainted questions to be addressed by the judge during the trial than to surface during deliberations as a matter for speculation.

Two attempts have been made to evaluate the impact of allowing jurors to ask questions. As part of the Second Circuit study described earlier, 6 judges presided over 26 trials in which jurors were allowed to submit questions in writing.[37] The reported level of questioning activity varied from trial to trial. In nine cases, no questions were submitted; in another nine cases, "several" questions were submitted. In one trial, jurors submitted 56 questions. In all but three cases, judges supported the procedure. More than two-thirds of the participating lawyers thought it was helpful.

As part of the Wisconsin project described earlier, jurors were permitted to ask questions in 33 out of the 63 trials sampled.[38] They asked an average of 2.7 questions. Significantly, jurors who were allowed to ask questions, compared to those who were not, were more satisfied with their state of information and with the thoroughness of the lawyers' examinations. Interestingly, lawyers whose cases were not assigned to the questioning procedure opposed it; yet those who were exposed to questions from the jury box liked it. Judges, too, expressed favorable opinions about the procedure.

We conclude this section on questions as we did its predecessor on note-taking. Common sense suggests that jurors stand to benefit from the opportunity to submit questions for witnesses. Unfortunately, in the absence of systematic research, we do not know what specific information-processing gains are to be expected. But it is clear that when courts experiment with the procedure, its predicted ruinous effects on the trial do not materialize. Again, we ask: why is there so much resistance?

American courts treat juries as passive recipients of information. Within this prevailing view, trial management theory dictates that jurors be prohibited from taking notes or asking questions of the witnesses. As we will see in Chapter 7, this passive-juror model also leads the courts to deny juries' requests to review transcripts of the testimony or receive a written copy of the judge's instructions. The rationales offered for these restrictions vary. What they have in common, however, is that they cast the individual juror into an uncomfortable bind: on the one hand, being expected to record information for subsequent retrieval; on the other hand, being denied the means with which to achieve that feat.

It is difficult to pinpoint precisely what motivates this model. It appears to be based on two internally inconsistent misconceptions about human cognition. The first is the brilliant-juror assumption that Judge Urbom alluded to in the passage quoted earlier. People are like the VCR—if the power is turned on and they are properly focused, the facts will be recorded for subsequent playback. Jurors may be brilliant, but they are also stupid. Based on the idea that people cannot be trusted to play a more active role in the acquisition of their own knowledge, it is said that jurors would take inaccurate and incomplete notes, distract themselves into oblivion, ask unintelligent and embarrassing questions, and so on. So the courts impose restrictions. The result, we think, is that jurors are handicapped in their information-processing efforts.

SUSPENDED JUDGMENTS: KEEPING HEARTS AND MINDS OPEN

As fact-finders, jurors are supposed to acquire information on a moment-by-moment basis. And yet, they are not supposed to act on that information, in a judgmental sense, until the trial presentation is over. In this section, we question whether people can suspend their judgments; whether it is reasonable to expect them to absorb the proceedings and evaluate the credibility of witnesses as they testify, without becoming committed to the "early returns." The answer, we think, is yes and no. It is natural for jurors to waver according to the ebb and flow of the testimony. But just as they should not favor a particular outcome because of prejudicial information that precedes the trial, they should not be frozen or locked into their judgments by information that appears *during* the trial. The importance of this objective is obvious. Because trials unfold over an extended period of time, those who form their opinions early will, by definition, be basing their decisions on an incomplete view of the evidence.

Judges and lawyers disagree on whether jurors can fulfill this aspect of their information-processing role. Some judges make it a point to deliver preliminary instructions in which they encourage jurors to weigh all the evidence before reaching a decision. Others choose instead to charge the jury after it has heard the evidence and arguments. This latter procedure is based, of course, on an assumption that people can keep their hearts and minds open enough for the final charge to make a difference. Trial lawyers also vary in their assumptions. Some lawyers agonize over their opening statements and make it a point to call their strongest witnesses first in order to capitalize on the power of first impressions. Others maintain that opening statements are less important than closing arguments and that the best witnesses should be saved for last.

Who is right? Do jurors commit themselves prematurely and, if so, do they then become deaf, dumb, and blind to the rest of the case? Or do jurors, humbled by the seriousness of their task and a heightened sense of responsibility, remain impartial until the final words of the trial are spoken? Sometimes people appear to violate the suspended judgment ideal. The 1984 drug trafficking trial of John DeLorean is a case in point. Finding that DeLorean had been entrapped by the government, the jury returned a not guilty verdict. Afterwards, when asked about their decision making, three jurors admitted to having formed a nearly unshakable belief in the defendant's innocence as soon as they heard the first government witness, an evasive FBI agent.[39] It remains to be seen whether this incident exemplifies the rule of juror decision making, or its exception. Thus, we question whether jurors are characteristically patient and reflective, or whether they are more impulsive in their "rush to judgment."

The Power of First Impressions

Everyone who is selected for jury duty knows that sooner or later he or she will be called on to form an opinion and defend it against others who might disagree. As the trial begins, jurors are thus bright-eyed and bushy-tailed, eager to unravel the mystery and reach the right verdict. Compared to uninvolved spectators, maybe they are too eager. Several years ago, social psychologist Robert Zajonc distinguished between people who merely observe an event (receivers) and those who must also communicate their observations to others (transmitters). Zajonc suggested that transmitters are pressured, for the sake of communication, to structure and simplify their observations even if that means suppressing information that is ambiguous or inconsistent with their overall impressions.[40] Research has shown that he was right.[41]

With jurors thus motivated by their ultimate task, there is the everpresent danger that they form premature opinions that serve as blinders through which they view the rest of the case. There is a voluminous literature in the psychology of impression formation that supports this view. In a classic study conducted over 40 years ago, Solomon Asch had subjects read a list of personality traits that characterized a hypothetical person, and then speculate on how much they would like that person. Half the subjects read that the individual was: intelligent, industrious, impulsive, critical, stubborn, and envious. The other half read the same list, but in the reverse order. Rationally speaking, subjects in the two groups should have felt the same way about their hypothetical person. But they did not. Subjects who read the original list, where the traits were ordered from the most to the least desirable, formed more favorable impressions than those whose list opened with the more negative traits. In other words, subjects' overall impressions were heavily determined by the first bits of information they received, a phenomenon that Asch called the primacy effect.[42]

Ever since this initial demonstration, and many others like it, social psychologists have been trying to explain why first impressions are so powerful. What they have found is that once people form an opinion or develop a theory, even if based on the limited early returns, they are unlikely to change their minds when confronted with subsequent contradictory information. We have all seen politicians who refuse to withdraw their support for programs and government policies that do not work. Even scientists, cloaked in the objectivity of their white lab coats, stubbornly defend their theories in the face of conflicting research data.[43] These instances of resistance are easy to explain. Politicians and scientists have a personal investment in their points of view. Having publicly committed themselves, and having spent time and money to further their positions, their pride, reputation, and funding may be at stake. But what about those of us who more innocently fail to revise our opinions, even to our own detriment? We wonder, for example, about the baseball manager who adheres to strategies that are ineffective, and about the trial lawyer who, as we saw in Chapter 3, repeatedly selects juries on the basis of false stereotypes. What accounts for this apparently nonrational and maladaptive human tendency? And, more to the point, what does all this imply about the decision-making process of the average juror?

Once an opinion is formed, the decision-making process can become frozen despite the heat generated by discrediting evidence.[44] There are four reasons for this phenomenon. To begin with, once a person has formed a belief, he or she may unwittingly adopt a biased *search* for information and, in doing so, procure false support for that belief. This strategy need not be conscious or deliberate. But it happens anyway. Recall the experiment conducted by Mark Snyder and William Swann, described in Chapter 4. They had pairs of college students, strangers to one another, participate together in an interview. Within each pair, one student was assigned to interview the other. Before doing so, the interviewers were told that their counterparts had shown signs of being either introverted or extraverted in their personalities. Although this information was invented by the experimenter, it had a marked effect on the interview process.

Subjects who thought they were interacting with an introvert asked introvert-like questions; those who were led to believe they were talking to an extravert asked extravert-like questions. In other words, subjects had unwittingly conducted interviews that were uniquely suited to confirm what they had already suspected, leaving them with an incomplete, one-sided view of the evidence.[45]

The fact that people are selective in their search for information provides a partial explanation for the power of first impressions. But first impressions have a way of perpetuating themselves even when people are forced to confront reality. Asch himself argued that the first words in a sequence, "intelligent" in one list and "envious" in the other, establish a clearly favorable or unfavorable first impression. Words that appear later are then interpreted in light of that impression. When a smart person is said to be critical, we assume that person has high standards; when an envious person is said to be critical, we think of sour grapes. The same trait takes on a different meaning depending on its context. In short, Asch proposed that people make snap judgments based on the first word in the series, and then *assimilate* subsequent information into that first impression. This hypothesis makes common sense. When a supposedly bright student fails an exam, rather than change our estimates of his intellect, we assume he must have been tired, ill, or preoccupied. And when a neighbor who is thought to be self centered and unfriendly offers to do a favor, rather than accept that gesture as a sign of goodwill, we become suspicious and look for ulterior motives. We have a remarkable tendency to see in others what we expect to see.[46]

Even more dramatic signs of closed-mindedness are evident. Some psychologists have found that information is more influential when it appears early rather than late because once people form an impression, they *discount* or reject facts that challenge their views.[47] Again, one may ask, what if people are forced to confront objective evidence that quite clearly contradicts their beliefs? Charles Lord and his colleagues asked that very question in an interesting experiment. A group of Stanford University students, half of whom favored the death penalty and half of whom did not, were asked to read about two purported research studies on the deterrent effects of capital punishment. The two studies they read about were at odds with each other. That is, one confirmed and the other disconfirmed the deterrence hypothesis. These mixed results should have made students on both sides of the issue less emphatic about their respective positions. But the reverse was true. Both sides accepted as valid the study that supported their views, while challenging as empirically unsound the nonsupportive evidence. Subjects became *more* rather than less certain of their positions, thereby *increasing* the overall level of disagreement between the two sides. That is quite a paradox. When faced with evidence that is equivocal at best, people on both sides manage to find support for their own views.[48] It's like what happens when voters watch American presidential debates. By nearly a 10 to 1 margin, those who saw the 1960, 1976, and 1980 debates believed that their preferred candidates had won.[49] What, then, might this imply about jurors who form opinions early in the trial?

There is yet a fourth cognitive mechanism by which first impressions can take on a life of their own. Once people form an opinion, even if they encode subsequent information accurately and without distortion, there is always the possibility that when it comes time to make a decision, they will *misremember* the evidence as having been more supportive than it actually was. Consistent facts will be remembered as such; inconsistent facts will be altered or forgotten. As we saw in Chapter 4, human memory is malleable and ever changing. Like the archaeologist who reconstructs extinct animal species from the presence of bone fragments, people reconstruct events they have seen from fragments of sensory information. The question is whether that reconstruction is accurate or biased by our expectations. More to the point, we ask, do jurors who have formed their opinions fill in the missing details of their trial memories in ways that favor their own tentative decisions? We have reason to believe that they do.

Elizabeth Loftus's eyewitness testimony research, showing that people reconstruct their memories for an event around their beliefs about that event supports this notion. Several other experiments do too. In one study, for example, subjects observed a videotape of a woman having a birthday dinner with her husband. Those subjects who were led to believe that she worked as a waitress remembered her drinking beer and owning a television. Those who watched the same film but thought she was a librarian remembered her wearing glasses and owning classical records. Subjects' recollections of the woman's behavior were thus consistent with their stereotypic impressions of her. In fact, these recollections were all untrue.[50]

Back in the Courtroom

First impression biases can be costly inside the courtroom. And we have every reason to believe that they exist. In one of the first studies of its kind, in 1940, H. Weld and E. Danzig had 41 mock jurors watch a live mock trial and make judgments 18 times during the presentation. As expected, subjects' opinions fluctuated predictably according to the testimony. However, Weld and Danzig also found that at least 25 percent of their jurors reached decisions early on, before the trial was over. As they put it, "thereafter the effect of the testimony was merely to change their certainty."[51]

It is easy to see, in concrete terms, how jurors might begin to close their hearts and their minds before all the evidence is in. Within a trial, any number of things can happen that would lead the average person prematurely to form an opinion. Seeing an unattractive criminal defendant enter the courtroom in prison clothing, learning that he or she had confessed, or was positively identified by an eyewitness, and hearing an effective opening statement are just a few examples. The consequences can be devastating. Thus, once an eyewitness testifies with confidence it becomes difficult to undo the damage when that witness is later discredited on cross examination. The same is often true of confession evidence. Once jurors learn that a defendant has confessed, they are unlikely to discount that confession when it is later revealed that coercive situational pressures were brought to bear on the suspect.

Consistent with what psychologists know about how first impressions distort our perceptions, it appears that even new evidence becomes tainted by one's beliefs. We know, for example, that whether people interpret an individual's statements as truthful or deceptive may depend more on their expectations than on the individual's behavior. When an honest man pauses before speaking, we perceive him as careful; when a dishonest man reacts the same way, we suspect him of falsification.[52]

In the trial context, David Saunders and his associates found that once jurors hear the testimony of an eyewitness, whether it is subsequently discredited or not, they come to accept the state's circumstantial evidence and become more critical of the defendant's testimony.[53] Many skillful lawyers are undoubtedly aware of this phenomenon. One attorney advises prosecutors to have their witness make an in-court identification early in the trial in order to activate in jurors' minds a concrete visual image of the defendant committing the acts described in subsequent testimony.[54]

It may be possible to minimize the jurors' tendency to form rigid first impressions through minor alterations in trial procedure. For cases that extend for more than a day, judges could remind the jury periodically to make a conscious effort to keep an open mind until the case is over. Research using Asch's list of trait adjectives has shown that the primacy effect is mitigated by this type of instruction.[55]

There is an even bolder solution, one that was used in the 1984–1985 libel case of General William C. Westmoreland against CBS. Because the trial promised to be long and complex, straining the jury's patience and capacity, Federal Judge Pierre Leval permitted the lawyers to make "interim summations." It was a novel idea. Over the course of the five-month trial, each side was allotted a total of two hours between the opening and closing arguments to interrupt the presentation of evidence and make what Judge Leval called interim summations. Although attorneys were free to use the time as they saw fit, on the average their summations ran from two to five minutes.

In the aftermath of the trial, both sides had nothing but praise for the technique. They liked being able to halt the accumulation of evidence from time to time in order to clarify key points. They also believed that it served the interests of a suspended judgment ideal. As CBS lawyer David Boies put it, "One of the advantages, particularly for defendants, was that it permitted you to keep the jurors' minds open" while the other side presented its case. "The ability of the plaintiff to condition the jury during the first several months is critical. Interim summations gives the defense an opportunity to counter that."[56] Judge Leval's innovation could prove to be the single best way to ensure that jurors suspend judgment until all the evidence is in. It makes psychological sense[57], and is easy to implement.

NOTES

1. Cited in Frank, infra note 2.

2. *The Mind of the Juror*. A similar view was advanced by Judge Jerome Frank (1949) in *Courts on Trial: Myth and Reality in American Justice*. Princeton: Princeton University Press.

3. It has been suggested that evidence and bias are inversely weighted, so that decreasing jurors' attention to the former will enhance the damaging effects of the latter. See M. Kaplan and L. Miller (1978), Reducing the effects of juror bias. *Journal of Personality and Social Psychology*, Vol. 36, pp. 1443–1455.

4. For an extensive discussion of this issue, see J. Hartwick, B. H. Sheppard, and J. H. Davis (1982), Group remembering: Research and implications. In R. Guzzo (Ed.), *Improving Group Decision Making in Organizations: Working From Theory*. New York: Academic Press.

5. H. Kalven and H. Zeisel (1966), *The American Jury*. Boston: Little, Brown.

6. *Zenith Radio Corp. v. Matsushita Electric Industrial Corp.* (1979), 478 F.Supp. 889.

7. *In re Japanese Electronic Products Litigation* (1980), 631 F.2d 1069.

8. *In re U.S. Financial Securities Litigation* (1977), 75 F.R.D. 702.

9. *In re U.S. Financial Securities Litigation* (1979), 609 F.2d 411.

10. See *Ross v. Bernhard*, 396 U.S. 531, p. 538.

11. Supra note 7, p. 1086.

12. Supra note 9, pp. 429–430, 432.

13. For a thorough discussion of these issues, see R. O. Lempert (1981), Civil juries and complex cases: Let's not rush to judgment. *Michigan Law Review*, Vol. 80, pp. 68–132.

14. *In re Asbestos Litigation Coverage Cases*, Judicial Council Coordinated Proceeding No. 1072.

15. M. A. Galante (1985), Megatrials. *The National Law Journal*, Vol. 7, No. 28, p. 35.

16. Ibid, p. 37.

17. 458 F.Supp. 423, p. 447.

18. See S. Greenhouse (1985), Business and the law: Complex suits and jury trials. *New York Times*, June 4, 1985, p. D2.

19. "Most district judges have sufficient familiarity with jury trials, either as judges or as practitioners, to make an informed judgment on the extent of a jury's capabilities," supra note 7, p. 1088.

20. See D. W. Ell (1978), The right to an incompetent jury: Protracted commercial litigation and the Seventh Amendment. *Connecticut Law Review*, Vol. 10, pp. 775–800.

21. Quoted in J. S. Granelli (1982), Long trials play havoc with courts. *The National Law Journal*, December 27, p. 10.

22. G. Bermant et al. (1981), *Protracted Civil Trials: Views from the Bench and the Bar*. Washington, D.C.: Federal Judicial Center.

23. 463 F.Supp. 983.

24. J. S. Cecil (1982), *Demographic characteristics of jurors in protracted civil trials*. Unpublished report.

25. E. A. Lind (1982), *Final Report of an Evaluation of Jurors' Trial Experiences*. Washington, D.C.: Federal Judicial Center.

26. G. L. Spence (1986), How to make a complex case come alive for a jury. *American Bar Association Journal*, Vol. 72, April, pp. 62–66.

27. A. H. Goldstein, Jr. (1985). Nothing is too complex. *American Bar Association Journal*,

Vol. 71, November, p. 40.

28. See supra note 7, p. 1088.

29. W. K. Urbom (1982), Toward better treatment of jurors by judges. *Nebraska Law Review*, Vol. 61, p. 425.

30. *Kemner v. Monsanto Co.*; see M. Middleton (1986), Still playing in Belleville, it's the longest trial ever. *The National Law Journal*, Vol. 8, No. 25, pp. 1, 47–49. (This suit was settled in October 1987 with a jury award to the plaintiffs.)

32. Ibid., p. 415.

33. *Report of the Committee on Juries of the Judicial Council of the Second Circuit* (1984).

34. S. Penrod (1985), *Evaluating techniques to improve juror performance*. Paper presented at the American Judicature Society Conference on the American Jury and the Law. Wingspread, Wisconsin.

35. One additional project is worth mentioning here. Law professor Arthur Austin took an in-depth look at two juries that sat through an antitrust case in Cleveland. He found that "none of the rationales cited for the prohibition against notes held up." For example, a reenactment of the deliberations suggested that notetakers were not disproportionately influential. Austin also reviewed jurors' notes and found that they were thorough, and included descriptions of witnesses and comments about their credibility; see A. D. Austin (1985), Why jurors don't heed the trial. *The National Law Journal*, August 12, 1985, pp. 15–19.

36. *U.S. v. Chiarella*, 184 F.2d 903, p. 907.

37. Supra note 33, pp. 51–59.

38. Supra note 34.

39. S. Brill (1984), Inside the DeLorean jury room. *The American Lawyer*, December, pp. 1, 94–105.

40. R. Zajonc (1960), The process of cognitive tuning in communications. *Journal of Abnormal and Social Psychology*, Vol. 61, pp. 159–167.

41. For example, H. Leventhal (1962), The effects of set and discrepancy on impression change. *Journal of Personality*, Vol. 30, pp. 1–15.

42. S. E. Asch (1946), Forming impressions of personality. *Journal of Abnormal and Social Psychology*, Vol. 41, pp. 258–290. Also see E. E. Jones and G. R. Goethals (1971), *Order effects in impression formation: Attribution context and the nature of the entity*. Morristown, NJ: General Learning Press.

43. See A. G. Greenwald, A. R. Pratkanis, M. R. Leippe, & M. H. Baumgardner (1986), Under what conditions does theory obstruct research progress? *Psychological Review*, Vol. 93, pp. 216–229.

44. A. W. Kruglanski and T. Freund (1983), The freezing and unfreezing of lay inferences: Effects on impression primacy, ethnic stereotyping, and numerical anchoring. *Journal of Experimental Social Psychology*, Vol. 19, pp. 448–468.

45. M. Snyder & W. B. Swann (1978), Hypothesis testing processes in social interaction. *Journal of Personality and Social Psychology*, Vol. 36, pp. 1202–1212.

46. For example, see D. L. Hamilton & M. P. Zanna (1974), Context effects in impression formation: Changes in connotative meaning. *Journal of Personality and Social Psychology*, Vol. 29, pp. 649–654; also see T. Hayden & W. Mischel (1976), Maintaining trait consistency in the resolution of behavioral inconsistency: The wolf in sheep's clothing? *Journal of Personality*, Vol. 44, pp. 109–132; J. M. Darley & P. H. Gross (1983), A hypothesis-confirming bias in labeling effects. *Journal of Personality and Social Psychology*, Vol. 44, pp. 20–33.

47. These explanations are fully articulated by N. H. Anderson (1981), *Foundations of Information Integration Theory*. New York: Academic Press, pp. 179–191.

48. C. G. Lord, L. Ross, & M. R. Lepper (1979), Biased assimilation and attitude polarization: The effects of prior theories on subsequently considered evidence. *Journal of Personality and Social Psychology*, Vol. 37, pp. 2098–2109.

49. D. R. Kinder & D. O. Sears (1985), Public opinion and political action. A chapter ap-

pearing in G. Lindzey & E. Aronson (Eds.), *The Handbook of Social Psychology*, 3rd ed. NY: Random House.

50. C. E. Cohen (1981), Person categories and social perception: Testing some boundaries of the processing effects of prior knowledge. *Journal of Personality and Social Psychology*, Vol. 40, pp. 441–452. It remains to be seen whether people selectively retrieve information that supports a belief formed *after* encoding; e.g., see M. Snyder & S. Uranowitz (1978), Reconstructing the past: Some cognitive consequences of person perception. *Journal of Personality and Social Psychology*, Vol. 36, pp. 941–950; also see L. F. Clark & S. B. Woll (1981), Stereotype biases: A reconstructive analysis of their role in reconstructive memory. *Journal of Personality and Social Psychology*, Vol. 41, pp. 1064–1072.

51. H. P. Weld & E. R. Danzig (1940), A study of the way in which a verdict is reached by a jury. *American Journal of Psychology*, Vol. 53, pp. 518–536; also see H. P. Weld & M. F. Roff (1938), A study in the formation of opinion based upon legal evidence. *American Journal of Psychology*, Vol. 51, pp. 609–628.

52. R. E. Kraut (1978), Verbal and nonverbal cues in the perception of lying. *Journal of Personality and Social Psychology*, Vol. 36, pp. 380–391.

53. D. M. Saunders, N. Vidmar, & E. C. Hewitt (1983), Eyewitness testimony and the discrediting effect. A chapter appearing in S. Lloyd-Bostock and B. Clifford (Eds.), *Evaluating Witness Evidence*. London: John Wiley.

54. M. Ficaro (1982), Prosecution of violent crimes, a paper presented in a seminar to the National College of District Attorneys, Colorado Springs, CO. Cited in E. F. Loftus & J. Goodman (1985), Questioning witnesses. A chapter appearing in S. Kassin & L. Wrightsman (Eds.), *The Psychology of Evidence and Trial Procedure*. Beverly Hills: Sage Publications.

55. A. S. Luchins (1957), Primacy-recency in impression formation. A chapter appearing in C. Hovland (Ed.), *The order of presentation in persuasion*. New Haven, CT: Yale University Press, pp. 33–61.

56. See R. Arthurs (1985), Mini-summation lauded in libel case. *Legal Times*, February 25, pp. 1, 6.

57. When research subjects are asked to stop and recall the information already presented before making their judgments, the primacy effect disappears; see N. H. Anderson & S. Hubert (1963), Effect of concomitant verbal recall on order effects in personality impression formation. *Journal of Verbal Learning and Verbal Behavior*, Vol. 2, pp. 379–391.

7

INTERPRETING THE LAW

When comedian Groucho Marx died in 1977, he left two houses, a Mercedes-Benz, municipal bonds, and other gifts worth more than $400,000, to Erin Leslie Fleming, a companion of seven years. The Bank of America, as executor of Marx's estate, charged that Fleming had manipulated the aging comedian or, in the court's words, "used undue influence, fraud, duress, or menace, or breach of fiduciary duty" to procure the property. Fleming, an actress, claimed it was voluntarily given. After 10 full days of deliberation, the jury voted against Fleming and awarded the bank nearly a half million dollars. Her attorney asked the judge to throw out the verdict—not because the jury could not follow the evidence, but because it failed to understand the meaning of love.[1]

Knowing all the facts as presented in court comprises only half of the jury's information processing task. In order to make judgments of guilt or liability, the jury must match its beliefs about the disputed event against the standards of conduct formalized in the laws of the land. Not needing to have passed a bar exam to serve on a jury, people obtain that education through their judge's instructions.

At some point in every trial, the presiding judge, acting as "master of ceremonies," informs the jury of its duties, its responsibilities, and about general and case-specific matters of law and procedure. This ritual is indispensable. Acting as liaison between the judicial system and its citizenry, the judge charges the jury in order to constrain its decision-making power, ensure procedural fairness, and promote the uniform application of the law across trials.

The specific functions of this ritual are numerous. To begin with, it is designed to transform average people into jurors, teaching them about the principles of law, evidence, trial procedure, and guiding them in the mechanics of decision making. Consider the following task-orienting instruction; one like it is used in virtually all trials:

> *Members of the jury: Now that you have heard the evidence and arguments, it becomes my duty to give you the instructions of the Court as to the law applicable in this case. It is your duty as jurors to follow the law as stated in the instructions of the Court, and to apply the rules of law so given to the facts as you find them from the evidence in the case.*
>
> *You are not to single out one instruction alone as stating the law, but must consider the instructions as a whole. Neither are you to be concerned with the wisdom of any rule of law stated by the Court. Regardless of any opinion you may have as to what the law ought to be, it would be a violation of your sworn duty to base a verdict upon any other view of the law than that given in the instructions of the Court; just as it would be a violation of your sworn duty, as judges of the facts, to base a verdict upon anything but the evidence in the case.*
>
> *Nothing I say in these instructions is to be taken as an indication that I have any opinion about the facts of the case, or what that opinion is. It is not my function to determine the facts, but rather yours. Justice through trial by jury must always depend upon the willingness of each individual juror to seek the truth as to the facts from the same evidence presented to all the jurors; and to arrive at a verdict by applying the same rules of law, as given in the instructions of the Court.[2]*
>
> *You will soon leave the courtroom and begin discussing this case in the jury room. As I told you earlier, the government has accused the defendant of committing a crime. But this is only a charge. The defendant is presumed to be innocent. Therefore, you may find him guilty only if you are convinced, beyond a reasonable doubt, that he committed this crime as charged. If you are not convinced beyond a reasonable doubt, you must find him not guilty.*
>
> *During the course of the trial you received all the evidence you may properly consider to decide the case. Your decision must be made solely on the evidence presented at the trial. Do not be concerned about whether evidence is "direct evidence" or "circumstantial evidence". You should consider all the evidence that was presented to you. At times during the trial, you saw lawyers make objections to questions asked by other lawyers, and to answers by witnesses. This simply meant that the lawyers were requesting that I make a decision on a particular rule of law. Do not draw any conclusion from such objections or from my rulings on the objections. These only related to the legal questions that I had to determine and should not influence your thinking. When I sustained an objection to a question, the witness was not allowed to answer it. Do not attempt to guess what answer might have been given. Similarly, when I told you not to consider a particular statement, you were told to put that statement out of your mind, and you may not refer to that statement in your deliberations.*

It is my job to decide what rules of law apply to the case . . . it is not the job of the lawyers. So, while the lawyers may have commented during the trial on some of these rules, you are to be guided only by what I say about them. You must follow all of the rules as I explain them to you. If you decide that the government has proved its case beyond a reasonable doubt, it will also be my job to decide what the punishment will be. You should not try to guess what the punishment might be. It should not enter into your consideration or discussions at any time.

The decision you reach in the jury room, whether guilty or not guilty, must be unanimous. You must all agree. Your deliberations will be secret. You will never have to explain your verdict to anyone.[3]

In addition to these rather basic instructions, judges direct the jury on various aspects of their in-court conduct. At their discretion and as needed, trial judges might direct jurors to accept certain facts stipulated as true, and to make certain presumptions, the most notable being that a criminal defendant be presumed innocent. They might direct jurors to refrain from drawing inferences from certain types of events. For example, jurors should not consider a criminal defendant's refusal to testify as proof of his or her culpability; nor should they be influenced by testimony subsequently ruled inadmissible and stricken from the record. Judges might advise the jury on how to evaluate the credibility of witnesses, including children on the one hand, and experts on the other. They might prohibit jurors from visiting the scene of a crime, discussing the case with others, taking notes, or asking questions during the trial. They might guide the jury in its deliberations, suggesting a means of electing a foreperson and taking ballots, and noting that jurors have a duty to consult with each other, express their views, and maintain an open mind. They might structure the jury's decision by having them answer a series of discrete factual questions before or concurrent with their general verdict. In some jurisdictions, they might even summarize or comment on the evidence.

First articulated by the U.S. Supreme Court in 1895, the main purpose of instructions is to inform the jury of relevant laws upon which their findings should be based.[4] Jurors are thus told when an act should be considered voluntary, negligent, or reckless; or what self defense, duress, and entrapment mean. They are told what first-degree murder is, and how it differs from second-degree murder and manslaughter; and what the differences are between larceny, theft, robbery, and burglary. Civil law is even more alien to the average person. Thus, jurors are informed on contracts to note the differences between implied, expressed, and written warranties. They are told the differences between comparative, contributory, and gross negligence; and between defamation, slander, and libel. And they are educated on the laws that govern real estate transactions, patents, copyrights, trademarks, trusts, estates, and securities. Taken together, the issues fill a demanding three-year law school curriculum. Depending on the case, jurors too must acquire knowledge enough to understand one or more of these issues. Their education is provided in the judge's instructions.

ECCENTRICITIES OF THE INSTRUCTION RITUAL

The courts want juries to comply with their judges' instructions. With that reasonable assumption as a point of departure, we ask: so why do they cling to psychologically unsound methods of communication?

Timing the Instructions

Consider the placement of instructions along the time-line of a trial. A judge's duty to direct the jury is continuous. It begins when the venire is impaneled, and it ends when the jury is discharged after its verdict. If there is a general principle, it is one of flexibility: the jury should be instructed as needed, when needed.[5] Although the procedure is not regimented by law, most judges instruct the jury at the close of the trial, right before it retires to deliberate.[6] The rationale for this custom is what psychologists call the "recall readiness" hypothesis—that immediate past events are remembered better than remote ones, especially when the sequence of information unfolds over a long period of time.[7] In order for an instruction to influence jurors, it should be salient, available in memory, and fresh in their minds when they deliberate.

As sensible as this reasoning sounds, think about it. When was the last time you learned the rules of a game *after* you played it? This reasoning contradicts the weight of research on primacy effects, as described in Chapter 6. It also has generated criticism in judicial circles. Judge E. Barrett Prettyman's position is instructive:

> *It makes no sense to have a juror listen to days of testimony only then to be told that he and his conferees are the sole judges of the facts, that the accused is presumed innocent, that the government must prove guilt beyond a reasonable doubt, etc. What manner of mind can go back over a stream of conflicting statements of alleged facts, recall the intonations, the demeanor, or even the existence of the witnesses, and retrospectively fit all these recollections into a pattern of evaluations and judgments given him for the first time after the events; the human mind cannot do so. The fact of the matter is that this order of procedure makes much of the trial of a lawsuit mere mumbo jumbo.[8]*

Advocates for the use of preliminary instructions are guided by two arguments. The first is that people are more efficient as information processors when they have a unifying theme or schema within which to organize their input. Providing jurors with a legal framework before they hear the evidence and arguments should enable them to appreciate the relevance of facts as they appear, and should facilitate their comprehension and recall of the most significant information.[9] The second argument is that jurors form opinions as the trial unfolds, often drawing conclusions before all the evidence has been presented. If true, then it follows that directives issued after the evidence could conceivably fall on deaf ears.

At what point in the trial should a judge instruct the jury in order to maximize their adherence to the law? In an attempt to test the primacy and recency hypotheses, we conducted a mock jury experiment in which we varied the timing of the so-called "requirements of proof" instruction.[10] A mandatory, clearly defendant-oriented instruction, the requirements of proof instructions tell jurors that the accused is presumed innocent, that the burden of proof is on the prosecution, and that all elements of the crime must be proven beyond a reasonable doubt.

One-hundred seven subject jurors watched a videotape of a staged trial based on an actual case in which the defendant, Ronald Oliver, was charged with stealing a car and transporting it across state lines. As presented, the government's case was based on the testimony of a used car salesman who identified the defendant as the person who stole the car from the lot, and a highway patrolman who stopped Oliver for speeding and later made the arrest. The defendant, on the other hand, maintained that he was driving an acquaintance's car and had no knowledge that it had been stolen. The total presentation consisted of opening statements, the examination of three witnesses, and closing arguments. All subjects watched the same event, except for our manipulation of the judge's instructions. Depending upon the experimental condition to which they were randomly assigned, subjects heard that instruction either before the evidence, after the evidence, or not at all.

As it turned out, 63 percent of those who were never instructed on the requirements of proof voted guilty. Compared to that baseline, the rate of conviction remained stable, at 59 percent, when the instruction followed the evidence. When it preceded the evidence, however, the conviction rate was reduced significantly to 37 percent. Further analysis revealed the reason why the postevidence instructions were ineffective. Approximately half the subjects in each condition made judgments at six discrete points during the trial. Looking at these data, we found that subjects' final verdicts were fairly predictable from their midtrial positions. That is, they tended to reach tentative decisions at some point before the trial was over.[11] These data demonstrate that adherence to judges' instructions might hinge on their placement within the trial. "Better late than never" may apply to some areas of life, but not to the practice of instructing juries.

Virtually all courts provide their juries with preliminary instructions concerning procedural matters. When it comes to guidance of a more substantive nature, however, that practice is more the exception than the rule. Jurors often listen to days, or weeks, of testimony before learning the specifics of their task. Some judges argue that until all the evidence is disclosed, they cannot fully draft their substantive instructions. That is true only in a very limited sense. Through the various pretrial activities, judges do acquire enough knowledge about the parties' cases to prepare a significant portion of that charge.[12] Our study, buttressed by the weight of current psychological theory and research, suggests that every effort should be made to do so. Preliminary instructions, because they provide a title and table of contents to the trial, are not a substitute for the final charge, but a supplement to it. There is no reason why juries could not be charged twice in order to ensure the information-processing advantages afforded on each occasion.[13]

Access to Written or Taped Instructions

One of the more archaic oddities of the instruction ritual is that many courts refuse to provide their juries with a written copy of the charge.[14] Originally, it was thought that allowing written instructions would divide the group along literacy lines, enabling those who were able to read to become interpreters of the law, and exert undue influence over the other members.[15] Although no longer a relevant argument, this idea has transformed into the hypothesis that, literacy considerations aside, the presence of written instructions in the jury room would still enable the more intelligent, verbally facile jurors to use the written word to dominate the decision-making process. There is also, we should add, a pragmatic, administrative argument: that it would cost the court additional money (a) to have the instructions typed and copied and (b) because their availability would encourage jurors to obsess over their contents, thereby increasing the length of their deliberations.[16]

Judges who provide written instructions point to the fact that juries frequently request a rereading or clarification of at least a portion of the charge. It makes good sense. Educational psychologists, interested in the didactic values of different methods of communication, have found that students comprehend and remember more material when they obtain it through reading texts than through listening to lectures.

Research on the effects of written instructions, though sparse, confirms the obvious. In one study, mock jurors watched a trial, deliberated with or without written instructions, and then completed a test of their comprehension. Subjects who had access to the written material understood the legal terms and substantive law better than those not provided with that material.[17] In another study, juries provided with written instructions were less confused, wasted less time arguing about legal terms, devoted more time to discussing relevant facts, and, in the end, exhibited greater confidence in the accuracy of their decisions.[18] Finally, in an in-court experiment, real juries were either provided or denied access to written instructions. Contrary to the hypothesis that it would prolong the length of deliberations, the two groups of juries did not differ in the amount of time it took them to return a verdict. In fact, those who had the written instructions available spent an average of only 25 minutes reading and discussing them.[19]

Judges' customary reluctance to allow a written copy of their instructions into the jury room is an interesting behavioral phenomenon in its own right. Research is consistent with the commonsense prediction that it facilitates the jury's processing of information. The literacy argument does not bear current relevance and there is no evidence to suggest that it unduly prolongs the deliberation process. The economic argument is not all that compelling either. Because judges usually read verbatim from already typed instructions, they need only provide copies—at a nominal cost. Besides, both the literacy and economic arguments are obsolete in the face of proposals calling for juries to receive audiotape recordings of the final charge. In a study conducted by the Second Circuit, three judges furnished 14 juries with tapes of their instructions. All participants who were polled—the judges, attorneys, and jurors—reacted with enthusiasm.[20]

GARBLED VERBIAGE AND VERBAL GARBAGE

On the issue of whether jurors comply with instructions, there is an interesting paradox. On the one hand, the legal community operates on the assumption that jurors are at the edge of their seats, that they scrutinize every word of the charge, and that their verdicts may be completely altered by its language. Virtually all leading trial advocacy books advise lawyers to make strenuous efforts to submit specifically phrased instructions to be included in the charge.[21] For judges, the leading trial-management manuals recommend that they employ what are known as "pattern instructions," standardized canned phrases previously approved by appeals courts for their technical accuracy. So important is the language of the judge's charge that an incorrect, omitted, or misstated instruction can be, and often is, sufficient cause for the reversal of a jury's verdict.

On the other hand, many judges and lawyers challenge the assumption that juries hang on every word of the judge's charge. Critics have long maintained that jurors do not adhere their verdicts to the law, in part because they cannot understand the instructions. Judge Jerome Frank was especially harsh in his evaluation of the jury's comprehension skills: "What a crop of subsidiary semi-myths and mythical practices the jury system yields! Time and money and lives are consumed in debating the precise words which the judge may address to the jury, although everyone who stops to see and think knows that these words may as well be spoken in a foreign language."[22]

Do juries understand and apply judges' instructions? Until recently, this empirical question did not have a satisfactory answer. Anecdotes aside, research had yielded hopelessly equivocal results. In 1937, 843 former jurors completed a questionnaire about their trial experiences. Of these, 72 percent said they fully understood their judges' instructions.[23] Ten years later, a survey of 185 former jurors reported a comprehension rate of 60 percent.[24]

It is difficult to know what conclusions to draw from these results. Self-report data of this sort are notoriously unreliable. Because people cannot appraise the state of their own knowledge, and because people are biased toward favorable self-presentation, these kinds of results are ambiguous at best. Besides, do the 72 and 60 percent figures signal comprehension or confusion? Perhaps jurors were able to grasp the gist of the judge's message without perfect comprehension. And perhaps jurors understand the instructions better after group discussion than when they are alone. Self-report surveys cannot inform us on these issues.

Recent research clearly documents the magnitude of the problem and its ramifications. In an archival study, Laurence Severance and Elizabeth Loftus reviewed the court records of 405 criminal and civil jury trials in Washington. They found that about a quarter of the juries interrupted their deliberations to request a clarification of the judge's charge. The courts' reactions were interesting, to say the least. Almost without exception, judges refused to paraphrase or in any way explain the problematic instructions. Instead, they directed their juries to reread them.[25]

In an excellent series of studies, Bruce Sales, Amiram Elwork, and James Alfini brought actual pattern instructions into the laboratory for investigation.[26] In one experiment a representative sample of jurors appeared at a local courthouse and watched a four-hour videotape of a Michigan trial concerning an automobile accident. Each party to the lawsuit claimed that the other drove recklessly, speeded through an intersection, and, therefore, was responsible for the accident. Approximately one third of the subjects received the standard Michigan instruction on negligence. A second group received a version of the instruction that the authors had rewritten to meet various criteria for comprehensibility. A third group received no instruction at all. Immediately after the trial presentation, subjects reached a verdict, made a decision on whether the plaintiff, the defendant, or both were negligent, and then filled out a series of comprehension questionnaires.

The results of this study confirmed critics' greatest fears about the jury's competence, or lack thereof. On measures of comprehension, those who heard the traditional instruction scored significantly lower than those who received the rewritten version of the same material. In fact, the former understood no more about negligence law than their uninstructed peers. Moreover, their inability to understand the instruction impaired the accuracy of their verdicts. Under Michigan's contributory negligence law, a plaintiff is entitled to recover damages only if the jury finds that the defendant alone was to blame. If the jury concludes that the plaintiff shared in any way in the fault, or that neither party was at fault, then it is supposed to find for the defendant. As it turned out, 40 percent of the uninstructed subjects reached verdicts that were logically inconsistent with their own negligence findings. Those who were educated by the pattern instruction exhibited no improvement; their rate of error was 38 percent. In short, subjects did not benefit at all from the judge's standard instruction.[27]

Additional research provides further cause for alarm. Reasoning that the deliberation process could compensate for individual jurors' failures, Elwork and his colleagues conducted additional experiments in which subjects deliberated in 6-person groups before completing the questionnaires. Still, they found that comprehension scores on a test of the pattern instructions were low and that subjects misunderstood critical points of law. In fact, the pattern instructions had an adverse effect on the dynamics of deliberation. In one study, for example, 16 mock juries heard the standard Michigan instruction, while 15 received the rewritten version of that charge. Having unobtrusively videotaped the deliberations, Elwork and his colleagues observed that by creating confusion about the law, the pattern instructions increased the likelihood that one or two members would proclaim their expertise and dominate their group's discussions. Symptomatic of this effect was that pattern-instructed juries, uncertain as to their task, often expressed a need to select as forepersons members who had previous experience on a jury.

Finally, this research revealed a variety of adverse effects on the contents of juries' discussions. Compared to groups that had received the rewritten instruction, pattern-instructed juries were more likely to discuss legally inadmissible topics such as whether the defendant's insurance company would pay the damages. Conversely, they were less likely to address the most important point of law, namely, that the case involved a contributory negligence standard. In short, Elwork and his colleagues found that the collective wisdom of the group did not correct for the failings of judges' instructions. In the end, deliberation had become a part of the problem, not the solution.

On the question of jury competence, critics of the civil jury find support in these data for their position. But is that the ultimate conclusion to be drawn from the results? We think not. As the vast majority of scholars would agree, *the problem is not jury comprehension, but the comprehensibility of judges' instructions.* There is nothing inherently wrong with juries. Although critics might argue otherwise, the empirical literature suggests that instructions need not be esoteric and inaccessible to the layperson. The language of the law exceeds in complexity the concepts it is intended to convey.

It is no secret that lawyers suffer from an inability or a reluctance to communicate clearly to others. Described by one playwright as ''a grand conglomeration of garbled verbiage and verbal garbage,''[28] jury instructions are no exception. ''We lawyers,'' notes Richard Wydick, ''cannot write plain English. We use eight words to say what could be said in two. We use old, arcane phrases to express commonplace ideas. Seeking to be precise, we become redundant. Seeking to be cautious, we become verbose.''[29] To that, federal district judge William Schwarzer adds, ''the same is true of judges whose English often carries the additional burden of pomposity.''[30]

What precisely are the problems associated with currently available jury instructions? Before we describe how they violate the basic principles of clear communication, let us consider the following rather typical instruction:

When I use the words ''proximate cause'' I mean, first, that there must have

*been a connection between the conduct of the defendant which the plaintiff
claims was negligent, and the injury complained of by the plaintiff, and second,
that the occurrence which is claimed to have produced the injury was a natural
and probable result of such conduct of the defendant.*

If these definitions appear indigestible for leisurely reading, consider the
plight of the juror who, after sitting through days or weeks of testimony, is
suddenly bombarded by a rapidly fired succession of long-winded instructions
such as this, orally presented, and without further explanation.

Recent analyses of current jury instructions have identified several problems
of a psycholinguistic nature.[31] To begin with, there is a serious lexical problem.
Jury instructions are riddled with legal jargon and words that otherwise do not
find their way into everyday conversation. The term "proximate cause," awk-
wardly defined earlier, is a case in point. Experiments in the psychology of
learning and memory have shown that familiar words are encoded and recalled
more efficiently than novel words. We know how familiar a word is by how
frequently it appears in print, as sampled in E. L. Thorndike and I. Lorge's
classic, *The Teacher's Word Book of 30,000 Words.*[32] When it comes to jury
instructions, we find that low-frequency words are commonly used in place of
more familiar alternatives. For example, the words "veracity" and "credibility," so often used in the courtroom, each appear only once per million words
of writing.

Grammatical construction contributes even more confusion to jury instructions. Sentences are often long and structurally complex. Consider the following
definition of negligence gleaned from the *Book of Approved Jury Instructions
(BAJI)*:

*One test that is helpful in determining whether or not a person was negligent is
to ask and answer whether or not, if a person of ordinary prudence had been in
the same situation and possessed the same knowledge, he would have fore-
seen or anticipated that someone might have been injured by or as a result of
his action or inaction.*[33]

This sentence contains nine subordinate clauses. To make matters worse, many
jury instructions contain double and triple negatives. Phrases such as "without
which the injury would not have occurred," or "innocent misrecollection is not
uncommon," both appearing in *BAJI*, would lead even the attentive listener to
pause. As one would expect, as grammatical complexity increases, through the
inclusion of self-embedded clauses, multiple negations and the like, people's
ability to encode, comprehend, and recall the relevant information diminishes
markedly.[34]

A third problem with jury instructions is that they are often not organized
well for presentation. The final charge consists of many specific instructions,
each consisting of several statements. Rather than embed sentences within para-

graphs, and paragraphs within instructions, in a hierarchical, logically ordered series, however, judges are often careless about how they package the information for the jury. As with the lexical and syntactic problems described earlier, experiments have shown that organizational factors can affect people's ability to comprehend and recall information.[35]

With jury instructions so unintelligible to the average person, two obvious questions present themselves. First, why are they so poorly written? Second, how can they be improved?

To answer the why question, one must place current practice in a historical context. The instruction ritual is of twentieth century vintage. Prior to that, juries often decided issues of law as well as fact. It was not until 1895 that the U.S. Supreme Court declared "it is the duty of juries in criminal cases to take the law from the court and apply that law to the facts as they find them to be from the evidence."[36] This ruling thus imposed on judges the obligation to communicate the law to their juries. As the volume of litigation increased through subsequent years, this obligation became a hardship. Trial judges wrote their own, often idiosyncratic instructions. And yet, precision was essential; more and more verdicts were being reversed on appeal because juries were not accurately instructed on the law. In response to a need for standardization, in 1938, a committee of California judges and lawyers published *BAJI*—the first complete set of "pattern" instructions.[37] Today, the vast majority of states use pattern instructions. In some, it is mandatory.[38]

Excuses, Excuses

Pattern instructions need not be incomprehensible. However, drafting committees—composed of legal experts—are motivated almost exclusively by the need to be accurate and technically precise as a means of protecting judges against successful appeals. Indeed the authors of the fourth edition of *BAJI* stated flatly that "the one thing an instruction must do above all else is correctly state the law. This is true regardless of who is capable of understanding it."[39]

Regardless of who is capable of understanding it? To be sure, this rather radical statement borders on the absurd. It is, however, an opinion occasionally voiced by others. In 1979 the Florida District Court of Appeals actually discouraged a trial judge from describing legal concepts to the jury in simplified language, even though he did not misstate the law.[40] Other committees are not nearly as flippant about comprehensibility concerns. Still, the *BAJI* quote does reflect the prevailing view which favors accuracy over clarity. As strange as it may sound, by and large, *jury instructions are written by lawyers for lawyers.* And why not? An instruction that is legally erroneous or misleading makes its way into the trial record as a possible basis for appeal. Yet jury confusion attributable to an unintelligible instruction does not. Clearly, we think, the adequacy of jury instructions should be evaluated equally in technical and human terms. As Robert Nieland put it, "A technically correct charge which is misunderstood by its audience may serve to assuage the consciences of appellate court judges, but it is as effective as no instruction at all in guiding jurors to a correct decision in the case."[41]

In recent years there has been a growing trend toward simplifying legal language. New York enacted the first "plain English" law in 1977. Under the terms of this law, many consumer contracts must be written in coherent non-technical language. Other states have since followed suit. Yet despite these legislative efforts, the judiciary has done surprisingly little to include the trial courts in that movement. Considering how well documented the problems are, and considering that we know how to write better instructions, there is no excuse for inaction. And yet despite all that we know, most drafting committees are still composed of only judges, lawyers, and law professors. Amiram Elwork and Bruce Sales recently observed that there is still a widespread disbelief that jury instructions are beyond comprehension.[42] Is that the reason for the unfortunate status quo or are there other less obvious factors operating to maintain it? We think there are.

Most judges acknowledge the difficulties but claim that there is a necessary tradeoff between accuracy and clarity. Jury instructions, they argue, contain delicate "terms of art" that cannot be readily translated into plain English; thus, the problem is one of conceptual complexity, not linguistic construction. In its clearest form, this argument asserts that some legal concepts are so difficult for the average person to understand that no amount of simplification will solve the problem. The same is often said of economics. But to that John Kenneth Galbraith stated flatly that "there are no important propositions that cannot be stated in plain language."[43]

Robert and Veda Charrow addressed this very issue in an interesting empirical study.[44] They had experienced California trial attorneys rate the legal and conceptual complexity of 52 *BAJI* instructions. They then compared these ratings with the degree to which comprehension performance improves on rewritten versions of these same instructions. The Charrows reasoned that if comprehension problems were caused by conceptual complexity, then instructions rated as inherently difficult would show relatively little improvement when simplified in only linguistic terms. But the opposite was true. The greater the conceptual difficulty, the greater the improvement when the material was rewritten. In short, the classic explanation that jury instruction problems are due to complicated law is not a valid reason; it is an excuse.

It is as if the courts prefer not to communicate clearly to their juries. Two possible explanations of this odd predicament present themselves. First, as is evident from the massive volumes of appellate cases, the law, often subject to multiple interpretations, is often unsettled. As such, efforts to rewrite certain already approved instructions could raise thorny legal issues. Second, the courts are sometimes ambivalent about the wisdom of certain rules. Reasoning that jury instructions can be seen as an attempt to balance competing interests, Law Professor Wallace Loh made this argument concerning limited admissibility instructions.[45] The rules of evidence prohibit prosecutors from dragging a defendant's criminal record into the trial. The reason is that this information would prejudice the jury and that it is unfair to hold a defendant accountable for his or her past. However, because we know that many offenders are recidivists and that, as an actuarial matter, there is a significant correlation between past and present behavior, this rule denies the jury access to probative information. As a compromise between decision-making accuracy and the values of procedural fairness, the rules of evidence thus strike a balance between wholesale acceptance and rejection of prior record. It achieves this balance by admitting the evidence, but then directing the jury to consider it only for establishing the defendant's credibility as a witness, not for determining his or her guilt. Can jurors really use such damaging information for one purpose but not another? Common sense suggests not. Loh's review of mock jury research on the question suggests that this rule does achieve a compromise—conviction rates are highest under unlimited admissibility circumstances, lowest under complete exclusion, and at an intermediate level when subjects receive the limited admissibility instruction.[46] In short, perhaps incomprehensible instructions, like the limited admissibility rule, reflect an ambivalence concerning their desired impact.

The "Beyond a Reasonable Doubt" Dilemma

Probably the clearest illustration of how American courts obfuscate the law, for better or for worse, is in how they define the phrase "beyond a reasonable doubt." It is thought to be one of those terms of art. In a recent trial, jurors went home, looked the term up in a dictionary, and discussed its definition during deliberations the next day. For that, the jury's verdict was reversed by an appeals court.[47]

A trial can be viewed as a search for probabilities. Since no judge or jury can ever reconstruct with absolute certainty the truth about some past event, they form a more or less confident opinion of what happened. Thus, every juror is ultimately faced with the question, how certain must I be to vote guilty? What constitutes an acceptable margin of error? To guide people, the courts have articulated three standards of proof.

In our legal system the complaining party, whether it is the plaintiff in a lawsuit or the government in a criminal prosecution, always carries the burden of proving its claim against the defendant. How heavy a burden that is depends on the consequences of an erroneous decision. In most civil cases, where mistaken judgments against the plaintiff and defendant are about equally undesirable, the jury is instructed that in order to vote for the complaining party, it must be satisfied with his or her case by "a preponderance of the evidence." Variously defined, this term is designed to convey the idea that if the jury concludes that the claim is probably more true than untrue, or that the plaintiff's case is stronger than the defendant's, then its verdict should favor the plaintiff. In contrast to this relatively lax criterion, criminal actions are guarded by a more stringent standard of proof. Because societal values dictate that false convictions are less desirable than false acquittals, that it is far worse to imprison the innocent than to let the guilty go free, the courts demand a higher degree of certainty to protect the accused. In 1798 this standard became crystallized in the familiar phrase, beyond a reasonable doubt. Finally, in certain civil actions that entail serious consequences for the losing defendant, an intermediate standard is applied. In cases involving civil commitment, for example, the jury is instructed to adopt a "clear and convincing evidence" criterion, one that is more demanding than a preponderance, but less demanding than a reasonable doubt.

The standard of proof is conveyed to the jury as part of the judge's instructions. The question is, how they should be defined. Over the years, thousands of pages of appellate court opinions and law review articles have analyzed the language and the psychology of various trial court instructions. Take the reasonable doubt standard as an example. An early, often used definition was first provided in 1850: "It is that state of the case, which after the entire comparison and consideration of all the evidence, leaves the minds of jurors in that condition that they cannot say they feel an abiding conviction, to a moral certainty, of the truth of the charge."[48]

As with other instructions, the fact that this explanation sounds confusing, or that it raises more questions than it answers, barely matters on appeal. Never mind that jurors cannot understand it. What really bothers the experts is when, after placing a definition for scrutiny under the microscope, they can detect in the phraseology a bias toward over- or understating how much doubt is to be considered reasonable. Thus, the statement that "a reasonable doubt must be substantial rather than speculative," or that "it is not necessary to prove the defendant guilty beyond all possible doubt," or that it is "a doubt for which you can give a reason" have been roundly criticized. They make convictions sound too easy. At the same time, the statement that a jury must have "a strong and abiding conviction of guilt" is also viewed with disfavor. It makes guilty verdicts sound almost impossible. But what about the apparently innocuous statement that it is "the kind of doubt on which you would be willing to act"? Although this description is more subtle, it has been called dangerous because it refers to the jurors personally. Needless to say, reasonable doubt instructions have evolved, quite literally, through trial and error. The following current instruction is among those that appear to have survived the major objections:

> *A reasonable doubt is a doubt based upon reason and common sense—the kind of doubt that would make a reasonable person hesitate to act. Proof beyond a reasonable doubt must, therefore, be proof of such a convincing character that a reasonable person would not hesitate to rely and act upon it in the most important of his own affairs.*[49]

Does it matter to the outcome of a jury trial how the reasonable doubt test is defined, or do jurors already have an intuitive grasp of it? It is interesting that in some federal and state jurisdictions, judges are not required to define the concept at all. Reasoning that the more detailed the explanation the greater the likelihood of error, an increasing number of courts are taking that safe approach. As with the Rorschach inkblots, jurors are thus left entirely to their own projections of how high or low a standard is implied by the term. In a study of how people interpret legal standards of proof, Rita James Simon and Linda Mahan had 106 judges and 25 jurors convert "reasonable doubt" and "preponderance of the evidence" into numeric terms.[50] Specifically, they asked their subjects how high the probability would have to be that a defendant committed the crime in order for them to vote guilty. Judges clearly distinguished the two standards, demanding an 89 percent probability level in for criminal standard, and 61 percent for the civil standard. Jurors, on the other hand, were not at all sensitive to the difference, asserting probability values of 79 and 77 percent, respectively. In a more recent series of experiments, Dorothy Kagehiro and Clark Stanton had college students read about a civil case followed by a judicially approved instruction concerning one of the three legal standards.[51] They found that their subjects' verdicts were unaffected by the differing instructions, even though these concepts were explicitly defined.

In a 1979 opinion, former Chief Justice Burger expressed skepticism over whether juries make the necessary distinctions between the preponderance, clear and convincing, and reasonable doubt standards of proof.[52] The research suggests they do not. It goes without saying, of course, that if jurors are not responsive to the differences *between* standards, they couldn't possibly appreciate the fine instructional distinctions *within* a standard. Does it really matter, in other words, whether the judge tells the jury that a reasonable doubt is one on which they would "be willing" rather than "hesitate" to act? Obviously not. And yet, as the courts obsess over the precise wording of these definitions, one wonders, "how much the care lavished on their form by appellate courts has been lawyers' shibboleth . . . and how skeptical one may be of proposals for reform which depend for their effect upon the instruction that can be appreciated only by those who have training or experience enough to do so."[53] But does all this imply a failure of the jury, a failure of the instructions, or, perhaps, no failure at all?

For years, legal scholars and social scientists have debated the utility of expressing the standards of proof in quantitative terms. After all, there is nothing ambiguous about a standard that is stripped down to a naked number. As far as we know, this practice is forbidden in American courtrooms.[54] Thus, in 1985 a Massachusetts jury in its third day of deliberation sought a reinstruction on the meaning of reasonable doubt. In an effort to assist them, the judge placed the concept on the scales of justice, compared it to the preponderance standard, and said, "where is that if you put it on a 1–100 scale? I don't know. It's above

50 percent.'' The defendant was found guilty of murder. But an appeals court reversed the conviction, noting that ''the idea of reasonable doubt is not susceptible to quantification. It is inherently qualitative.''[55] Why reject what appears to be an opportunity for the ultimate in instructional clarity? In their experiments on the effects of varying the standard of proof through judicial instruction, Kagehiro and Stanton had half of their subjects receive quantified definitions in which the preponderance, clear and convincing, and reasonable doubt thresholds were represented, respectively, as 51, 71, and 91 percent levels of probability.[56] In contrast to their finding that verbal definitions had no bearing on decision making, the numbers made a substantial difference. Verdicts for the plaintiff were the most frequent under the preponderance standard, the least frequent under the reasonable doubt standard, and at an intermediate level under the clear and convincing test. Arguing that quantified instructions only clarify what is implicit in the law, Kagehiro and Stanton proposed that they be used in court.

Although we do not find this recommendation objectionable, we part company with this hard line on clarity for two reasons. First, ''if it ain't broke, don't fix it.'' It is by no means clear that real juries are as oblivious to the burdens of proof as suggested in the foregoing research. Perhaps for methodological reasons,[57] the research is inconsistent with the trends of real-world jury verdicts. Take Simon and Mahan's results as an example. Compared to judges, their jurors overestimated the burden implied by the preponderance standard, and underestimated that implied by the reasonable doubt test. That pattern should result in jurors' favoring the prosecution in criminal trials and the defense in civil cases. And yet, as shown by Kalven and Zeisel's research, that is precisely the opposite of how the legal community views its juries. Recall that Kalven and Zeisel found that, compared to judges, juries are more likely to exhibit leniency toward criminal defendants and generosity toward civil plaintiffs.[58] If anything, this pattern suggests that, whether by instruction, intuition, or simply an appreciation for the differential consequences of criminal and civil decisions, juries are already sensitive to variations in the standard of proof. As one juror put it, ''When you listen closely to the judge's definition, all it seemed to mean was that 'reasonable doubt' meant 'reasonable doubt.' I couldn't pin down what he was saying. But the funny thing was that when we reached the deliberations, we had the feeling there really was some quantity of evidence that had to be reached, like a vase that had to be filled to a certain mark before we could find the guy guilty.''[59]

UP AGAINST THE LAW

There have always been two competing views of what role the American jury should fulfill. One, the more limited view, is that the jury is no more than a finder of facts. It should resolve matters of evidence and then match its findings to the law. Having done that, the jury's verdict is little more than an actuarial matter. The alternative view is that the jury is a political institution—that because it serves as a conduit for community sentiment, it should do more than blind application of law to specific cases. Thus, it is argued, whether juries adhere their verdicts to judges' instructions should depend not only on whether they *understand* those instructions, but on whether they *agree* in conscience with them.

The Jury's Nullification Power

This distinction comes to life in a trial described in Paige Mitchell's book, *Act of Love*. Lester Zygmanik, age 23, was tried in New Jersey for the murder of his older brother George.[60] Earlier that year George had suffered a serious motorcycle accident that left him paralyzed from the neck down. In agony from his hospital bed, he pleaded with Lester that "I want you to promise to kill me. I want you to swear to God." Lester complied with the request. He entered his brother's hospital room one night, shot him in the head with a 20-gauge sawed-off shotgun, dropped the gun by the bed, and turned himself in. He confessed to the killing immediately and described it as an act of love for his brother. Lester Zygmanik was charged with first-degree murder, which in the state of New Jersey carries a mandatory life prison sentence.

If we apply the limited fact-finding model of the jury, and focus on the question of whether Lester's actions violated the law, then Lester Zygmanik is guilty as charged. No if's, and's, or but's. His actions were willful, deliberate and premeditated. At one point he told his lawyer that "I gave it a lot of thought. You don't know how much thinking I did on it. I had to do something I knew that would definitely put him away. And the only thing I knew that would definitely do that would be a gun. . . . I wanted to make sure he would definitely die."[61] In fact, Lester went so far as to pack the bullets with candle wax in order to compact the explosion and increase its deadly impact. A verdict of guilty seemed inevitable. The jurors, seven men and five women, were tough, conservative, blue-collar, and over 30 years of age. Both the law and the facts were unambiguous. The judge had even ruled that the term "mercy killing" could not be used in the trial.

But the jury saw its role differently. After deliberating for less than three hours, it found the defendant not guilty. The jurors had focused on the relationship between Lester and his brother, the defendant and his victim. In so doing they concluded that Lester had been overcome by grief and that he had acted out of selfless love. The message conveyed by the verdict was clear: in this instance, at least, the commitment to care for a loved one was more important than following the letter of the law. During the trial, Lester had testified that on the night of the killing, "I asked him if he was in pain. At this time, he couldn't speak at all. He just nodded that he was. He nodded yes. So I says, 'I am here to end your pain—is that all right with you?' And he nodded yes. And the next thing I knew, I shot him. . . . "[62]

But then there was the story of Roswell Gilbert, a 75-year-old retired electrical engineer. "My wife begged to die" is how newspaper headlines reported his trial. Gilbert's wife Emily, age 73, suffered from Alzheimer's disease and osteoporosis, both of which were incurable. She pleaded with her husband repeatedly to put an end to her pain and misery. She was in such a state, Gilbert told his attorney, that "hospitals wouldn't take her, [private] nursing homes wouldn't take her. . . . In a state hospital, they'd have to strap her down. She'd be dehumanized." So one day, as Emily sat on a sofa looking out a window in their tenth-floor condominium, he shot her twice in the back of her head. Tried for murder, Gilbert pleaded not guilty. Several witnesses, friends of the elderly couple, corroborated the claim that his wife had begged for her own death. Nevertheless, 10 women and 2 men in Fort Lauderdale, Florida, convicted Gilbert of first-degree murder punishable by life imprisonment. One of the jurors said later, "We had no choice. The law does not allow for sympathy."[63]

The Zygmanik and Gilbert verdicts well illustrate the contrasting views of how juries should reconcile the conflicts that occasionally arise when the law, or their obligation to apply it in a particular instance, clashes with their personal sense of justice. Gilbert's jury took its role as a limited finder of facts quite literally. Zygmanik's jury listened to a different voice, an inner voice of compassion. In this section we address the very controversial question, whether jurors should "nullify" the law, that is, set it aside, in order to make decisions that satisfy their own feelings of what is right and wrong. For the vast majority of cases, these goals are compatible with each other. But there are those few important occasions when they are not. How do jurors actually behave under these circumstances—do they necessarily strive for verdicts that are legally accurate or would they prefer to dispense outcomes that seem instinctively to be fair and equitable? And is their resolution of the conflict affected in any way by what the judge says of their nullification power?

These fundamental questions are not of recent vintage. In fact, they predate the Constitution. Those who favor the jury's nullification power cite as its American birth the 1735 trial of John Peter Zenger, the only printer in the colonies to publish material that had not been authorized by the ruling British government. Under the law, printing anything as such without authorization was a criminal act even though the material printed was true. Andrew Hamilton, Zenger's young lawyer at the time, argued to the jury that it "had the right beyond all dispute to determine both the law and the facts."[64] The jury followed his advice, disregarded the judge's instructions, and acquitted Zenger.

This concept of a nullification-powerful jury persisted through the post-revolutionary era, in part out of a resentment felt toward crown-appointed judges.[65] Soon thereafter, however, its political importance diminished. Then in the 1895 case of *Sparf and Hansen v. the United States*, the Supreme Court made it official and defined the jury's role in the more limited terms. The Court declared that although they cannot be compelled to do so, juries are expected to receive the law from the judge's instructions.[66] Still, juries have been known to use their power on certain occasions. Before the Civil War, northern juries regularly failed to convict people charged with aiding escaped slaves, thereby nullifying the fugitive slave laws. During the 1920s and 1930s, juries refused to convict those who were charged with violating prohibition laws, thereby leading to their repeal. Then in the turbulent Vietnam era, with the government prosecuting antiwar activists on political conspiracy charges, questions about the jury's role were renewed once again.[67]

Unpopular laws are only one reason juries exercise their inherent nullification power. Sometimes they agree in principle with the spirit of a law but question whether its application in a particular trial serves the broader interests of justice. That is what happened in *Wisconsin v. Leroy Reed*, a trial in which TV cameras, for the first time ever, recorded the jury's deliberations.[68] Without belaboring the details, it was a classic nullification case. The defendant, a well-intentioned but dull-witted man, was charged with the illegal possession of a firearm. All jurors, seven men and five women, agreed that he should be convicted by law, but acquitted by justice. The defense attorney had asked for a nullification instruction, but the judge refused because, in his words, "to tell the jury they have that power would be, in my view, an invitation to anarchy." Thus uninformed, the jury debated its role for more than two hours. On one side, there were those who maintained that "technically, the man is guilty, guilty as sin" and that "I think this is a good law. And I don't want to say or do anything that suggests that I don't take that law seriously." Yet others argued that "I don't care what the law says. Has justice been done?" One juror said, rather emphatically, that "I am not a computer and I will not accept everything I am told. . . . I can't do that as a thinking and breathing human being." In the end, this jury found the defendant not guilty.

The pages of history are filled with cases such as this. Kalven and Zeisel reported that juries are generally reluctant to vote guilty in cases involving the defense of self or property. The 1987 trial of Bernhard Goetz, the New York City subway vigilante, is a case in point. Sometimes juries exhibit leniency when they believe that a defendant was mistreated by the police or had suffered enough in some other way. Along similar lines, jurors are notorious for obsessing over the consequences of their decisions for the involved parties.[69] So pervasive is this concern that judges in many states admonish criminal juries to leave sentencing considerations up to the court. Essentially, they are told, it is none of their business. Likewise, civil juries are instructed to determine questions of liability without worrying about whether the defendant has enough insurance to cover the damages.

On their own, juries often suspend the law and, instead, follow their own sentiments in order to achieve outcomes they find fair, just, and equitable. Nobody has to tell a group of people to think about a case in human terms. The question is, what should juries be *instructed* to do when they view a defendant's actions, as they would Robin Hood's, as moral but illegal? Should the courts inform them officially of their inherent power?

The prevailing view follows the U.S. Supreme Court's 1895 opinion that juries should be told to stick to law. In *United States v. Dougherty* (1972), for example, several members of the Catholic Clergy, collectively known as the D.C. Nine, were convicted by a jury for having ransacked the offices of Dow Chemical in protest of the company's manufacture of napalm. Their attorney had asked the trial judge to instruct the jury that it could acquit the defendants on moral grounds. The judge refused. The U.S. District Court of Appeals upheld that decision, noting that jurors "already 'knew' of their nullification powers from informal sources and to institutionalize these powers in routine judge's instructions to the jury would alter the system in unpredictable ways."[70] Would it?

Writing for the majority, Judge Harold Leventhal drew an analogy to highway speed limits. A posted speed limit of 60 mph, he argues, produces speeds of 10 or 15 mph in excess of that limit. Motorists know that some of this speed is tolerated even though they are not officially informed of that policy. If the limit were raised to the speeds actually tolerated, however, motorists would drive even faster. In reply to that argument, Law Professors Alan Scheflin and Jon Van Dyke, jury nullification proponents, maintain that instructions should not encourage juries to ignore the law, merely to suspend it in very specific situations. To carry through with the analogy, they say, the speed limit signs should read "The posted limit is 60 mph, but if emergency conditions exist, persons who drive faster may not be punished."[71]

Ultimately, the controversy raises an empirical question about human behavior. Are jurors affected by an instruction from the judge that sanctions their nullification power? If so, then a more political question is raised. Is that effect desirable? In two states, Indiana and Maryland, juries receive nullification instructions within the final charge. In Maryland courtrooms, for example, judges say something like the following:

> *Members of the jury: this is a criminal case and under the constitution and laws of the state of Maryland in a criminal case the jury are the judges of law as well as the facts in the case. So that whatever I tell you about the law, while it is intended to be helpful to you in reaching a just and proper verdict in the case, it is not binding upon you as members of the jury and you may accept or reject it. And you may apply the law as you apprehend it to be in the case.*[72]

With the reigns of government loosened, some might fear that the juries of Maryland and Indiana would run amok. Compared to their counterparts in other states, some might expect their verdicts to be erratic, predictable only by sentiment, and in disregard of the law. In 1975, political scientist Gary Jacobsohn surveyed 44 Maryland judges about their experiences and views of the nullification instruction. He found that very few respondents disapproved of it. In fact, most felt that it had "not been a significant factor in the output of the trial process."[73] Were they right?

Social psychologist Irwin Horowitz addressed this very question in a fascinating study of mock juries. He had 270 people participating in 45 groups listen to one of three criminal trials. One was an ordinary murder case in which the defendant was alleged to have killed a grocery store owner during a robbery. The second was a euthanasia case involving a nurse who, at the request of a terminally ill cancer patient and his family, ended the patient's life. The third was a drunk driving case in which the defendant was a male college student who had killed a pedestrian in a high-speed automobile accident. In all trials the defendant's guilt was clearly implicated by the evidence. After hearing a case, each jury received either a standard instruction, the Maryland nullification instruction, or a more radical nullification instruction—one that is not actually used in American courtrooms. This latter instruction emphasized the jury's role as a community conscience and invited them rather pointedly to vote for acquittal "if they feel that the law, as applied to the fact situation before them, would produce an inequitable or unjust result."

The results were clear. The radical nullification instruction had a dramatic effect. Compared to the standard charge, it increased the likelihood that jurors would vote for acquittal in the euthanasia case, but it increased their tendency to vote for conviction in the drunk driving case. Juries who received the radical instruction also spent more of their deliberation time exchanging personal experiences and discussing the instruction itself; they spent less time reviewing the evidence. Interestingly, the Maryland nullification instruction had none of these effects. In fact, jurors who received it seemed as unaware of their nullification power as those who were not informed. Just as the Maryland judges had suspected, it appears that their instruction does not alter either the process or the outcome of jury trials.[74] As one judge from Jacobsohn's survey put it, "When the jury is told that they are judges of the law, I doubt that they have any grasp of what is meant."

Is that a desirable result? It depends on who you ask. To those who favor a limited view of the jury's role, the Maryland results are perfect. Jurors are told of their power, but they are unaffected by it. To those who favor the jury's right to nullify the law, however, an ineffective instruction means that juries are still not well informed of their right to moderate outcomes according to conscience. From their standpoint, it is only the more radical instruction that achieves its objectives.

Horowitz's study, however, leaves us wondering about the wisdom of using a nullification instruction that alters the jury decision-making process. One problem, expressed by others, is that jury nullification is like a door that can swing both ways.[75] Just as it can license jurors to acquit the guilty, it is argued, it can enable them to convict those who are innocent. Horowitz's drunk driving case is a good example. Second, it is conceivable that when nullification is made salient, the jury's attention becomes diverted from the external to the internal, from the evidence onto their sentiments. Horowitz's analysis of the deliberation process revealed that this too may be a problem.

Whether or not juries should be encouraged to nullify the law is a difficult question to answer in the abstract. Inevitably, our judgments depend on how we feel about particular cases. And inevitably, our opinions change according to those feelings. Should juries nullify the law when the defendant is charged with the bombing of an abortion clinic? Should all-white southern juries be permitted to acquit KKK defendants who are guilty of racially motivated murder? On the other hand, what about the Zenger and Zygmanik trials? And what about the fugitive slave laws, prohibition, and the Vietnam anti-war conspiracy cases? Chances are, most people would like to see juries nullify some of those laws but not others. It is more a matter of political ideology, we think, than one of jurisprudence.

Deep Pockets, Empty Pockets

Criminal juries are not the only ones that are known to moderate their decisions according to an instinctive sense of equity and justice. It has become fashionable, especially among insurance companies and large corporations, to say that we have become a litigious society and that the civil jury is partly to blame. Jury awards are out of control, we are told. That was certainly the gist of what appeared in newspaper headlines when the Houston jury, in 1985, awarded Pennzoil $10.53 billion in its suit against Texaco. There are many aspects to the charge that the jury is a bleeding heart for civil plaintiffs. It has been said that people are predisposed to favor the plaintiff in their judgments of liability, that they award inflationary sums of money, that their awards are as unpredictable as lottery numbers, and that they are particularly generous toward individuals with "empty pockets" at the expense of corporations and others who are endowed with "deep pockets."

Some of these charges appear to be justified, others do not. To begin with, there is no evidence to support the claim that juries are generally biased toward plaintiffs in their judgments of fault and liability. When Kalven and Zeisel compared judges and juries in civil trials, they found, as they had in the criminal domain, a 78 percent rate of agreement in their verdicts. In the remaining cases, where they disagreed, judges favored the plaintiff 10 percent of the time, juries 12 percent of the time—an even split. Judges and juries did diverge, however, when it came to monetary damages. On the average, jury awards were 20 percent higher.[76]

It is not that juries are erratic or unevenly generous in their awards that has stirred insurance companies and the corporate world into a frenzy. It is that they appear to distribute their awards according to who the litigants are and the financial resources they have at their disposal. In specific terms, it is widely believed that juries grant excessive amounts of money when individual plaintiffs manage to sue defendants who can afford to make the payments. Those with the so-called deep pockets include the government, large corporations, and others who are covered by liability insurance. Like Robin Hood, civil juries are accused of using the courts as a means of taking from the rich and giving to the poor.[77]

At this point, there is reason to believe that perhaps juries do take these kinds of factors into account. The Rand Corporation's Institute for Civil Justice recently published the results of a series of studies on the topic.[78] Tracking the records of more than 9000 civil jury trials held in Chicago between the years 1960 and 1979, investigators found that plaintiffs receive larger awards for the same injuries when they resulted from accidents at the workplace than in an automobile. Injuries from defective products and medical malpractice are also generously compensated. The price of whiplash or a broken neck depends on how that injury is sustained and who is being blamed for it. Consistent with that pattern, it also turned out that government and corporate defendants paid substantially larger damage awards than individuals, especially when the plaintiff was seriously injured. It is always possible, of course, that cases involving government and corporate defendants are different in other important ways from those involving individual defendants. For that reason, we are left to conclude that these findings "do not necessarily mean that juries treated types of litigants differently."[79]

Mock jury experiments, however, support the conclusion that people do in fact take litigants' financial conditions into account. In one study, subjects' awards to a plaintiff increased when they found out through inadmissible testimony that the defendant was insured for the damages. That increase was especially dramatic among those who were admonished to disregard that information.[80] In another study, subjects read a negligence case and were led to believe that the defendant was either Mr. Jones or The Jones Corporation. Even though all subjects received exactly the same facts, plaintiffs were awarded larger sums of money when they were thought to have been injured by a corporation than by an individual.[81]

This "deep pockets" effect, like jury nullification, illustrates how people react when faced with clashing values. Is it fair for civil juries to moderate the distribution of awards according to characteristics of the litigants, or should justice be blind to such factors? It depends on how you define justice. From a legal standpoint, awards should be strictly contingent upon the attribution of responsibility. In human terms, however, people use additional rules to evaluate the fairness of outcomes. It is conceivable, for example, that as representatives of their community, juries are expressing the sentiment that certain impersonal defendants, like corporations and the government, should be held accountable to a high standard for their conduct. Likewise, it is conceivable that juries operate by a "needs rule" which dictates that resources be allocated, at least in part, according to need.[82] Is this justice? Again, it depends on how you feel about the values expressed by the jury's decision.

NOTES

1. Court asked to overturn verdict on Marx estate (1983), *New York Times*, April 16, Section 1.

2. These instructions were taken from the often-used manual written by E. J. Devitt and C. B. Blackmar (1977), entitled *Federal Jury Practice and Instructions* (3rd ed.). St. Paul: West Publishing.

3. These instructions were taken from the *Federal Judicial Center Committee to Study Criminal Jury Instructions* (1982), Pattern Criminal Jury Instructions. Washington, D.C.: Federal Judicial Center.

4. *Sparf v. United States*, 156 U.S. 52.

5. R. L. McBride (1969), *The Art of Instructing the Jury*. Cincinnati: W. H. Anderson.

6. In some states the charge is delivered before closing arguments; in others, after. The Federal Rules of Civil and Criminal Procedure both provide that the judge must instruct the jury after counsel's closing arguments.

7. E. E. Jones and G. R. Goethals (1971), *Order effects in impression formation: Attribution context and the nature of the entity*. Morristown, NJ: General Learning Press.

8. E. B. Prettyman (1960), Jury instructions—first or last? *American Bar Association Journal*, Vol. 46, p. 1066.

9. Amiram Elwork and his colleagues obtained support for this hypothesis, finding that jurors' interpretations of case facts were altered when they received substantive preliminary instructions. See A. Elwork, B. D. Sales, and J. J. Alfini (1977), Juridic decisions: In ignorance of the law or in light of it? *Law and Human Behavior*, Vol. 1, pp. 163–189.

10. S. M. Kassin and L. S. Wrightsman (1979), On the requirements of proof: The timing of judicial instruction and mock juror verdicts. *Journal of Personality and Social Psychology*, Vol. 37, pp. 1877–1887.

11. For further discussion of the notion that jurors make intermediate judgments while the trial is in progress, see R. Hastie & B. Park (1986), The relationship between memory and judgment depends on whether the judgment task is memory-based or on-line. *Psychological Review*, Vol. 93, pp. 258–268.

12. Indeed, none of the three federal judges who participated in an "experiment" on preliminary instructions sponsored by the Second Circuit reported being ill equipped to prepare their instructions at that early stage; see *Report of the Committee on Juries of the Judicial Council of the Second Circuit* (1984), pp. 40–50.

13. The federal courts have viewed the practice of administering pre-evidence instructions favorably, so long as the jury is again fully instructed at the close of the proceedings; see *United States v. Ruppel* (1982), 666 F.2d 274.

14. In the federal courts, it is a matter left to the trial judge's discretion; for a review of state court procedures, see R. G. Nieland (1979), *Pattern Jury Instructions: A Critical Look at a Modern Movement to Improve the Jury System*. Chicago: American Judicature Society.

15. This view was clearly articulated in *Smith v. McMillen* (1862), 19 Ind. 391.

16. For example, see McBride, supra note 5.

17. H. Sigworth and F. Henze (1973), cited in Nieland, supra note 14, p. 29.

18. R. F. Forston (1975), Sense and nonsense: Jury trial communication, *Brigham Young Law Review*, pp. 601–637.

19. S. Penrod, supra note 6.34.

20. Supra note 6.33, pp. 84–89.

21. For example, R. E. Keeton's (1973), *Trial Tactics and Methods* (2nd ed.). Boston: Little, Brown.

22. Supra note 6.2, p. 181.

23. W. B. Wanamaker (1937), Speech given at the Cincinnati Conference, printed in Trial by Jury (1979), *University of Cincinnati Law Review*, Vol. 11, p. 119.

24. J. C. Hervey (1947), Jurors look at our judges, *Oklahoma Bar Association Journal*, Vol. 25, pp. 1508–1513.

25. L. J. Severance and E. F. Loftus (1982), Improving the ability of jurors to comprehend and apply criminal jury instructions. *Law and Society Review*, Vol. 17, pp. 153–197.

26. See Elwork et al., supra note 4.43, and A. Elwork, B. D. Sales, and J. J. Alfini (1982), *Making Jury Instructions Understandable*. Charlottesville, VA: Miche; also see R. P. Charrow and V. R. Charrow (1979), Making legal language understandable: A psycholinguistic study of jury instructions. *Columbia Law Review*, Vol. 79, pp. 1306–1374.

27. It is worth noting that only 13 percent of those presented with the clarified, rewritten instruction fell prey to that inconsistency error.

28. M. J. Asken (1978), *Psychology in the Courtroom: Jury Instructions and the Myth of Jury Decision by Legal Principle*. Doctoral dissertation, West Virginia University.

29. R. Wydick (1978), Plain English for lawyers, *California Law Review*, Vol. 66, p. 727.

30. W. W. Schwarzer (1981), Communicating with juries: Problems and remedies. *California Law Review*, Vol. 69, p. 743.

31. The most complete analyses can be found in the Charrow and Charrow article, supra note 26, and in B. D. Sales, A. Elwork, and J. J. Alfini (1978), Improving comprehension for jury instructions. In B. Sales (Ed.), *Perspectives in Law and Psychology: The Criminal Justice System*, Vol. 1, pp. 23–90.

32. Originally published in 1944 by the Bureau of Publications, Teachers College of Columbia University.

33. Typically cited by its initials, *BAJI*, it was written by the Judges of the Superior Court of Los Angeles County, California, and originally published in 1938 by Wolfer. Its sixth edition was published in 1977 by the West Publishing Company.

34. For example, K. I. Forster and L. A. Ryder (1971), Perceiving the structure and meaning of sentences. *Journal of Verbal Learning and Verbal Behavior*, Vol. 10, pp. 285–296; P. B. Gough (1965), Grammatical transformations and speed of understanding. *Journal of Verbal Learning and Verbal Behavior*, Vol. 4, pp. 107–111.

35. Ibid.

36. Supra note 30, p. 102.

37. Supra note 32.

38. See Nieland, supra note 14.

39. *BAJI* (Fourth Edition, 1954), cited in R. Winslow (1962), The instruction ritual, *Hastings Law Journal*, Vol. 13, p. 456; according to Nieland, the evidence on whether the use of pattern instructions has reduced the frequency of instruction-related appeals is mixed, supra note 14.

40. *Davis v. State*, 373 So. 2d, 382.

41. Supra note 14.

42. See: Jury instructions, in S. Kassin and L. Wrightsman (Eds., 1985), *The Psychology of Evidence and Trial Procedure*. Beverly Hills: Sage Publications.

43. J. K. Galbraith (1978), Writing, typing, and economics, quoted in R. Wydick, supra note 29, p. 756.

44. Supra note 29.

45. W. D. Loh (1984), *Social Research in the Judicial Process: Cases, Readings, and Text*. New York: Russell Sage Foundation.

46. See also R. L. Wissler and M. J. Saks (1985), On the inefficacy of limiting instructions: When jurors use prior conviction evidence to decide on guilt. *Law and Human Behavior*, Vol. 9, pp. 37–48.

47. Juror's use of dictionary helps defendant win reversal (1983). *The National Law Journal*, Jan. 3, p. 43.

48. *Commonwealth v. Webster* (1850), cited in E. W. Cleary (Ed.), *McCormick's Handbook of the Law of Evidence*, Second Edition. St. Paul, MN: West, p. 799.

49. Devitt and Blackmar, supra note 2, Part 2, p. 310.

50. R. J. Simon and L. Mahan (1971), Quantifying burdens of proof: A view from bench, the jury, and the classroom. *Law and Society Review*, Vol. 5, pp. 319–330.

51. D. K. Kagehiro and W. C. Stanton (1985), Legal vs. quantified definitions of standards of proof. *Law and Human Behavior*, Vol. 9, pp. 159–178.

52. See *Addington v. Texas* (1979), 441 U.S. 418, pp. 424–425.

53. A. P. Sealy and W. R. Cornish (1973), Juries and the rules of evidence. *Criminal Law Review*, April, pp. 208–223.

54. In *United States v. Clay*, 476 F.2d 1211 (1973), the U.S. Court of Appeals for the Ninth Circuit specifically directed its judges to remove from their definitions all references to "balancing" or "probabilities". Likewise, in *United States v. Anglada*, 524 F.2d 296 (1975), the U.S. Court of Appeals for the Second Circuit advised that judges should not instruct juries that the standard is quantitative rather than qualitative.

55. See A. I. Coon (1985), Mass. judge erred in quantifying "reasonable doubt." *The National Law Journal*, October 21, p. 8.

56. Supra note 50.

57. Most notably, subject jurors did not deliberate and arrive at a group-level decision concerning the applicable standards; yet there is reason to believe that this process results in an increased appreciation for the reasonable doubt standard in criminal cases (see G. Stasser, N. L. Kerr, and R. M. Bray (1982), The social psychology of jury deliberations: Structure, process, and product. In N. Kerr and R. Bray (Eds.), *The Psychology of the Courtroom*. New York: Academic Press).

58. See Kalven and Zeisel, supra note 1.19.

59. S. Wishman (1986), *Anatomy of a Jury: The System on Trial*. New York: Times Books, p. 249.

60. P. Mitchell (1976), *Act of love: The killing of George Zygmanik*. New York: Knopf.

61. Ibid. at p. vii.

62. Ibid. at p. 195.

63. Associated Press (1985, May 10). Man, 75, gets life for wife's death. *Kansas City Times*, p. A-4.

64. J. Alexander (Ed., 1973), *A brief narration of the case and trial of John Peter Zenger*. Boston: Little, Brown, p. 78.

65. C. Rembar (1980), *The law of the land*. NY: Simon & Schuster.

66. 156 U.S. 51.

67. For an excellent historical review, see A. Scheflin & J. Van Dyke (1980), Jury nullification: The contours of a controversy. *Law and Contemporary Problems*, Vol. 43, pp. 52–115; also see M. R. Kadish and S. H. Kadish (1973), *Discretion to Disobey*. Stanford, CA: Stanford University Press; C. Rembar (1980), *The Law of the Land*. NY: Simon & Schuster.

68. Inside the Jury Room (1986), appearing on the PBS show, *Frontline* (produced by Al Levine and Steve Herzberg).

69. Several experiments have shown that even mock jurors, whose decisions are not of real consequence, are markedly affected in their verdicts by what they believe will happened to the convicted defendant; e.g., see E. Z. Gallun (1983), *The effect of the insanity defense and its consequences on jury verdicts*. Unpublished thesis, Williams College; also see N. L. Kerr (1978), Severity of prescribed penalty and mock jurors' verdicts. *Journal of Personality and Social Psychology*, Vol. 36, pp. 1431–1442.

70. 473 F.2d 1113, at p. 1135.

71. Supra note 67, p. 66.

72. Scheflin & Van Dyke, supra note 67; p. 83.

73. G. Jacobsohn (1976), The right to disagree: Judges, juries, and the administration of criminal justice in Maryland. *Washington University Law Quarterly*, pp. 571–607.

74. See I. A. Horowitz (1985), The effect of jury nullification instruction on verdicts and jury functioning in criminal trials. *Law and Human Behavior*, Vol. 9, pp. 25–36.

75. See G. Simson (1976), Jury nullification in the American system: A skeptical view. *Texas Law Review*, pp. 288–526.

76. H. Kalven (1964), The dignity of the civil jury. *Virginia Law Review*, Vol. 50, pp. 1055–1075.

77. The insurance industry complains that it is being used in the courts as a "social welfare"

system. This view is expressed by F. D. Watkins (1976), Social inflation: Our next trial. *Insurance Magazine*, Vol. 77, p. 42.

78. M. A. Peterson & G. L. Priest (1982), *The civil jury: Trends in trials and verdicts, Cook County, Illinois, 1960–1979*; M. A. Peterson (1984), *Compensation of injuries: Civil jury verdicts in Cook County*; A. Chin & M. A. Peterson (1985), *Deep pockets, empty pockets: Who wins in Cook County jury trials*. All published in Santa Monica, CA: Rand Corporation.

79. Ibid., at p. v.

80. D. Broeder (1959), The University of Chicago jury project. *Nebraska Law Review*, Vol. 38, pp. 744–760.

81. V. P. Hans (1987), *Perceptions of corporate versus individual responsibility for wrongdoing*. Paper presented at the annual meeting of the American Psychological Association, New York City, August.

82. For a review of the varying conceptions of justice, see G. S. Leventhal (1976), Fairness in social relationships. A chapter appearing in J. Thibaut, J. Spence, & R. Carson (Eds.), *Contemporary Topics in Social Psychology*. Morristown, NJ: General Learning Press.

8

INSIDE THE JURY ROOM

Think for a moment about Henry Fonda's role as Juror #8 in *Twelve Angry Men*. In this classic film the defendant is a young, uneducated Puerto Rican boy from a poverty-stricken home. He is charged with the stabbing death of his physically abusive father. The viewer sees this defendant, as well as his judge and lawyer, only in the opening minutes of the film. The scene then shifts from the courtroom to the jury room. As the title suggests, it is an all-male jury. Among them is a garage owner filled with racial prejudice; a conservative stockbroker, calm, and reserved, but clearly fixed in his opinion; a wise-cracking salesman eager to vote so he can get out to a baseball game; a young Madison Avenue advertising man, constantly vacillating in his opinion; and an immigrant watchmaker, openly appreciative of his life in a democracy. Among the remaining seven jurors is Henry Fonda's character about whom the viewer knows next to nothing.

Almost as soon as the door closes behind them, the jury is prepared to find the defendant guilty. After selecting a foreman, they open by taking a show-of-hands vote. The result is an 11 to 1 majority in favor of conviction, with Fonda the lone dissenter. After some discussion, Fonda makes it clear that although he does not necessarily believe the defendant to be innocent, he does harbor enough doubt to warrant a critical review of the evidence. With that, they go around the table for each of the jurors to air his views. Consistently, Fonda manages to raise a reasonable doubt, question the accuracy of witnesses, and suggest alternative explanations. Then just as tension mounts over the apparent stalemate,

Fonda offers a deal: If he is still the only dissenter after a secret ballot, he would capitulate to the majority's will. A vote is taken, and the result is that Fonda gains an ally—10 to 2 in favor of conviction.

At this point, with the sides clearly drawn, the deliberation takes on a more serious, down-to-business tone. All aspects of the evidence against the defendant are scrutinized. Was the eyewitness who claims to have seen the murder from her bedroom window across the street credible? What about the downstairs neighbor, an elderly man, who claims to have heard the defendant scream "I'll kill you," followed by the sound of a fall—did he, as testified, run into the hallway in time to see the defendant running out? And what about the boy's story that he had spent the night at the movies, despite his inability to remember what film he had seen? And then there is the murder weapon that was found nearby—a knife similar to the one purchased but supposedly lost by the defendant. How unique was that knife and what were the odds that it could have resembled the defendant's by coincidence? On each item of evidence, alternatives were suggested. Led by Fonda, an increasing number of jurors questioned whether the eyewitness, awakened from her sleep, could have been wearing her glasses. They questioned whether the downstairs neighbor could have identified the defendant's voice over the rumbling sounds of the elevated subway outside the building. They reenacted the neighbor's limp-ridden walk from his bedroom into the hallway, timed it, and questioned whether it was possible. Periodically, the foreman would call for a vote. On each successive occasion, the number of not-guilty votes increased. Eventually, they reached an 11 to 1 majority in favor of acquittal. That left one man who, under pressure to defend his rigid position, revealed his prejudice against a young defendant who painfully reminded him of his defiant son. Finally, frustrated and unable to overcome the jury's reasonable doubt, he too reverses his vote.

Now consider the dynamics of a real jury that, in 1974, acquitted John Mitchell and Maurice Stans of charges that they had conspired to obstruct an SEC investigation of President Nixon's reelection campaign funds. Real life does not ordinarily imitate art. But, then again, this was not an ordinary trial. Taking place in New York City, it was one of the highly publicized Watergate-related cases. The defendants were a former U.S. Attorney General and a former Secretary of Commerce, both members of Nixon's cabinet. The government's case against the defendants was strong. But a few weeks into the trial, a juror became ill and was replaced by Andrew Choa, an alternate juror. Choa was a vice president at the First National City Bank, the second largest in the country. In contrast to the other jurors, he was a college graduate, a graduate of Harvard Business School, a world traveler, and well informed about Watergate. Politically, he was a dedicated Republican and supporter of Richard Nixon; as an acquaintance put it, Choa was "to the right of Ivan the Terrible."

Thanks to *New York Times* reporter Martin Arnold, we know something about how the jury reached its verdict.[1] By interviewing some of the jurors, including Choa, Arnold was able to reconstruct portions of the deliberation process. It turned out that the first formal vote resulted in an 8 to 4 majority in favor of conviction. Although Choa was in the minority, he eventually managed to convert the others to accept his views. The story of his role in the group is interesting. The jury was sequestered in a local hotel during the trial so as to be shielded from outside influences. At one point, they wanted to see the St. Patrick's Day parade but were not allowed to mingle with the street crowds. Choa arranged for them to watch the parade from one of the branch offices of his bank. Occasionally, he took the group to movies shown in the bank's private auditorium, paid minor expenses for entertainment when money from the court was temporarily unavailable, and even provided baseball bats obtained from the bank. As the *New York Times* reporter put it, Choa had become the jury's "social director."

Having accepted all these favors, one wonders how easy it would have been for the eight college-uneducated jurors to resist Choa's efforts to influence them. Several times, we are told, he persuaded the jury to request a rereading of the testimony and instructions. We do not know specifically what information he wanted to have repeated. But we do know that the requests were written by Choa and signed by the foreperson. One of the most damaging pieces of evidence against the defendants was a memorandum written by Robert Vesco, a financier and fugitive from justice, to Don Nixon, the President's brother. In that memo Vesco threatened to disclose his secret $200,000 cash contribution to CREEP (the Committee to Re-elect the President) unless the SEC dropped another case against him. Apparently, when Choa dismissed this evidence as "trash" the jury agreed. Finally, Choa seemed to be well aware of tactics that would further increase his measure of influence. During the deliberations, he was initially circumspect. He later said he had deliberately chosen a seat at the jury table that would insure his being called on last. Indeed, even while declaring "I did not want to influence my fellow jurors" he must have known that the person who speaks last often carries a voice of authority. Choa was recently contacted by Paula DiPerna, a journalist, in Hong Kong where he now works. His reply to the claim that he single-handedly turned the majority around was, "My major role was to keep the jury focused on the judge's instructions."[2]

Now compare your reactions to *Twelve Angry Men* and the Mitchell-Stans trial. In both cases the jury opens with a strong majority in favor of conviction. And in both cases, it is reversed toward a unanimous acquittal through the workings of a single, highly influential juror. So why do we react favorably to Fonda's efforts, and unfavorably to Choa's? Why is Fonda cast as the hero, and Choa as the villain? To be sure, these stories differ in several important respects. One is fiction; the other is reality. One is a run-of-the-mill case against a youthful minority defendant; the other is a nationally visible trial involving two powerful figures. In one, the key juror is a lone dissenter; in the other, he has three allies. Are these differences enough to account for our reactions to these two successful protagonists? We think probably not.

What most distinguishes Fonda and Choa is the extent to which their methods of influence comport with our vision of an ideal deliberation. Fonda entered the jury room as just another juror. Unknown to the group in name or occupation, he was simply juror #8. Admittedly unable to prove the defendant's innocence, he nevertheless managed to convert his peers through a series of rational and persuasive arguments concerning the quality of the state's evidence. Choa, on the other hand, entered the jury room as a man of known status. With the jury having been sequestered (that is, kept under security and housed in a hotel in order to be protected from outside influences) for several weeks, he had already emerged as the group's social director. He was also the most educated of the jurors and, as a bank vice president, he brought his expertise in case-relevant financial matters. From the little we know about the deliberations, it appears that Choa used his status to exert influence through social pressure.

THE IDEALS OF JURY DELIBERATION

Our comparison of *Twelve Angry Men* and the Mitchell-Stans jury provides a nice framework for illustrating the ideals of jury deliberation. It is often said that the distinctive power of the system is that the jury functions as a *group*. Is it? How do jurors carrying different opinions manage to converge on a single verdict? What distinguishes a jury from any other arbitrary collection of individuals? Indeed, what does transpire behind the closed doors of the jury room? We will see that although the jury meets in total privacy, the courts have articulated a clear vision of what the dynamics of deliberation should look like. Basically, there are three components to this ideal.

The first component is one of independence and equality. No juror's vote counts for more than any other juror's vote. A 12-person jury should thus consist of 12 *independent* and *equal* individuals, each contributing his or her own personal opinion to the final outcome. The courts attempt to foster this ideal in a number of ways. For example, judges instruct jurors to refrain from discussing the trial with each other until they retire for their deliberations. In this way, each juror develops his or her own unique perspective on the case, uncontaminated by others' views. This ensures not only the independence of individual members but also the diversity of the group as a whole.

Unlike other task-oriented groups, the jury's role is ideally structured to advance the cause of equal participation. The cardinal rule of jury decision making is that verdicts be based only on the evidence introduced in open court. By limiting the task as such, jurors are discouraged from basing their arguments on private or outside sources of knowledge. Because they experience the same trial, and because they are provided with identical information, jurors are placed on an equal footing. To further promote equality, the courts often exclude from service people who are expected to exert a disproportionate amount of influence over other jurors. Lawyers or others who are particularly knowledgeable about trial-relevant subjects are thus excluded despite their otherwise welcome expertise.[3] Several years ago, Edmund G. Brown, then Governor of California, was among those picked at random from a pool of 219 prospective jurors in Sacramento. At least publicly, nobody questioned his impartiality. But wouldn't his presence on the panel overwhelm other jurors? During the voir dire, the defense lawyer asked a prospective juror, "Would you hesitate to disagree with him in deliberation?" she replied, "No, I've disagreed with him before." In the end, Brown was seated on the jury and elected foreperson.[4]

The second component of the deliberation ideal is an openness to informational influence. Once inside the jury room, jurors have a duty to interact and discuss the case. They should share information, exchange views, and debate the evidence. Thus, when an Indianapolis juror locked herself in the ladies' room after 20 hours of deliberation and refused to talk after having been called a "big mouth," the judge was forced to declare a mistrial.[5] Two essential characteristics of an ideal jury follow from the requirement of deliberation. One is that jurors maintain an open mind, that each juror withhold judgment until "an impartial consideration of the evidence *with his fellow jurors*."[6] Openmindedness is such an important aspect of an ideal deliberation that if a juror dies before a verdict is announced, then the jury cannot return a verdict even if all the remaining jurors indicate that the deceased had agreed with their decision. The reasoning behind this rule is that "the jurors individually and collectively have the right to change their minds prior to the reception of the verdict."[7]

The second is that consensus should be achieved through an exchange of information. Jurors should scrutinize their own views, be receptive to others', and allow themselves to be persuaded by rational argument. One juror advances a proposition; the others either accept it, challenge it, or modify it on publicly defensible grounds. As the Supreme Court put it almost a century ago, "The very object of the jury system is to secure unanimity by a comparison of views, and by arguments among the jurors themselves. . . . It cannot be that each juror should go to the jury-room with a blind determination that the verdict shall represent his opinion of the case at that moment; or that he should close his ears to the arguments of men who are equally honest and intelligent as himself."[8]

The third component of the deliberation ideal follows from the second. Although juries should strive for a consensus of opinion, it should *not* be achieved through heavy-handed normative pressure. Obviously, jurors who dissent from the majority position should not be beaten, bullied, or harangued into submission. Indeed "no juror should surrender his honest conviction as to the weight or effect of the evidence solely because of the opinion of his fellow jurors, or for the mere purpose of returning a verdict."[9] The reason for discouraging juries from securing unanimity through social pressure is simple. Jurors are expected and, in fact, instructed to vote with their conscience. If they change their minds because they are genuinely persuaded by new information, fine. But if they comply with the majority just to avoid being rejected or to escape an unpleasant experience, then their final vote will not reflect their true beliefs. In the Supreme Court's words, "the verdict must be the verdict of each individual juror, and not a mere acquiescence in the conclusion of his fellows."[10]

A Social-Psychological Analysis

It is rare for all jurors to agree on a verdict at the outset of their deliberations. For that reason, the process of deliberation is, by and large, a study in persuasion and social influence. With that in mind, the legal system is clear in its prescriptions for how its juries should manage the inevitable tension between minority and majority viewpoints; between individual expression and independence on the one hand, and the collective need for consensus, on the other. How should jurors influence and be influenced? What kinds of pressure comport with the ideals of deliberation? Before evaluating the extent to which juries meet the courts' standards, let us look at the psychology of group influence.

In a now classic series of experiments, social psychologist Solomon Asch confronted people with the following awkward situation. Subjects were scheduled in small groups to participate in a study of visual discrimination. Upon their arrival, they were seated around a table and instructed that they would be making a series of simple judgments. Presented with a single vertical line on one board and three lines of varying length on another, subjects were asked to decide which of the three comparison lines was the same as the standard. Because the task was straightforward, the experimenter remarked, he would save time by having subjects announce their judgments out loud in order of their seating position. Actually, there was only one real subject in the group—the others were ''confederates'' posing as subjects but working for the experimenter. The first two judgments passed uneventfully. The discriminations were simple and all subjects agreed on the correct answer. Then on 12 of the next 16 trials, the first confederate gave what clearly seemed to be the wrong answer. The next four did the same. With all eyes on the subject, how does he respond? Much to Asch's surprise, subjects conformed with the incorrect majority 37 percent of the time. Only when they had an ally, or even another member who dissented from both their own and the others' judgments, were subjects able to resist the pressure to conform.[11] More recent research, motivated by psychologist Bibb Latane's *social impact theory*, corroborates this basic finding.[12]

Asch's study raised important questions, the first being, why did people conform as often as they did? By interviewing his subjects, Asch discovered that they followed the majority for different reasons. Some claimed they actually agreed with what the majority had reported; others became uncertain of their own perceptions; still others maintained their original beliefs but went along anyway. Shortly after Asch's initial demonstration, social psychologists Morton Deutsch and Harold Gerard repeated the experiment with one significant modification. In one condition, subjects were separated by partitions and prevented from communicating with one another. And instead of publicly announcing their answers, they indicated their judgments by pressing a button. Do people still conform, even when protected by their anonymity within the group? The answer is, yes and no. Deutsch and Gerard found that subjects who participated in this anonymous condition were less likely to follow the incorrect majority than those who were in the face-to-face situation created by Asch. But they were still more likely to make incorrect judgments than a group of subjects who completed the line-judgment task alone.[13]

Deutsch and Gerard concluded from this study that people are influenced by others for two distinct reasons—informational and normative. Through *informational* social influence, people conform because they want to be correct in their judgments and expect that when others agree with each other, they must be right. Thus in Asch's visual discrimination task, it is natural for subjects to assume that ten eyes are better than two. Through *normative* social influence, however, people conform because they fear the negative consequences of appearing deviant. Wanting to be accepted and well liked, they avoid behaving in ways that make them stick out like a sore thumb. And for good reason. Decision-making groups often reject, ridicule, and punish individuals who frustrate a common goal by adhering to a deviant position.[14]

The distinction between normative and informational social influence is critical not just for an understanding of why people conform, but because it produces two very different types of conformity: public compliance and private acceptance. The term *public compliance* refers to a superficial change in behavior. Often, people will publicly vote with the majority, even though privately they continue to disagree. "To get along, go along," as they say. In contrast, as the term *private acceptance* indicates, there are times when people are genuinely persuaded by others' opinions. In these instances, they change not only their overt behavior, but their minds as well.[15] Obviously, public compliance is a weaker and less stable outcome of social influence than private acceptance. The individual who complies without truly sharing the group's views is likely to revert to his or her own real attitude as soon as the promise of reward or threat of punishment are no longer in effect (for example, when he or she is not being observed).

The social psychology of group influence provides a framework and, as we will see, an empirical literature with which we can evaluate the ideals of jury deliberation. As the courts have long recognized, an ideal jury enters the jury room with diverse opinions and open minds. Through a vigorous exchange of viewpoints, a majority faction develops. It then strives toward unanimity through a process of informational influence until the final holdouts come to accept that position. In the ideal, then, a jury's final verdict reflects each individual's vote of conscience. In contrast to this information-acceptance model, there is what might be called the normative-compliance model of deliberation. It is characterized by the use of heavy-handed social pressure that leads dissenters to publicly support the jury's verdict while privately harboring reservations. As the poet Ferlinghetti put it, "Just because you have silenced a man does not mean you have changed his mind." In this less-than-ideal model, the jury completes its task unanimous in vote but not in conscience.

There are important reasons to protect individual jurors from the kinds of normative pressure that would force merely their compliance. To begin with, justice itself is undermined when a jury renders a verdict not supported even by its own membership. Criminal defendants should not be convicted by juries that are plagued by a reasonable doubt within its membership. There is also danger that people's perceptions of justice are undermined as well by deliberations that follow a normative-compliance model. How much faith in the legal system can a juror have after voting against his or her conscience? The following case illustrates the point.

In 1981 a Miami jury deliberated for more than six hours on whether four defendants had paid undercover agents $220,000 for 15 pounds of cocaine. At one point the jurors reported they were deadlocked, so the judge asked that they try further to reach agreement. Three hours later they returned with verdicts: three convictions and an acquittal. When the judge began polling them in open court as to whether they agreed in conscience with their decisions, the very first juror said, "no." The judge sent them back to the jury room. A few minutes later, they returned with the same verdicts. Polled again, the first juror agreed, but juror #5 said, "No, it's not my verdict." Again, the judge sent them back. This time, they returned and confirmed the verdicts. But one of the defense lawyers said, "We noticed juror #11 kick the back of juror #5's chair when it was her turn." Polled separately, jurors 1 and 5 both repudiated their verdicts. Sent back a fourth time, the jurors deliberated half an hour more, returned with the same verdicts, and stood by them. Then when the trial had ended, jurors 1 and 5 approached two of the defendants and apologized for their convictions. According to their report, two jurors insisted on concluding that night because they had vacation plans. One of them swung at another juror, and four who initially had voted for acquittal were "browbeaten into submission."[16]

Now that we have a clear image of the informational-acceptance and normative-compliance models of deliberation, we should add that they rarely appear in their pure form. Most decision-making groups achieve a consensus of opinion through a combination of forces.[17] Juries are no exception. As Kalven and Zeisel noted, the deliberation process "is an interesting combination of rational persuasion, sheer social pressure, and the psychological mechanism by which individual perceptions undergo change when exposed to group discussion."[18] With that reality in mind, it is clear that the ideals of deliberation should be stated in relative terms: *A jury verdict meets the courts' standards if, following a vigorous exchange of information and a minimum of normative pressure, it accurately reflects each of the individual jurors' private beliefs.*

BEHIND CLOSED DOORS: WHO SAYS WHAT TO WHOM?

If only the walls of the jury room could talk, what would they say? By carefully observing mock jury deliberations, by interviewing actual jurors, and by analyzing trial verdict records, it is possible to piece together what transpires during deliberations. How is the foreperson elected? Who does the talking? What is said, and to whom is it said? How and when are votes taken? How do factions develop? These are among the many questions jury researchers have tried to answer.

Leaders, Participants, and Followers

Juries should consist of 12 independent and equal individuals, each contributing to the final outcome. Let us consider whether that is a realistic ideal. Many trial lawyers do not think so. Robert Duncan, an experienced Kansas City attorney, asserts that "most juries consist of one or two strong personalities with the rest more or less being followers. Thus, often the jury trial actually consists of a one or two person jury."[19] Looking at the empirical literature, it is clear there is an element of truth to that observation. In virtually all kinds of small-group discussions, the rate of participation among individual members is very uneven—a few people do almost all the talking.[20] Exactly the same pattern seems to characterize how juries function. In one study more than 800 people watched a reenactment of a murder trial and then participated in one of 69 mock juries. By videotaping the deliberations and then counting the number of statements contributed by each juror within each group, the experimenters were able to measure how equally the individuals had participated in their respective groups. The results of this analysis were clear. In each group a few jurors controlled the discussion, while the others spoke at a much lower rate. In fact, most groups included as many as three members who remained virtually silent through deliberations, speaking only to cast their votes. Add to that pattern the fact that the more a juror speaks, the more he or she is spoken to and the more persuasive he or she appears to the others, and it is apparent that dominance hierarchies develop in juries just as they do in other groups.[21]

With juries stratifying into leaders, participants, and followers, it is natural to ask—what constitutes leadership on a jury, or any other kind of group for that matter? What kinds of people emerge as leaders, and under what circumstances? Social scientists have two ways of answering that general question. One is to focus on stable personal qualities that distinguish those in power from everyone else. The idea is that leaders are born, not made; that the history of nations and social movements is a history of great individuals; that to identify leaders, one must study their abilities, their character, their appeal, and their personality. The second approach is to focus on transient situational forces that propel certain individuals into positions of power and leadership. From this perspective, leadership is determined by current events, the needs and resources of a particular group, and the nature of the task that needs to be performed. A person who is prepared to lead in one situation may be ill equipped in another group at another time.[22]

When it comes to small decision-making groups, everyday observation and empirical research have shown that leadership consists of two discrete components or—to put it differently—there are two types of leaders. In order to achieve a specific objective, groups need a *task-oriented* leader, one who takes charge, defines a substantive and procedural agenda, establishes a network of communication, and drives the group toward its destination. For the maintenance of interpersonal harmony, however, groups need a *socioemotional* leader, one who reduces tensions created by decision-making conflicts, provides emotional support to individual members, and helps to increase the cohesiveness and morale of the group as a whole.[23] Both task and socioemotional roles are important. Within a group's life cycle, the relative needs for the two types of leadership change according to circumstances.

Turning to the jury, it is common for people to assume that the foreperson is the jury's leader. That is true only in a limited sense. The foreperson holds a position of responsibility that cannot be denied. Selected for the role by the judge, by random assignment, or by the jury itself, the foreperson announces the verdict in open court and acts as a liaison between the judge and jury. Although a leader in this formal sense, however, the foreperson is not necessarily the most influential juror in either a task-oriented or socioemotional sense. Neither Henry Fonda nor Andrew Choa was assigned that role, but both emerged through their deliberations as opinion leaders.

Who are these forepersons and how are they selected? Research shows that juries spend little time at it. Forepersons are often chosen by acclamation and without dissent. People do not seem to seek the position actively. In fact, chances are that the first juror who says "what should we do about a foreman?" is immediately chosen.[24] It is interesting that although the selection process is rather casual, its outcomes follow a predictable pattern. To begin with, the foreperson is, quite literally, a *foreman*. All sexist language aside, men are more likely to be selected than women. This finding was not particularly shocking when it appeared in the 1950s, at a time when traditional sex roles were intact. But the bias toward male forepersons continues even in today's era of greater equality for women. Apparently, people assume (erroneously, we might add) that men make better leaders than women.[25] To illustrate how dramatic the difference is, a recent study of 179 trials held in San Diego revealed that although 50 percent of the jurors were female, 90 percent of the forepersons were male.[26]

Other systematic patterns are evident too. For example, forepersons tend to be better educated and hold higher status jobs than the average juror. Those who have previous jury experience are also selected at a higher-than-expected rate.[27] Then there is an interesting, less obvious selection bias. In 1961, jury researchers Fred Strodtbeck and L. H. Hook published a paper entitled "The social dimensions of a 12-man jury table."[28] Looking at the most common geometrical layout, the rectangular table, they discovered that foreperson selections were predictable from where jurors were seated. Those who sat at the heads of the table were by far the most likely to be chosen, whereas those located in the middle were the least likely. Since it also turns out that jurors of higher status naturally tend to take more prominent seats, it appears that this dimension adds even further to the development of a dominance hierarchy within the jury.

Research has thus shown that although juries are casual about their choice of a foreperson, the selections follow systematic patterns. But research has also shown that it does not really matter who fills that role. To be sure, the foreperson is usually the most active member of the jury. Several of the Chicago Jury Project studies reported in the 1950s and 1960s found that, on the average, the foreperson accounts for approximately 25 percent of the statements made during deliberations.[29] It turns out, however, that although forepersons carry a disproportionate amount of influence over the process of deliberation, they do not have the same kind of impact over its outcome. In one study, for example, forepersons contributed a great deal at first on primarily procedural matters (calling for votes or rereading judges' instructions), but then behaved like the more average participants as the deliberations progressed.[30] Another study revealed that while forepersons raised organizational matters at five times the rate of other jurors, they were less likely to express an opinion concerning the verdict.[31] This latter result suggests that it may be more accurate to think of the foreperson not as the jury's leader, but as a referee or moderator. Indeed, Martin Balsam's character in *Twelve Angry Men* fits that role perfectly.

If the foreperson does not lead the jury to its verdict, who does? The answer to this question is simple. By and large, the same characteristics that are associated with foreperson selections are also related to opinion leadership: sex, employment status, jury experience, and seating position. Male and female jurors, for example, play very different roles in the jury room. Consistent with traditional sex roles, men assume a primarily task-oriented role, offering information and expressing opinions; women assume the more socioemotional role, agreeing with others' statements, offering support, and helping to reduce interpersonal tensions.[32] Needless to say, male jurors are rated by their fellow panelists as more persuasive than their female counterparts.[33]

Experienced and novice jurors are not equivalent in their levels of participation, either. When Dale Broeder interviewed jurors after their trials, he came across several experienced jurors who had taken on an air of expertise and tried to control the rest of the group. As an example, he described a woman who, immediately upon entering the jury room, cut paper ballots, explained that it was standard procedure to open with a secret vote, and "did everything but suggest that she be elected foreman."[34] More controlled research with mock juries lends support to Broeder's observations. In one study, subjects who had previously served on a real jury talked more during deliberations than those who had not.[35] These kinds of effects appear even when the subject's experience consists of having earlier participated in a mock jury. In this situation, the first author, in collaboration with Ralph Juhnke, found that new subjects reportedly participated less and made less persuasive comments than their more experienced peers. We also found that new subjects conformed to their groups more when they deliberated with others of experience than when they participated in fully inexperienced groups.[36] Finally, consistent with the more situational theories of leadership, we suspect that individual jurors will lead or follow depending upon their suitability and expertise for a particular trial. It is probably not a coincidence that the Mitchell-Stans jury turned to Andrew Choa, a banker, for guidance on evidence of a financial nature. In principle, all jurors are supposed to be created equal. In practice, however, this egalitarian ethic is seldom if ever realized. The fact of the matter is that dominance hierarchies develop that mirror the differences of status in the real world. Thus, despite the forces designed to place all jurors on an equal footing and neutralize individual differences, juries still consist in predictable ways of leaders, participants, and followers.

The Sounds of Deliberation

Imagine that you just sat through a full trial, having listened to several witnesses, lawyers, and the judge. You still have not communicated your thoughts and impressions to anyone else, nor do you know what the others on the panel are thinking. You may have formed some opinions, and you are probably filled with questions. Finally, the door of the jury room closes, and you find yourself with 11 strangers. Where do you begin? How do juries structure their discussions and what do they talk about? In short, what are the sounds of deliberation? Kalven and Zeisel offer the following colorful description:

> There is at first, in William James' phrase about the baby, the sense of buzzing, booming, confusion. After a while, we become accustomed to the quick, fluid movement of jury discussion and realize that the talk moves with remarkable flexibility. It touches an issue, leaves it, and returns again. Even a casual inspection makes it evident that this is interesting and arresting human behavior. It is not a formal debate; nor, although it is mercurial and difficult to pick up, is it just excited talk.[37]

Social psychologists interested in how groups solve problems describe the process as passing through series of stages.[38] According to this view, a group begins in an open ended, not very well defined *orientation* phase. During these opening moments, the group defines its task and perhaps even a strategy for discussion. Questions are raised, issues are explored, and tentative views are expressed in general terms. Formally or informally, a vote is eventually taken. Differences of opinion are thus revealed, factions develop, and the group enters an *open conflict* phase. At this point, the discussion takes on a more focused, serious tone. With individuals taking sides in a debate, only points of disagreement are addressed. During this critical and often lengthy period, discussion is best characterized in social influence terms, with both informational and normative pressures operating. In most groups, a sizeable majority eventually emerges, and a mutually acceptable decision appears imminent. When that happens, the group enters a period of *conflict resolution and reconciliation*. If one or two individuals continue to hold out in the face of attempts to convert them through rational argument, then they become the targets of increasing pressures to conform. If and when unanimity is achieved, the group then goes through a period of reconciliation designed to heal the wounds of battle, express support and reassurance, and affirm its satisfaction with the final outcome.

Judges and lawyers are forever wondering about what jurors talk about in their deliberations. Do they stick like glue to the evidence, or do they allow themselves to wander onto topics prohibited by the judge? How much time do they spend talking about their own personal experiences? To answer these kinds of questions, sociologist Rita James Simon transcribed 10 mock-jury deliberations and then classified all statements made according to their content.[39] She found that jurors spent most of their time talking about trial evidence and their reactions to that evidence. After that they were most likely to talk about procedures for deliberating, experiences from their daily lives, and the judge's instructions. For all categories, Simon found that jurors' statements were, for the most part, relevant, accurate, and helpful for reaching a verdict.[40]

The problem with Simon's analysis is that it represents the deliberation process in static rather than dynamic terms. Do juries' discussions really sound the same in the opening and closing moments? Obviously not, according to the stage-like analysis described earlier. And what do juries do with their statements about evidence, instructions, procedure, and so on? Surely, the decision-making process does not consist of an unrelated string of sentences. More recent studies of jury deliberation are providing answers to these questions. In one study, psychologists Reid Hastie, Steven Penrod, and Nancy Pennington had more than 800 people participate in mock juries and deliberate until a verdict was reached. On the average, deliberations lasted for almost two hours. In order to monitor how discussions change from beginning to end, each deliberation was divided into five units of time. This analysis revealed a very consistent pattern about how juries operate.[41]

As a first step, they spend a good deal of time exchanging views about the case facts and the credibility of the various witnesses. Then they struggle to make sense of the evidence by transforming it into a story of what probably happened. Storytelling, they found, is an important part of deliberation. Confronted with fragments of evidence, juries try to reconstruct the events in question. As with other stories, what they usually come up with is a linked series of episodes that has a beginning, a middle, and an end. To construct these narratives, juries lean heavily on the evidence they find most compelling. Wanting to establish a coherent story, they might then fill in missing details, make inferences about the actors' goals, motives, and intentions, and reject evidence that is incompatible with their views.

As the deliberations progress, jurors become increasingly focused on the judge's instructions concerning the law, the requirements of proof, and the kinds of verdicts they could reach. They might argue about the differences between first and second degree murder, or about how to interpret the concept of an implied contract, or about how much doubt should be considered reasonable. In short, juries appear to shift, generally, from a concern for fact-finding (the "what happened?'' stage) to an application of the law (the "what do we do now?" stage).[42]

The Drive Toward Unanimity

So far, the deliberation process sounds quite rational and orderly. Juries find facts, construct stories, and apply legal principles. But the jury does not speak with one voice. Indeed it is not a "collective mind" but a collection of individuals. Often, individual jurors express a legitimate disagreement with prevailing opinion. Others are ineloquent in their dissent, but just plain stubborn. How do juries ever achieve a consensus and, in the end, a unanimous verdict?

Before trying to answer that question, it is important that we first take the mystique out of popular, romanticized images of jury dynamics. To begin with, the stories of Henry Fonda and Andrew Choa are atypical. The majority almost always wins. Thus, to predict the outcome of deliberations with a fair degree of certainty, one need only know where the 12 individuals stand before they enter the jury room. Kalven and Zeisel found convincing support for this phenomenon in their research. Through posttrial interviews with jurors in 225 criminal juries, they were able to reconstruct how juries split on their very first vote. In all but 10 cases, there was at least a slight majority favoring a particular verdict. Out of these, only six juries reached a final decision that was not predictable from this initial breakdown. From that rather striking result, Kalven and Zeisel concluded that "the deliberation process might well be likened to what the developer does for an exposed film: It brings out the picture, but the outcome is predetermined. . . . The deliberation process, though rich in human interest and color appears not to be at the heart of jury decision making."[43]

Though not a frequent occurrence, minorities sometimes manage to prevail. There are two rather distinct strategies that enable nonconformists to turn others around. One strategy, identified by Serge Moscovici and his colleagues, is to adopt right from the start a staunch, consistent, and unwavering position. Confronted with this self-confident opponent, those in the majority will sit up, take notice, and rethink their own positions.[44] There is a second, very different strategy that can be taken. Based on the fact that dissent often breeds hostility, Edwin Hollander maintains that people who challenge the majority immediately, without having first earned the others' respect, run the risk of becoming alienated and powerless. Based on his own research, Hollander concludes that individual dissenters become influential by first conforming to the majority and establishing their credentials as accepted members of the group. Having accumulated enough "idiosyncrasy credits" (or brownie points), the individual is in a better position to exert influence.[45] In light of our comparisons between *Twelve Angry Men* and the Mitchell-Stans jury, it is interesting that Henry Fonda succeeded by taking Moscovici's consistency approach, whereas Andrew Choa succeeded by accumulating Hollander's idiosyncrasy credits. Indeed, research has shown that, under the right circumstances, both strategies are effective.[46]

There is more to the "majority wins" rule than meets the eye. Legal scholars have long maintained that a unique strength of a trial by jury is that the verdict is reached through an interaction of individuals. That is why jurors are required to deliberate rather than simply vote, as in a political election. Underlying this requirement is the belief that through a comparison and contrast of competing views, extreme opinions cancel each other out, resulting in a relatively balanced final outcome. The logic is simple: bring together a group of conservatives and liberals, and they will make moderate decisions. Psychologists used to share this belief that groups moderate individuals' unchecked impulses. But we now know that the reverse is true. In the first test of the original hypothesis, James Stoner had individuals read a series of stories, each about a fictional character who faces a dilemma: How much risk is he or she willing to take in order to obtain a highly attractive outcome? What if there is only a 10 percent chance of succeeding—is that a risk worth taking? What about 30, 50, or 70 percent? Subjects were asked to read each scenario and then advise the characters on how much risk they should take. Afterwards, participants were assembled into groups to discuss each of the problems until they could agree on a course of action. Consistently, the groups made riskier decisions than the average individuals had made on their own.[47] Almost immediately, however, additional research showed that for certain types of dilemmas, groups gravitate toward caution in their decision making.[48]

Faced with these apparently contradictory findings, social psychologists conducted additional research. As a result, we now know that when a dilemma elicits relatively risky decisions from individuals, groups shift toward even more extreme risk taking; for dilemmas that attract relative caution from individuals, groups shift toward extremely cautious decision making. This pattern of results is referred to as the *group polarization phenomenon*, defined as follows: "The average post-discussion response will tend to be more extreme in the same direction as the average of the pregroup responses."[49] In plain terms, put a group of moderate liberals together and they will make very liberal decisions; put a group of moderate conservatives together and they will make highly conservative decisions. The question is, what does this imply about juries—how are the judgments of individuals transformed by group interaction? Is there a tendency to shift toward conviction or acquittal? Large or small civil awards?

To test whether group polarization applies to jury decisions, social psychologists David Myers and Martin Kaplan had people read traffic felony cases and, for each one, indicate how guilty they thought the defendant was. In some of the cases they read, the evidence against the defendant was strong; in others it was weak. Afterwards, subjects discussed the cases in six-person groups and then indicated again their opinions of the defendant's guilt. The results fit the group polarization pattern perfectly. In cases where the evidence was strong, subjects became *more* likely to find the defendant guilty after talking to others about it. Conversely, when the evidence was weak, subjects became *less* likely to find the defendant guilty after discussion.[50]

There is one interesting wrinkle in this pattern when it comes to juries: in addition to polarizing opinions, the deliberation process consistently produces a bias toward *leniency* for the criminal defendant. All other things being equal, individual jurors are more likely to vote guilty than are juries; they are also more likely to favor conviction before than after deliberation. Thus, when jurors are initially split in their vote, their group typically returns a not-guilty verdict. And when an initial majority favors conviction by only a 7 to 5 margin, the jury often votes for acquittal or remains deadlocked. Apparently, with jurors appreciating the gravity of their task and taking seriously the concept of "beyond a reasonable doubt," it is easier to defend an acquittal than a conviction.[51]

Alternate Routes: Informational and Social Pressure

Group polarization tells us that, although there are occasional exceptions, a jury's verdict is an exaggeration of its members' predeliberation opinions. This happens, of course, through a combination of forces. Some are desirable; others are not. It is difficult, however, to disentangle the effects of informational and normative influence. When jurors speak, what they say often conveys two messages. They provide information that could persuade others but, at the same time, they also reveal where they stand on the verdict. Suppose a juror says "I don't understand how the witness could have seen the defendant at 5:30, if his wife claims he returned home, which is almost half an hour away, at 5:45." A second juror then adds, "And how could the defendant have been on that street so early, anyway, when he was at work that day?" These statements contribute information *and* they indicate a preference, without a formal vote, for a not guilty verdict. If a third juror subsequently changes his vote from guilty to not-guilty, is that because he came to accept the position implied by the arguments, or is it because he came to realize that, like in Asch's situation, he held an unpopular opinion?

We turn to Kaplan's program of research for an answer. To test the relative effects of informational and normative influence processes, Kaplan developed an artificial but interesting method of "deliberation." Subjects read either a strong- or weak-evidence version of a manslaughter case and indicated whether they thought the defendant was guilty or not. In order to control the subsequent discussion, Kaplan had jurors, each seated in their own cubicles, communicate with each other by passing notes. Actually, all the original notes were intercepted and replaced with others written by the experimenter. Now imagine that you are a subject in this experiment and you believe the defendant is guilty. You write down your opinion, you write down the facts you used to form that opinion, and then you receive notes from other jurors who supposedly did the same. After reading all the notes, you find out that your colleagues either agree or disagree with your verdict. You also learn about facts that either support or refute that verdict. Finally, you are asked again for your judgment. What influences whether you adhere to or change your original position? How do you react if the facts you read about support your guilty verdict, but the other jurors favor an acquittal? Conversely, what if you were supported by others' opinions but not by the facts? Consistently, subjects were more responsive to new, substantive information than they were to the strictly normative pressures.[52]

Research on other decision-making groups yields the same comforting conclusion: people change their minds and their votes according to information and rational argument.[53] That does not mean, of course, that interpersonal forces are inoperative, especially in situations that involve truly important decisions. Kaplan and others are unwilling to close the door on the normative-compliance component of jury decision making. We would have to agree.

Informational and normative influences are not endpoints of a single continuum; they are two independent dimensions. The drive toward unanimity is not characterized by one or the other, but by both. With that in mind, we reiterate our working definition of the ideal deliberation as one in which the informational influences are strong and the normative influences are weak. Some degree of social pressure is inevitable and perhaps even desirable. It is a fact of life not just on juries, but in the board room, the classroom, the social club, and the laboratory. The question is, how much pressure is too much? Opinions differ. We certainly part company with an Ohio judge who said, ''When you get twelve people in one room, and they all have to reach one decision, things happen. I've known fist fights to break out in the jury room. Abuse that one juror gives to the other is not a reason to turn over a just verdict.''[54] A just verdict? How can a verdict be just when one or more jurors was coerced into the final vote? Consistent with a social-psychological perspective, a simple rule applies: Normative influence exceeds an acceptable level whenever it leads people to vote against their true beliefs.

Research has shown that juries fulfill at least half of the deliberation ideal: they are responsive to informational influence. But then there is the other half. One cannot help but wonder about the pressures toward uniformity, and about jurors who appear to abandon their true convictions in order to avoid the role of being deviant. Stories can be found to illustrate both the more and less desirable versions of the deliberation process. Thus, following one trial in which the jury acquitted the defendant of rape and murder, several jurors expressed their pride and satisfaction with the way they had reached a verdict. As one participant put it, ''It was not an easy decision to come to. I honestly think the verdict could have gone either way. And even if there was a little shouting, we all tried to listen to what other people are saying. There were shifts of opinion, but we tried not to pressure anyone.''[55]

In contrast, jurors sometimes succumb under the weight of inordinate pressure. Take as an example a 1986 trial of two New York City police officers charged with torturing a prisoner with an electric stun gun. Concluding two days of deliberation, a jury of seven women and five men announced a verdict of guilty. Afterwards, one of the jurors reported in an affidavit that she had agreed to the verdict only because she had been intimidated and abused for holding out.

"When I argued that the defendants had to have engaged in 'knowing and intentional' conduct before they could be found guilty of any of the crimes charged, the foreman screamed at me words to the effect: 'How would you like a policeman to do this to you?' and, thereupon, he squeezed my left thigh. This physical touching put me in fear of further physical abuse, so I voted guilty on the first count that the jury took up for consideration."[56]

As we have argued throughout this book, isolated anecdotes and case studies do not provide an adequate basis for evaluating the jury system. Every story has its counterpart. What, then, is the incidence of undue normative pressure? How frequently do jurors exhibit public compliance without private acceptance? In one study, interviews with former jurors revealed that as many as 10 percent of those sampled admitted that they felt pressured into their verdict, and had lingering doubts even as the vote was announced.[57] Since people are generally reluctant to admit their own weaknesses, this figure might even underestimate the problem.

As we will see in Chapter 9, the courts have the power to manipulate the often delicate balance between informational and normative influences. And the balance *is* delicate. On the one hand, judges urge jurors to vote independently and according to conscience; on the other hand, they urge them toward compromise and agreement. Let us explore the kinds of trial procedures that can promote and frustrate the ideals of deliberation.

NOTES

1. M. Arnold (1974), How Mitchell-Stans jury reached acquittal verdict. *New York Times,* May 5, p. 1.
2. P. Diperna (1984), *Juries on Trial.* New York: Dembner Books, p. 89.
3. As Osborn noted, "In a lawsuit involving a bridge, no bridgebuilder or anyone who knows anything about bridges is allowed to serve"; See *The Mind of the Juror* (1937), p. 18.
4. As ye sow, so shall ye reap (1979). *National Law Journal,* June 29, p. 39.
5. J. Mellowitz (1985), Temper fugit. *The National Law Journal,* January 14, p. 43.
6. See the American Bar Association Project on Minimum Standards for Criminal Justice (1968), *Standards relating to trial by jury,* Section 5.4.
7. E. J. DeVitt & C. B. Blackmar (1977), *Federal Jury Practice and Instructions* (Vol. 1). St. Paul, MN: West Publishing, p. 166.
8. *Allen v. United States* (1896), 164 U.S. 492, pp. 501–502.
9. See the American Bar Association Project, supra note 6.
10. *Allen v. United States,* supra note 8, p. 501.
11. See S. Asch (1952), *Social Psychology.* Englewood Cliffs, NJ: Prentice-Hall.
12. B. Latane (1981), Psychology of social impact. *American Psychologist,* Vol. 36, pp. 343–356; as the theory relates specifically to group judgment situations, see B. Latane & S. Wolf (1981), The social impact of majorities and minorities. *Psychological Review,* Vol. 88, pp. 438–453.
13. M. Deutsch & H. B. Gerard (1955), A study of normative and informational social influence upon individual judgment. *Journal of Abnormal and Social Psychology,* Vol. 51, pp. 629–636.

14. For example, see S. Schachter (1951), Deviation, rejection, and communication. *Journal of Abnormal and Social Psychology*, Vol. 46, pp. 190–207; for a review, see J. M. Levine (1980), Reaction to opinion deviance in small groups. In P. Paulus (Ed.), *Psychology of Group Influence*. Hillsdale, NJ: Erlbaum.

15. Several psychologists have made this distinction over the years; e.g., see H. Kelman (1961), Processes of opinion change. *Public Opinion Quarterly*, Vol. 25, pp. 57–78. Kelman distinguished three types of conformity—compliance and two forms of private acceptance, identification and internalization.

16. Reported in O. Friedrich (1981), We, the jury, find the. . . . *Time*, September 28, pp. 44–56.

17. For example, some of Asch's subjects reported feeling pressured to make the wrong judgment, while others came to reevaluate their own perceptions.

18. Kalven and Zeisel, supra note 1.19, p. 489.

19. Personal communication.

20. F. Stephan & E. Mishler (1952). The distribution of participation in small groups: An exponential approximation. *American Sociological Review*, Vol. 17, pp. 598–608.

21. See Hastie et al. (1983), supra note 2.25.

22. For a review of these approaches, see E. P. Hollander (1985), Leadership and power, a chapter appearing in G. Lindzey & E. Aronson (Eds.), *Handbook of Social Psychology* (Vol. 2). New York: Random House.

23. R. F. Bales (1958), Task roles and social roles in problem solving groups, a chapter appearing in E. E. Maccoby, T. M. Newcomb, & E. L. Hartley (Eds.), *Readings in Social Psychology*. NY: Holt, Rinehart & Winston.

24. See, for example, F. L. Strodtbeck, R. James, & C. Hawkins (1957), Social status in jury deliberations. *American Sociological Review*, Vol. 22, pp. 713–719.

25. See M. B. Jacobson & J. Effertz (1974), Sex roles and leadership perceptions of the leaders and the led. *Organizational Behavior and Human Performance*, Vol. 12, pp. 383–396; also see B. Rosen & T. H. Jerdee (1973), The influence of sex-role stereotypes on evaluations of male and female supervisory behavior. *Journal of Applied Psychology*, Vol. 57, pp. 44–48.

26. N. L. Kerr, D. L. Harmon, & J. K. Graves (1982), Independence of multiple verdicts by jurors and juries. *Journal of Applied Social Psychology*, Vol. 12, pp. 12–29.

27. Ibid.

28. *Sociometry*, Vol. 24, pp. 397–415.

29. Ibid.

30. C. Hawkins (1960), *Interaction and coalition realignments in consensus-seeking groups: A study of experimental jury deliberation*. Unpublished doctoral dissertation, University of Chicago.

31. Hastie et al., supra note 2.25.

32. F. L. Strodtbeck & R. Mann (1956), Sex role differentiation in jury deliberations. *Sociometry*, Vol. 19, pp. 3–11; for a more recent replication of these results, see C. Nemeth, J. Endicott, & J. Wachtler (1976), From the '50s to the '70s: Women in jury deliberations. *Sociometry*, Vol. 39, pp. 293–304.

33. Hastie et al., supra note 2.25.

34. See Broeder, supra note 3.22.

35. Hastie et al., supra note 2.25.

36. See Kassin & Juhnke, supra note 2.34.

37. Kalven and Zeisel, supra note 1.19, p. 486.

38. See, for example, R. F. Bales & F. Strodtbeck (1951), Phases in group problem-solving. *Journal of Abnormal and Social Psychology*, Vol. 46, pp. 485–495.

39. R. James (1959), Status and competence in jury deliberations. *American Journal of Sociology*, Vol. 64, pp. 563–570.

40. J. Kessler (1973), An empirical study of six- and twelve-member jury decision-making processes. *University of Michigan Journal of Law Reform*, Vol. 6, pp. 712–724.

41. R. Hastie, S. D. Penrod, & N. Pennington (1983), *Inside the Jury*. Cambridge, MA: Harvard University Press.

42. For a more extensive discussion of this story model of jury deliberation, see N. Pennington & R. Hastie (1986), Evidence evaluation in complex decision making. *Journal of Personality and Social Psychology*, Vol. 51, pp. 242–258; also see J. A. Holstein (1985), Jurors' interpretations and jury decision making. *Law and Human Behavior*, Vol. 9, pp. 83–100.

43. Supra note 1.19, pp. 489, 496.

44. See S. Moscovici (1985), Social influence and conformity. A chapter appearing in G. Lindzey & E. Aronson (Eds.), *Handbook of Social Psychology* (Vol. 2). NY: Random House.

45. See E. P. Hollander (1985), Leadership and power. In G. Lindzey & E. Aronson (Eds.), *Handbook of Social Psychology* (Vol. 2). NY: Random House.

46. For a review, see A. Maass & R. D. Clark III (1984), Hidden impact of minorities: Fifteen years of minority influence research. *Psychological Bulletin*, Vol. 95, pp. 428–450.

47. J. A. F. Stoner (1961), *A comparison of individual and group decisions involving risk*. Unpublished master's thesis, Massachusetts Institute of Technology.

48. F. Nordhoy (1962), *Group interaction in decision making under risk*. Unpublished master's thesis, Massachusetts Institute of Technology.

49. See S. Moscovici & M. Zavalloni (1969), The group as a polarizer of attitudes. *Journal of Personality and Social Psychology*, Vol. 12, pp. 125–135.

50. D. G. Myers & M. F. Kaplan (1976), Group-induced polarization in simulated juries. *Personality and Social Psychology Bulletin*, Vol. 2, pp. 63–66.

51. For an excellent review of this leniency bias, see: G. Stasser, N. L. Kerr & R. M. Bray (1982), The social psychology of jury deliberations: Structure, process and product. In N. Kerr & R. Bray (Eds.), *The Psychology of the Courtroom*. New York: Academic Press.

52. For a review of this research, see M. F. Kaplan, & C. Schersching (1981), Juror deliberation: An information integration analysis. In B. Sales (Ed.), *The Trial Process*. New York: Plenum.

53. See, for example, E. Burnstein, & A. Vinokur (1977), Persuasive argumentation and social comparison as determinants of attitude polarization. *Journal of Experimental Social Psychology*, Vol. 13, pp. 315–332.

54. Quoted in K. Myers (1984), An erratic juror causes mistrial in murder case. *The National Law Journal*, March 5, p. 10.

55. Quoted in S. Wishman (1986), *Anatomy of a Jury: The System on Trial*. New York: Times Books, p. 250.

56. J. P. Fried (1986), Juror asserts she was pressured to vote guilty in stun-gun case. *New York Times*, June 7, p. 10.

57. See R. James (1959), supra note 39.

9

CONTROLLING THE DELIBERATIONS

Normative influences operate in the jury room as a direct result of internal group dynamics. But there may be added pressures from both inside and outside the courtroom. Although juries deliberate in complete secrecy, their verdicts are a matter of public record, and are watched closely by others. There are two sources of outside normative influence on the jury: (a) *external*, from the news media, interested nonparties, and the community they are called on to represent, and (b) *court-generated*, emanating from the judge. In order to guard the delicate balance between informational and normative pressure, juries should be protected from unacceptable levels of intimidation from both sources.[1] The question is how?

GUARDING THE JURY'S CONSCIENCE

Nobody had to tell the John Hinckley jurors that they were under the public's microscope. The same can be said for those who sit on any case that attracts widespread attention. In certain trials the pressure is built into the jury's decision-making task. Consider the 1984 trial in which Israeli General Ariel Sharon sued *Time* magazine for libel. In that case the jury was sequestered from the moment they were instructed until they concluded their deliberations 10 days later. The reason? According to former Judge Abraham Sofaer, who presided over the trial, "A massive barrage of commentary appeared in the press, consisting of highly opinionated articles and news reports. Some reporters were so eager to talk to the jurors that they called their homes during deliberations, despite my warnings, and on occasion ran after them in the streets even when the jury was in the custody of U.S. marshals."[2]

Some lawyers don't want their juries to be sequestered. Its purpose, of course, is to shield the jury from prejudicial, inflammatory information and from the opinions and passions of a relatively uninformed public. At times it seems a necessary safeguard. But in and of itself does being sequestered bias the jury's decision? Some lawyers think it does. In Claus von Bulow's second trial, in Providence, Rhode Island, the judge sequestered the jury over the objections of chief defense counsel, Thomas Puccio. According to Puccio, a sequestered jury favors the prosecution because jurors end up blaming the defendant for their being isolated from family and friends. Is that true? In the von Bulow case, the judge told the jurors that the decision to sequester them was hers alone, that she—and not the lawyers—was to blame for the inconvenience. Puccio estimates that "nine out of ten defense lawyers say it is not helpful to the defense." As far as we know there is absolutely no empirical evidence on the matter, one way or another.

It could be argued, of course, that, although sequestering a jury does not systematically direct it toward conviction or acquittal, it does compromise the integrity of the decision-making process. It is probably safe to say that sequestered jurors are anxious about their exile. Even though people are regularly excused from sequestered juries for reasons of hardship, those who do serve might be all too eager to return home. Of course, the opposite could be true as well. Judge Charles Alberti tells the story of an experience he had in a criminal trial held in Boston. The case, he thought, was clearcut. But the jury, sequestered in a local hotel, was still deadlocked after several hours of deliberation. One night, while doing a room check, the court officer discovered that there were three jurors, two males and one female, engaged in some kind of sexual activity. They were separated and warned against further contact. Bright and early the following morning, the jury returned its verdict.[3]

Relatively few juries are sequestered during their deliberations; even fewer for the full life of a trial. It is a practice that is stressful to those who serve and expensive for the government. However, sometimes it is necessary.[4] And, as we said, we know of no hard evidence to suggest that it adversely affects either the process or outcome of their decision making.

A more recent development in trial management, also designed to protect jurors from coercive outside forces, is to conceal their identities and even, at times, to furnish them with police protection. Anonymous jurors were first used in the 1977 trial of Leroy "Nickey" Barnes, a Harlem narcotics dealer. Since then, the technique has been employed in other criminal cases, particularly against members of organized crime or terrorist groups. For example: In 1983, five American supporters of Puerto Rican independence were brought to trial in Brooklyn, New York. They were members of FALN, which stands for Fuerzas Armadas de Liberacion Nacional, or Armed Forces of National Liberation. At the time, FALN had already claimed responsibility for about 100 bombings nationwide, including a recent bombing of the courthouse in which the trial was held. According to the FBI, the organization was one of the most active terrorist groups in the country. When the trial opened, under tight security, the panel of prospective jurors was identified only by the numbers 1 through 175.[5]

As with sequestration, anonymity arouses passionate objection. When it was first used, a U.S. appeals court upheld the practice, noting that "all safety measures should be taken for the protection of prospective jurors." Psychologically, it makes sense. As with subjects in Asch's conformity experiments, jurors are better able to resist normative pressure when their judgments are made anonymously. However, civil libertarians and defense lawyers argue that the practice undermines the presumption of innocence by conveying the impression that the defendants are dangerous. One lawyer referred to it as "a red flag" that waves over a case.[6] It is an interesting issue, but one that has not been subjected to empirical research. In the FALN case, the judge informed prospective jurors that their identities would be kept secret for reasons unrelated to the defendants in their trial. Did jurors believe the judge, or did they in fact associate the protective measures with the defendants? If it is possible to keep people from drawing such inferences, then it is reasonable to expect that anonymity would enable jurors to vote according to conscience and without a fear of reprisal.

It is bad enough that juries are sometimes subject to normative influences emanating from outside the courtroom. It is intolerable when that pressure is applied from the judge's bench. The following incident is unusual in that respect. In 1982, in Atlanta, Anthony "Amp" Wiley was convicted of sexually molesting and then killing a woman and torturing her female companion. This brutal crime aroused anger in the community. It took the jury less than two hours to find Wiley guilty of all charges. It then deliberated on whether to impose the death sentence (in Georgia, only a jury can assign the death penalty). After seven hours, the foreman reported a 10 to 2 deadlock. According to news accounts of the trial, the judge then said, "I would remind you that during jury selection you stated you were not opposed to capital punishment." The jury deliberated further and then returned with an 11 to 1 impasse. The judge was so incensed that before dismissing the jury he asked the foreman to identify the holdout in open court. The district attorney told reporters that this named juror had singlehandedly thwarted justice. After the trial this juror had acid thrown into his locker at work and received several death threats over the phone.[7] Upon learning of the jury's vote, did the judge have a right to remind the panel that they were death qualified and, in so doing, nudge them toward a verdict? And did he have the right to express his own opinion of their final decision? Certainly not, if jurors are to be free from public scorn, abuse, and harassment.

AS A MATTER OF POLICY

It used to be the case that judges could force juries in all sorts of ways to resolve their disagreements and reach a verdict. In England, during the nineteenth century, juries that were unable to achieve unanimity "were locked up in a cart, without meat, drink, fire, or candle, and followed the judge from town to town. Only their verdict could secure their release."[8] American juries were subjected to the same kinds of coercion. One jury was loaded onto an oxcart and bounced around until they reached a verdict. Others were denied food and drink. In one case the judge threatened that any juror found to have "stubbornly refused to do his duty" would be sent to jail for contempt of court. Although these kinds of drastic measures became unpopular, some twentieth century judges continued to take direct action against deadlocked juries. Thus, food rations were reduced, jurors were forced to pay for their meals, heat was turned off during the winter, and deliberations were extended through the night, leaving jurors without sleep. Needless to say, these methods produced results: usually, a hasty conference followed by a verdict. We should add that pressures from the bench are not lessons from ancient history. Although judges today could not get away with the same kinds of egregious tactics, they can still exert a measure of influence over deliberations, albeit in more subtle ways. According to Kansas City lawyer Robert Duncan, who has been involved in almost 1000 trials, juries often believe (because their judges fail to inform them otherwise) that they are going to be held in the jury room until they reach a verdict. This problem, he notes, is accentuated when the deliberations take place well beyond normal business hours.[9] It obviously does not take a psychologist to see that, under these circumstances, a juror's vote of conscience might give way to more basic human needs.

Blasting the Jury with Dynamite

Imagine yourself as the judge in the following, not atypical, situation. The jury has just sat through the trial of a revenue agent charged with accepting bribes. The trial was not particularly long and, as you can tell from experience, the issues are not that complex. But the jurors cannot seem to agree on a verdict. After several hours of deliberation, the foreman sends you following message: "Jury hopelessly deadlocked. No change in sight." What should you do at this point—should you do nothing in the hope that time will soften the jurors' positions? Should you take direct action in an effort to encourage a unanimous verdict? Or, should you just accept the jury as hung and declare a mistrial?

This very situation confronted Judge Thomas Murphy in a 1965 trial. In response, he called for a conference with lawyers for both sides and showed them the jury's note. This is what then transpired:

Prosecutor: I would request an Allen charge.
Defense: Oh, no, your Honor.
Judge: What do you mean no? I would give it to my mother.
Defense: That is highly questionable.
Judge: Take your exception, gentlemen, and bring the jury in.

With that, Judge Murphy read to the jury the *Allen* charge, a special instruction that had been approved by the U.S. Supreme Court. The jury thus reconvened and promptly returned a verdict of guilty.[10] What rules are there about deadlocked juries? At what point is a split jury officially declared "hung"? And what is this *Allen* charge that was so favored by the prosecutor and so dreaded by the defense?

The hung jury is an interesting phenomenon. It is considered a valuable means of ensuring the integrity of the deliberation process. But it also represents a failure of the system to produce a final outcome. Although it has been argued that juries should not be permitted to hang,[11] the nation's courts have made it clear that juries have the right to not reach a decision. According to Kalven and Zeisel, hung juries occur in about 5 percent of all criminal jury trials. When they do occur, they tend to be in cases that are close, and where the minority consists of a group of individuals rather than a single holdout. However infrequent and whatever the cause, judges do not like hung juries. They result in mistrials which, in turn, means wasted time, money, and often a new trial. So what can judges do to prevent it? They can read the *Allen* Charge, a special instruction that casts a spell on the deadlocked jury.

The *Allen* Charge gets its name from *Allen v. U.S.*, an 1896 Supreme Court decision in which the instruction was first approved.[12] It works so well that lawyers have given it many names, including the "shotgun instruction," the "third-degree instruction," the "nitroglycerin charge," the "hammer instruction" and, most popularly, the "dynamite charge." Unlike the magic of an incantation, judges can differ somewhat in the language they use to convey the message of the *Allen* instruction. Essentially, it says to jurors the following:

> *That in a large proportion of cases absolute certainty would not be expected; that although the verdict must be the verdict of each individual juror, and not a mere acquiescence in the conclusion of his fellows, yet they should examine the question submitted with candor and with a proper regard and deference to the opinions of each other; that it was their duty to decide the case if they could conscientiously do so; that they should listen, with a disposition to be convinced, to each other's arguments; that, if much the larger number were for conviction, a dissenting juror should consider whether his doubt was a reasonable one which made no impression upon the minds of so many men, equally honest, equally intelligent with himself. If, upon the other hand, the majority was for acquittal, the minority ought to ask themselves whether they might not reasonably doubt the correctness of a judgment which was not concurred in by the majority.[13]*

Other, similar instructions are available. Some appeal not only to the spirit of openmindedness and concession but also to the importance of a verdict to the parties, the public, and the court.

Think about the jury that, after hours or even days of deliberation, is unable to reach a verdict. Having already discussed the case at great lengths, the jurors are called into the courtroom and read this supplemental instruction. Their state of information and their arguments over the evidence remain unchanged. What then transpires back in the jury room, in light of this latest directive? How are the majority and minority factions within the group affected? And what happens to that delicate balance between informational and normative influences?

These are important empirical questions, but sadly they are all without answers. There are no studies comparing deadlocked juries blasted with the dynamite charge to those left to their own devices. Nor are there studies of how juries deliberate before versus after receiving this kind of instruction. To begin with, we wonder if the dynamite charge is really as effective as its reputation suggests. Even in the absence of hard data, 90 years' worth of anecdotes seems to compel the tentative conclusion that it is. The real question is not *whether* this instruction is effective, but *why* is it, for the right or wrong reasons?

One view, shared by many judges and scholars, is that the dynamite charge unfairly points a finger at the minority of jurors. As one court described it, "The dissenters, struggling to maintain their position in a protracted debate in the jury room, are led into the courtroom and, before their peers, specifically requested by the judge to reconsider their position. . . . The charge places the sanction of the court behind the views of the majority, whatever they may be, and tempts the minority juror to relinquish his position simply because he has been the subject of a particular instruction."[14] And yet others maintain that it is okay to pressure the holdouts. One judge thus argued that "They may properly be warned against stubbornness and self-assertion."[15] These judges may be writing about the same instruction, but are they writing about the same minority faction?

What seems to drive those who strongly favor or oppose the dynamite charge is their image of the holdouts in deadlocked juries. Proponents of the instruction base their opinion on the belief that juries hang because of an obstinate, uncooperative, and closed-minded individual, the chronic nonconformist. Opponents, on the other hand, base their views on the belief that juries hang as a genuine response to close and difficult cases in which the evidence allows for well-reasoned disagreement. Which side is right? The problem is, both are right. And for that reason, the dynamite charge offers the solution to one problem, and the exacerbation of another.

Obviously, not all juries, deadlocked or otherwise, are created equal. According to Kalven and Zeisel's research, most hung juries occur in close cases, a fact that lends support to the more rational image of the phenomenon. Thus, jurors disagree after deliberating precisely when their open exchange of information reveals an ambiguous case. But there are also exceptional trials in which the hung jury fits the first, nonrational profile. One researcher thus cited an incident in which a single juror "'sang, looked out the window, made jokes, and refused to talk about the case or to go along with the majority view.'"[16] What all this suggests is that there are properly hung juries marked by legitimate disagreement over information, and there are improperly hung juries plagued by the failures of normative influence. With that in mind, the law's objective should be to blast improperly hung juries into a verdict, while leaving the others untouched.[17]

Does the dynamite charge, an instruction that turns the volume up on normative pressure, achieve these dual objectives? Or, does it indiscriminately blast all deadlocked juries, proper and improper alike? In the words of law professor Paul Marcus, should it be "permanently defused"?[18] More importantly, is there an alternative? In the absence of research on these questions, we are reluctant to take a strong position. But what we do know—that most juries hang because of close cases, and that previously deadlocked juries often return a verdict shortly after being blasted—suggests that the dynamite charge may be too explosive. The good news is, there *is* an alternative. Several years ago, the American Bar Association proposed an instruction to replace the dynamite charge. It is intended to be included as part of a judge's final instruction, before the start of deliberations, though it could then be reread later if needed. Imagine yourself in the minority faction of a divided jury. Does this instruction sound less coercive, less likely to make you feel targeted if reread by the judge? We think so:

> *It is your duty, as jurors, to consult with one another and to deliberate with a view to reaching an agreement, if you can do so without violence to individual judgment. Each of you must decide the case for yourself, but do so only after an impartial consideration of the evidence with your fellow jurors. In the course of your deliberations, do not hesitate to reexamine your own views and change your opinion if convinced it is erroneous. But do not surrender your honest conviction as to the weight or effect of evidence solely because of the opinion of your fellow jurors, or for the mere purpose of returning a verdict.[19]*

The ABA instruction provides an interesting alternative to the *Allen* charge because it emphasizes jurors' duty to consult with one another, and to be accountable to defend their positions. To the extent that nonparticipating jurors follow this directive, it succeeds in encouraging further exchange of views and, as such, increasing informational rather than normative influence. To date, many courts use the ABA instruction, but many do not—perhaps out of the belief that the dynamite charge blasts the jury more effectively. They may be right, and they have the sanction of a 90-year-old Supreme Court ruling. But at what cost to the properly divided jury?

Jury Shrinkage: How Small Is Too Small?

In Boulder, Colorado, lawyer Melvin Tatsumi represented a defendant who was facing trial for criminal mischief. Fearing "the mob mentality of twelve people," he requested a one-person jury. The judge went along with the idea, but the district attorney rejected it: "a jury of one is a contradiction of terms," he argued. A state appeals court agreed.[20] What number of people does it take to form a jury? Although the Constitution says nothing about the proper size of a jury, some have imbued the number 12 with an almost mystical quality. There were 12 tribes of Israel, Christ had 12 apostles, our calendar is divided into 12 months, our school system has 12 grades, and there are 12 units to a dozen.

Maybe we are wedded to that tradition only because the jury has worked as such since the *twelfth* century.[21] And maybe the number 12, in the U.S. Supreme Court's words, "is a historical accident, unnecessary to effect the purposes of the jury system and wholly without significance 'except to mystics.' "[22]

For years, state courts had decided jury-related issues for themselves. But then in 1968 the Supreme Court ruled that all states had to abide by the standards set by the constitution for federal criminal cases.[23] Since the federal courts had been required to use 12-person juries, those states that were permitting smaller juries became subject to challenge. That happened almost immediately in *Williams v. Florida* (1970).[24] In that case, the defendant Williams was convicted of armed robbery by a Florida jury of 6 persons, after having requested a full 12-person jury. He appealed the verdict to the U.S. Supreme Court and lost. In this landmark ruling, Justice Byron White, writing for the majority, took an interesting position. After concluding that there was no legal or historical reason for preferring a larger jury, he framed the issue in strictly practical terms: Does it make a difference? That is, do 6- and 12-person juries behave the same way?

In more specific terms, the Court questioned whether smaller juries reach different verdicts, whether they are less likely to provide a representative cross section of the community, and whether they deliberate with less vigor than traditional 12-person juries. For answers to these empirical questions, the Court turned to a review of available research. In the end (or, perhaps, right from the beginning), it concluded that the jury's performance does not depend on its size:

> *To be sure, the number should probably be large enough to promote group deliberation, free from outside attempts at intimidation, and to provide a fair possibility for obtaining a representative cross-section of the community. But we find little reason to think that these goals are in any meaningful sense less likely to be achieved when the jury numbers six, than when it numbers twelve— particularly if the requirement of unanimity is retained. And, certainly the reliability of the jury as a factfinder hardly seems likely to be a function of its size.[25]*

Three years later, in the case of *Colgrove v. Battin* (1973), the Supreme Court stood by its conclusion and extended the use of 6-member juries to federal civil trials.[26]

The *Williams* and *Colgrove* opinions were greeted with outrage by social scientists who felt that the Court had misrepresented their research findings. The reason: to justify a reduction in jury size motivated by a concern for cutting trial costs. Almost immediately, articles appeared with titles such as ". . . And then there were none: The diminution of the federal jury"[27] and "Ignorance of science is no excuse."[28] Part of the problem is that the Court buttressed its opinion not with experiments, as it had claimed, but with haphazard comparisons, the personal observations of court officials, and naturalistic studies so seriously flawed that psychologist Michael Saks said, "the quality of social science scholarship displayed in [the Court's] decisions would not win a passing grade in a high school psychology class."[29] To make matters worse, when the Court cited the right research, it drew the wrong conclusions from it. For example: One of the questions raised by a reduction in jury size is, does it affect the minority's ability to resist normative pressures toward public compliance? On that question, the Court concluded that size should not make a difference. Citing Solomon Asch's conformity experiments, as described earlier, it reasoned that "jurors in the minority on the first ballot are likely to be influenced by the proportional size of the majority aligned against them."[30] Is that true? Did Asch find that an individual's ability to resist normative influence depends on the *proportional* size of the majority? The minority in a 4 to 2 split might be as well insulated as its counterpart in an 8 to 4 jury, but what about the dissenter in a 5 to 1 jury, compared to his or her counterpart in a 10 to 12 jury? According to the Court's proportionality principle, both minorities in this 83-17 percent division are equally capable of withstanding normative pressures. But Asch's studies showed exactly the opposite: it is the *absolute,* not proportional, size that matters. The presence of a single ally is one of the most powerful determinants of an individual's ability to maintain his or her independence.[31]

Despite the Supreme Court's ill-guided use of psychology, it has, at least for now, settled the jury size issue. How much smaller can a jury get and still qualify as a jury? The Court realized in *Williams* that it had placed itself on a "slippery slope," that it would inevitably be faced with successively smaller juries until it is forced to declare a halt to the shrinkage. Sure enough, three states—Georgia, Louisiana, and Virginia—passed laws permitting 5-person juries in some trials. Then came the 1978 case of *Ballew v. Georgia.* Claude Ballew, the manager of an adult theater in Atlanta, was convicted by a 5-person jury for showing an allegedly obscene film called *Behind the Green Door.* On appeal, the U.S. Supreme Court reversed the verdict and declared six as the required minimum size for a criminal jury.[32] The Court's ruling in this case added to its already strained relations with the social science community. On the positive side, Justice Harry Blackmun's lead opinion included 10 pages of scholarly, well documented review of the relevant psychological literature. Citing 19 jury-size studies generated by the controversy, Justice Blackmun justified the 6-as-minimum rule. It is ironic that studies on the differences between 6- and 12-person juries were used to justify a ruling about 5- versus 6-person juries. Based on the Court's review of this research, it logically should have reversed *Williams* and reinstated the full 12-person tribunal. Not being called upon to confront the original *Williams* challenge, of course, it did not. Thus, as one commentator put it, the Court got off the slippery slope but was unwilling to climb back up.[33]

On the negative side, three justices—Powell, Burger, and Rehnquist—while they agreed with the ruling, filed a separate opinion in which they were critical of Justice Blackmun's "heavy reliance on numerology derived from statistical studies."[34] It is true that Justice Blackmun, with a background in mathe-

matics and tax law, was uniquely familiar with scientific reasoning and sta-
tistics. But, numerology? Numerology is defined as "The study of the occult
meanings of numbers and their supposed influence on human life!"[35] This statement expresses a disdain of scientific research based on ignorance. Describing
controlled studies of human behavior as numerology is like referring to case law
as a book of fairy tales. Indeed Justice Blackmun took a unique opportunity to
address his colleagues' criticism. Inserted within a footnote of his opinion, he
wrote, "Without an examination about how juries and small groups actually
work, we would not be able to understand the basis for the conclusion of Mr.
Justice Powell that 'a line has to be drawn somewhere.' "[36] He then confronted
the hypocrisy of Justices Burger and Rehnquist who, in *Williams* and *Colgrove*,
cited empirical research to justify the 6-person jury.

Having digressed somewhat from the main thrust of this section, let us look
at current practices. Today, as far as we know, at least 7 states permit juries of
less than 12 in felony trials, though never in capital cases. At least 24 states use
6-person juries for misdemeanors, and 22 states permit them in civil trials. With
practices that varied we return to our original question: does it make a difference? Suppose you were in court as the plaintiff in a lawsuit. Or, suppose you
were being tried for criminal assault in what you believed to be a self-defense
situation. Would you have any reason to prefer a jury of 12 rather than 6?

To begin with, the rates of conviction and acquittal appear to be unaffected
by group size. However, a problem might arise in cases that are plagued by a
potential for bias and the need for representativeness. As Michael Saks pointed
out, it is a statistical fact of life that when people are drawn at random from
heterogeneous populations, the size of the sample determines how well minority
groups are represented. Saks calculated, for example, that in a community that
has a 10 percent minority population, 72 percent of 12-person juries, but only 47
percent of 6-person juries, are likely to include at least one member of that
minority.[37] These figures are not trivial. It could be the difference between
having a Henry Fonda or an Andrew Choa on your jury or not. Combined with
what we know about individual juror bias, we assume that verdicts could, at
least on occasion, turn on the size of a jury.[38]

One must also wonder about dynamics within the jury room and whether the
ideals of deliberation are meaningfully affected by the size of the group. As the
Supreme Court made clear in *Williams*, it is not just the outcome of a jury trial
that is important, but the process as well. The right result should be achieved for
the right reasons. And the right reasons include juror independence, equality,
vigorous discussion of the evidence, and persuasion through informational
rather than normative social influence.

Looking at all of the relevant research on jury size and the deliberation
process, we must conclude with uncertainty about the net effect of shifting from
12- to 6-person juries on the deliberation process. As there are the disadvantages
described earlier, there are also some benefits of a smaller tribunal. For example, we noted that pecking orders develop in virtually all group decision-

making contexts, with some individuals dominating discussion and others falling into a relatively passive role. To the extent that this phenomenon reflects a hierarchy of influence during deliberations, it is almost like having a jury within the jury. As it turns out, this hierarchy, as measured by how often the individual members speak, becomes less pronounced as groups decrease in size. In 12-person mock juries, between 20 and 25 percent of individuals all but fade into the woodwork. In 6-person juries, only about 5 percent fail to participate.[39] The egalitarian ideal is thus achieved better in the smaller sized jury. In practical terms this means that 6- and 12-member juries are not *that* different from each other when we compare their respective number of *active* participants (that is, the "jury within the jury"). There is yet another fact about small groups that should be taken into consideration. Several studies have shown that as groups increase in size, individuals tend to form cliques that often talk or whisper amongst themselves rather than to the group as a whole. To the extent that this is true of juries, it raises the question of whether 12 jurors actually speak with that many independent voices.[40]

Turning to the quality of deliberations, and the balance between informational and normative influences, again the net effect of size is unclear. Twelve-person juries take longer to reach a verdict and recall more of the evidence than 6-person juries.[41] Does that mean that larger groups base their decisions on a more thorough consideration of the evidence? Not necessarily. Research on nonjury discussion groups ranging in size from two to 20 has shown that although the total number of contributions increases with group size, the amount of new information introduced appears to peak and then level off, coincidentally, at 6-person groups.[42] Consistent with the law of diminishing returns, the more participants the better—but only up to a point. And that point may be closer to 6 than to 12.

Less Than Unanimous Verdicts

About 10 years ago, lawyer Robert Duncan defended a man who was charged with murder and claimed he had acted in self defense. Although the evidence in his favor was strong, the jury was out for several hours, and at one point notified the judge that they were hopelessly deadlocked 11 to 1. After being sent back for further deliberations, they eventually returned a verdict of not guilty. Then, in Duncan's own words, "I left the courtroom and rode down on the elevator with the foreman of the jury. During that ride the foreman advised me that the holdout was a young 'hippie' girl and that they had finally arrived at a verdict through the process of not counting her vote. To my knowledge, this is the only 11 to 1 unanimous acquittal ever returned in the Circuit Court of Jackson County, Missouri."[43] This nonunanimous unanimous verdict is an anomaly, of course. Or is it? We would argue that whenever a juror complies under pressure with a jury's vote, but does not privately accept its verdict, the unanimity obtained is more apparent than real.

Today even the appearance of unanimity is often not necessary. In a pair of unprecedented decisions, both in 1972, the U.S. Supreme Court ruled that states may allow their juries to return verdicts without having to secure agreement from all of their members. In *Apodaca v. Oregon*, Robert Apodaca appealed his conviction on charges of assault with a deadly weapon by a jury vote of 11 to 1. As part of that same appeal, defendant Henry Morgan Cooper sought to reverse a burglary conviction by a jury vote of 10 to 2.[44] In the meantime, in *Johnson v. Louisiana*, the defendant appealed his conviction on robbery charges by a 9 to 3 majority verdict.[45] In both cases, decided on the same day, the Court upheld the nonunanimous verdicts. As it did in *Williams*, it asserted that there was neither a legal nor a historical basis for the unanimity tradition. It then concluded that, as a practical matter, juries function the same way regardless of whether or not they are held to a unanimous decision rule.

In evaluating whether nonunanimous juries fulfill the ideals of group deliberation, the Court argued that since most jury decisions follow from the majority of their individual members' initial votes, then verdicts should be unaffected by the change. It then speculated freely about social influence processes within the jury room, interactions between majority and minority factions, and the like. Just as we are not constitutional lawyers, it is clear that the justices of the high court are not social psychologists. Justice Byron White, author of the *Williams* decision, offered the following "theory" in *Johnson*:

> We have no grounds for believing that majority jurors, aware of their responsibility and power over the liberty of the defendant, would simply refuse to listen to arguments presented to them in favor of acquittal, terminate discussion, and render a verdict. On the contrary it is far more likely that a juror presenting reasoned argument in favor of acquittal could either have his arguments answered or would carry enough other jurors with him to prevent conviction. A majority will cease discussion and outvote a minority only after reasoned discussion has ceased to have persuasive effect or serve any other purpose—when a minority, that is, continues to insist upon acquittal without having persuasive reasons in support of its position.[46]

In dissent, Justice William Douglas proposed an alternative theory of jury decision making:

> Nonunanimous juries need not debate and deliberate as fully as most unanimous juries. As soon as the requisite majority is attained, further consideration is not required either by Oregon or by Louisiana even though the dissident jurors might, if given the chance, be able to convince the majority. . . . It is said that there is no evidence that majority jurors will refuse to listen to dissenters whose votes are unneeded for conviction. Yet human experience teaches us that polite and academic conversation is no substitute for the earnest and robust argument necessary to reach unanimity.[47]

Which of these portrayals of the jury is the more accurate? In contrast to how the jury shrinkage cases were handled, neither of these opinions cites relevant psychological research. Instead, they are based on intuition or, in Justice White's words, "longstanding perceptions about jury behavior."[48]

Imagine yourself on a jury that is told you need only achieve a 9 to 3 majority in order return a verdict. You open the deliberations with a vote and, lo and behold, you find that you already have the needed quorum. What next? Prepared to announce a decision, how does your jury proceed? According to Justice White, all jurors, including those in the minority faction, speak with an equal voice. So you probably deliberate with as much vigor and passion as you would if you needed to persuade the three dissenters. And you are just as open-minded to the possibility of being converted by their persuasive arguments. In short, you cannot tell the difference between this jury and any other. Consider as an alternative Justice Douglas's scenario. After the vote is taken, the jurors—all having seen *Twelve Angry Men*—begin to discuss the case. Those who are in the majority, of course, are secure in the knowledge that they are continuing on their own terms, and can terminate the deliberations at any time. In this jury room, all participants are not equal. The dissenters can join with the majority or not—either way, their votes are unimportant. So you talk about the case for a while, but without the tension created by the need for unanimity, your discussion seems relatively tame and superficial. Which of these scenarios sounds right? Are the ideals of deliberation intact despite a nonunanimous decision rule? Henry Morgan Cooper, one of the *Apodaca* appellants, probably does not think so. His jury deliberated for only 41 minutes before returning a 10 to 2 guilty verdict.

As with jury size, current practices are varied. The federal courts still require unanimous verdicts in all criminal and civil trials. But 6 states permit lesser verdicts in some criminal cases, and 31 states allow them for civil cases. Is the Supreme Court on another slippery slope? How much of a majority is sufficient for a verdict, anyway? Is 8 to 4 enough? What about 7 to 5? Thus far, the Court has articulated only one limitation. As it ruled in *Ballew* that juries must have at least 6 people, it ruled, in *Burch v. Louisiana*, in 1979, that a 5 to 1 verdict in criminal cases was impermissible.[49] The courts are thus free to shrink a jury in its size to 6 or in its decision rule, but not in both. It remains to be seen whether intermediate outcomes, like 7 to 2, are acceptable.

Thanks to Justices White and Douglas, the behavioral parameters of this controversy are clearly defined. Simply put, are unanimous and majority-rule juries equivalent in the extent to which they fulfill the ideals of deliberation? Several studies have addressed the question, and their results all converge on the same answer: no. In fact, the differences are substantial.[50]

Consider what happens, for example, when a jury begins its deliberation with the majority it needs to return a verdict. Charlan Nemeth had several hundred students at the University of Virginia read the testimony in a murder trial and then indicate whether they believed the defendant to be guilty or not guilty. These students then participated in mock juries three weeks later. Knowing what their verdicts would be, Nemeth constructed groups that would split 4 to 2 in their initial vote, favoring either conviction or acquittal. The groups were allotted two hours to reach a decision. Half were instructed to return a unanimous verdict, the other half were told that they needed a two thirds majority. Compared to those driven by the need for unanimity, majority-rule juries took less time to settle on a decision. Many of these groups, in fact, concluded their deliberations with the same 4 to 2 division they had begun with. When subjects were given an opportunity to evaluate the quality of their deliberations, those who had participated in majority juries were less satisfied overall, less certain of their verdicts, and less influenced by others' arguments.

In an even more extensive study, Reid Hastie and his colleagues recruited more than 800 people from jury pools in Massachusetts.[51] After a brief voir dire, these subjects were randomly assigned to participate in 69 mock juries, all of whom watched a videotape of a reenacted murder trial. An approximately equal number of juries were instructed to reach a verdict by either 12 to 0, 10 to 2, or 8 to 4 margin. Based on objective analyses of the deliberations as well as jurors' own subjective reports, the results were striking. Compared to unanimous juries, those that deliberated under a more relaxed rule spent less time discussing the case and more time voting. After reaching their required quorum these groups usually rejected the holdouts, terminated discussion, and returned a verdict within just a few minutes. Needless to say, people who participated in majority juries viewed their peers as relatively closed-minded, felt less informed about the case, and were less confident about the final verdict. Finally, Hastie and his colleagues observed that many of the majority juries were quite combative during their deliberations. Apparently, "larger factions in majority rule juries adopt a more forceful, bullying, persuasive style because their members realize that it is not necessary to respond to all opposition arguments when their goal is to achieve a faction size of only eight or ten members."[52]

It could be argued that since jury verdicts so often follow from the majority preference, litigants are unaffected by the change. There are two problems with that rationalization. First, even though most verdicts do follow the initial majority, they are not *all* predictable as such. Minority factions succeed in their efforts to persuade others about 10 percent of the time. In absolute terms, that amounts to a significant number of cases. It would be a mistake to dismiss these reversals as unimportant. Second, the Supreme Court has time and time again affirmed its commitment to the *process*, not just the outcome, of deliberation. That commitment is difficult, if not impossible, to resolve with research showing that the nonunanimous decision rule seriously compromises the ideals of deliberation. Henry Fonda, step aside. The jury has reached its verdict.

The Logistics of Voting

As we all know, polling the jury during its deliberations is a way to keep track of its progress en route to a verdict. It provides the group with a series of critical events or checkpoints that mark changes in consensus. Through voting, jurors monitor how effective their arguments are and acquire a sense of how they are aligned within the group as a whole. But polling the jury is more than just a way to *reflect* changes that have already taken place. It can also *cause* changes and become a "turning point" that might not otherwise have taken place.

This point is dramatically illustrated by the fact that the drive toward unanimity is like a snowball rolling down a hill. Once an individual defects from one position to another, he or she never looks back.[53] More importantly, others follow. In a study of 224 mock jury deliberations resulting in a unanimous verdict, Norbert Kerr discovered a startling fact: the first vote shift, whether it was toward conviction or acquittal, correctly predicted the final outcome 96 percent of the time. In other words, as soon as one juror publicly changes his or her mind, the final outcome can be predicted with a near certainty. Call it a bandwagon effect, or call it momentum. Either way, the first faction within the group to lose a supporter ultimately loses the verdict.[54]

Led by their forepersons, juries vary according to when and how often they vote. When they do, they use four different methods: (a) the *verbal go-around*, a commonly used Asch-like method in which jurors take turns announcing their verdict preferences; (b) the *verbal dissent*, where a verdict is asserted and only those jurors who disagree with it declare their dissension; (c) the *show of hands*, a similarly public procedure; and (d) the *written secret ballot*, the one method that is designed specifically to enable members to vote with anonymity. The most important distinction is between the three public methods and the secret ballot; jurors feel greater pressure to vote with the majority when they vote openly than in secret. Apparently, forepersons are aware of that fact and use it, when necessary, to secure a verdict. Research has shown that juries take secret ballots during the early phases of deliberation, but then shift to using more public methods when they have trouble reaching agreement. As you might expect, this shift is favored primarily by those who have voted with the majority. The same is true of how frequently juries vote. Knowing that it is a strategic way to exert normative pressure, those who are in the majority like to do it often.[55]

Polling the jury appears to have a particularly interesting effect on the tempo and style of deliberations. As we noted earlier, problem solving groups tend to begin their task in an exploratory, orientation phase. Then, usually following a formal vote, they enter a period of open conflict in which all members take sides in a more focused debate. With juries, because the initial vote marks the transition from the first phase of deliberation to the second, its timing can affect the dynamics of deliberation.[56] For example, while many juries talk in general terms before voting, others open with a poll before ever discussing the case. When that happens, they bypass the orientation phase and end up deliberating for a shorter period of time overall before returning a verdict. Are the ideals of deliberation achieved more or less as a result of the timing of the first vote? Is there a reason for the courts to prefer a particular procedure?

Tentatively, the answer is, yes. When juries open with a public ballot, their deliberations take on what has been called a "verdict-driven style," one that is starkly adversarial. With jurors committed right from the start to a predelibera- tion position, the battle lines are immediately drawn. As a result, jurors behave more like advocates than impartial fact-finders, citing only evidence that favors their verdict. In contrast, when juries spend time together before taking a formal vote, their discussions take on an "evidence-driven style," one that is more inquisitorial in its appearance. In these kinds of groups, jurors do not associate themselves early on with a particular verdict. Instead they engage one another more cooperatively, citing evidence without the concern for what it implies about a particular verdict.[57]

Generally speaking, when people publicly commit themselves to a position, it becomes difficult for them to switch sides without appearing weak or incon- sistent. They become more closed-minded and more resistant to changing their minds when faced with new information. That is what seems to happen when jurors take sides in a formal vote. Hastie and his colleagues divided mock juries into three groups according to how long it took them to take the first vote. They found that juries that voted within the first 10 minutes returned verdicts quicker than those who waited for at least 40 to vote. Moreover, people who participated in early-voting juries rated the others in their groups as less open-minded, less serious, and less persuasive. The implications of these results are clear. Indi- vidual jurors are supposed to decide the case for themselves only after an impar- tial consideration of the evidence with their fellow jurors. That is the point of deliberating. In order to further that objective, juries should be advised against voting prematurely. Although judges could offer that advice in their final in- structions, they do not.

NOTES

    1. Racially sensitive trials like those described in Chapter 2 are historically prominent ex- amples. In these cases, juries often functioned within a partisan or highly divided community that is vocal in its opinions.
    2. A. D. Sofaer (1985), Jury management in Sharon v. Time, Inc. *Chambers to Chambers: The Federal Judicial Center*, September 15, pp. 1–3.
    3. Personal communication, January 14, 1987.
    4. See J. Friendly (1985), Judge orders jurors sequestered in the retrial of von Bulow. *New York Times*, April 17.
    5. J. Capeci (1983), The no-name jurors. *The National Law Journal*, Feb. 21.
    6. Quoted in R. Smothers (1985), A mixed verdict on anonymous jurors. *New York Times*, October 13.
    7. D. Ranii (1982), Judge is criticized for identifying holdout juror. *The National Law Journal*, Jan. 4, pp. 2, 14.
    8. W. Blackstone, quoted in: *Walker v. U.S.* (1956), 342 F.2d 22, p. 28.
    9. Personal communication (1986).
    10. *U.S. v. Kenner* (1965), 354 F.2d 780.
    11. Icenogle (1961), The menace of the hung jury, *American Bar Association Journal*, Vol. 47, p. 280.

12. 164 U.S. 492.

13. Ibid. at p. 501.

14. *People v. Gainer* (1977), 19 Cal.3d 835, p. 50.

15. *People v. Randall* (1961), 9 N.Y.2d 413, p. 425.

16. See Hawkins, supra note 8.30, pp. 136–137.

17. Notes and Comments (1968), On instructing deadlocked juries. *The Yale Law Journal*, Vol. 78, pp. 100–142.

18. Supra note 17, p. 613.

19. American Bar Association Project on Minimum Standards for Criminal Justice (1968), *Standards relating to trial by jury*, Standard 5.4.

20. It would be easy to poll this jury (1985), *The National Law Journal*.

21. J. G. Forester, Jr. (1984), Return the 12-man jury. *Litigation*, Vol. 10, pp. 3–4, 64.

22. *Williams v. Florida* (1970), 399 U.S. 78.

23. *Duncan v. Louisiana* (1968), 391 U.S. 145.

24. Supra note 22.

25. Ibid., pp. 100–101.

26. 413 U.S. 149.

27. H. Zeisel (1971), *The University of Chicago Law Review*, Vol. 38, pp. 710–724.

28. M. J. Saks (1974), Vol. 10, 18ff.

29. Ibid., p. 18.

30. *Williams v. Florida*, supra note 22, p. 101.

31. In fact, Asch reported that minority resistance is greater in an 8-2 split (80-20 percent) than in a proportionally more favorable 3-1 split (75-25 percent); see Asch, supra note 8.11, pp. 398–399.

32. 435 U.S. 223.

33. E. D. Tanke, & T. J. Tanke (1979), Getting off a slippery slope: Social science in the judicial process. *American Psychologist*, Vol. 34, pp. 1130–1138.

34. *Ballew v. Georgia*, 435 U.S. 223, p. 246.

35. W. Morris, Editor (1976), *The American Heritage Dictionary of the English Language.* Boston: Houghton Mifflin, p. 901.

36. Ibid., p. 232.

37. M. J. Saks (1977), *Jury Verdicts*. Lexington, MA: D.C. Heath.

38. Actually, jury size is consistently related to the chances of obtaining a hung jury. Zeisel reported a hung jury rate of 2.4 percent in a sample of 290 six-person criminal juries, significantly fewer than the 5.6 rate observed for 12-person juries; supra note 27. This result makes sense, as shown in a mock jury study conducted by social psychologists Norbert Kerr and Robert MacCoun. These investigators found that the smaller a group is, the more likely it is to begin its deliberations at or near unanimity; see N. L. Kerr & R. J. MacCoun (1985), The effects of jury size and polling method on the process and product of jury deliberation. *Journal of Personality and Social Psychology*, Vol. 48, pp. 349–363.

39. See A. P. Hare (1976), *Handbook of Small Group Research* (2nd ed.). New York: Free Press; Hastie et al. (1983), supra note 2.25; and Saks (1977), supra note 37.

40. For a review, see E. J. Thomas & C. F. Fink (1963), Effects of group size. *Psychological Bulletin*, Vol. 60, pp. 371–384.

41. Saks, supra note 37.

42. See R. F. Bales, F. L. Strodtbeck, T. M. Mills, & M. E. Rosenborough (1951). Channels of communication in small groups. *American Sociological Review*, Vol. 16, pp. 461–468.

43. Personal communication, 1986.

44. 406 U.S. 404.

45. 406 U.S. 356.

46. Ibid., p. 358.

47. Ibid., p. 360.

48. Ibid., p. 362.

49. 441 U.S. 130.

50. The following is a sample of the more notable research efforts: Hastie et al., supra note 2.25, C. Nemeth (1977), Interactions between jurors as a function of majority vs. unanimity decision rules. *Journal of Applied Social Psychology*, Vol. 7, pp. 38–56; M. Saks, supra note 37.

51. Supra note 2.25.

52. Ibid., p. 112.

53. C. Hawkins (1962), Interaction rates of jurors aligned in factions. *American Sociological Review*, Vol. 27, pp. 689–691.

54. Reported in G. Stasser, N. L. Kerr, & R. M. Bray (1982), The social psychology of jury deliberations: Structure, process, and product. Appearing in N. Kerr & R. Bray (Eds.), *The Psychology of the Courtroom*. New York: Academic Press.

55. See Hawkins, supra note 53.

56. Hawkins, supra note 53; Saks, supra note 37; Hastie et al., supra note 2.25.

57. This distinction was articulated by Hastie et al., supra note 2.25; a similar distinction was made between juries that deliberate ''in factions'' and those that deliberate ''in unity,'' see Hawkins, supra note 53.

10

CLOSING ARGUMENTS

The American trial is a truly unique institution. In the words of Kalven and Zeisel, "it recruits a group of twelve laymen, chosen at random from the widest population; it convenes them for the purpose of a particular trial; it entrusts them with great official powers of decision; it permits them to carry out deliberations in secret and report their final judgment without giving reasons for it; and, after their momentary service to the state has been completed, it orders them to disband and return to private life."[1]

With the use of ordinary citizens empowered to determine the fate of individuals, corporations, and the government, social, political, and economic policy, it is easy to understand why the jury system is sanctified by so many. And yet it is a system that is, always has been, and always will be under siege. Criticisms of the Hinckley and Pennzoil juries, noted in Chapter 1, illustrate the point. Reactions such as these are to be expected. Although the names, dates, and places may change, the basic story line remains the same: Every verdict declares winners and losers. In a pluralistic society such as ours, that gives many jury decisions a "damned if you do, damned if you don't" quality.

The Big Dan's barroom rape trial held in New Bedford, Massachusetts, is a case in point. It was an appalling incident. In 1984, six Portuguese immigrants were charged with the gang rape of a woman on a barroom pool table for more than an hour while male patrons drank, gawked, and cheered without ever coming to the victim's rescue. The evidence was strong, and in the end some of the defendants were convicted. After the jury announced its verdicts, they were booed and jeered by a crowd of over 100 spectators, members of the local Portuguese community, as they left the courthouse. Two years earlier, an Atlanta jury had convicted Wayne Williams who was charged with the deaths and disappearances of 29 young blacks. Many Atlantans breathed a sigh of relief at the news. But others, including some of the victim's families, publicly scorned the jury's findings. As the mother of one victim said to a reporter, "With this conviction, Wayne Williams, at 23, became the thirtieth victim of the Atlanta slayings."[2] One can well imagine how people would have reacted to a jury verdict in the 1985 libel case of General William Westmoreland against CBS. Had Westmoreland not withdrawn his suit before the trial had ended, the jury would have been asked to arbitrate American history and decide, essentially, whether the government had deceived us during the Vietnam war. Either way, that jury was destined to become a lightning rod for that emotional controversy.

We have maintained throughout this book that juries cannot be evaluated by case studies, autobiographical accounts, and news stories, no matter how vivid and compelling they may seem. Likewise, the wisdom of their verdicts should not be evaluated by the results of public opinion polls. Jurors are people and decision making is their behavior. Their performance thus raises concrete, empirical questions. By bringing psychology to bear on questions of how the jury should function, we think certain modifications in trial practice and procedure naturally present themselves. It is a good system, but it can be better.

THE IMPARTIAL JUROR

In order for jury trials to produce fair and accurate outcomes, those chosen to make the decisions should be impartial. We opened Chapter 2 by questioning this ideal. After evaluating the assumptions on which it is based, we conclude that there is a problem. People exhibit a remarkable ability to set aside their individual biases while seated in the jury box. Researchers have found that juries almost always vote with the evidence when it clearly favors a particular verdict. Even in close cases, where the evidence can reasonably support different verdicts, the impact of pretrial biases is usually modest and unreliable. So far so good. But in certain types of cases, the subject matter awakens deep-seated personal values over which people adamantly disagree. Rape, the death penalty, politics, and racial prejudice are among these sensitive topics. In trials that involve these kinds of emotional issues, we have reason to believe that individual juror bias is a force to be reckoned with. Add to that the situational problem of pretrial publicity, discussed in Chapter 3, and it is clear that the ideal of an impartial jury rests heavily on the shoulders of an effective voir dire.

We are thus led to the ultimate question of how effectively the legal system screens its candidates for jury service. There are two schools of thought on the matter. One view is that, in the long run, the most effective way to ensure impartiality is by impaneling representative juries. Proponents of this approach emphasize the early stages of selection—the need to use multiple sources to compile eligibility lists, to crack down on exemptions from service, and to curtail or eliminate peremptory challenges. Consistent with that model, Justice Marshall recently called for a complete ban on the use of peremptory challenges.[3] The problem is that this approach, in its pure form, does not adequately protect the litigant whose day in court takes place in a biased community. The second view is that the best way to ensure the impartiality of a jury is to allow the opposing parties to reject prospective jurors suspected of bias. Proponents of this approach favor an open voir dire conducted by attorneys without constraints on their time or the scope of their inquiries. The unfettered use of peremptory challenges is the centerpiece of this approach.

Prevailing practices fall somewhere between these extremes. We do not have a definitive answer to the question of whether the voir dire is an effective safeguard. But its problems are readily apparent. The first is *abuse*. Peremptory challenges are sometimes used to produce racially skewed juries. Although the Supreme Court recently ruled in *Batson v. Kentucky* against that all-too-common practice, it remains to be seen how it will be affected. Aside from the discrimination issue, lawyers openly subvert the process by using it to influence prospective jurors. In reaction to that practice, many courts have placed the voir dire inquiry within the judge's control. That policy results in a quicker voir dire and preempts the illegitimate use of influence techniques. If it could be demonstrated that judges elicit useful information at least as effectively as lawyers do, then this policy wins hands down.[4]

Toward that goal, judges should be encouraged to take steps to improve their interviewing skills. They should ask open-ended questions, develop areas of inquiry from the general to the specific, pace the examination, and so on.[5] They should also be wary of possible sources of bias that prospective jurors are unlikely to admit in response to direct, pointed questions. Psychologists have long recognized that people portray themselves in socially desirable ways, especially when questioned about interracial attitudes.[6] As criminal lawyer Seymour Wishman put it, "the question 'Can you be fair?' almost always gets an affirmative answer that tells nothing about the juror. Even Adolf Hitler would have answered that he would be fair, and perhaps he would have thought he was telling the truth."[7]

On a related matter, Massachusetts Superior Court Judge Charles Alberti believes from his own experience that jurors are more willing to admit their prejudices when questioned individually in judge's chambers, than when queried in open court in front of their peers.[8] This is an interesting and important observation. In the federal system and in most state courts, the voir dire is conducted *en masse*, that is, with the panel as a whole. And yet common sense would suggest that people are reluctant to make negative self disclosures in public. Imagine being one of 12 or 28 prospective jurors and being asked to raise your hand if you feel that you are so prejudiced against black people that you could not be fair. To expect people to make such admissions, even when they are warranted, is unrealistic. Indeed a recent study of actual cases showed that more biased jurors were eliminated (that is, more challenges for cause were granted) through individually conducted than *en masse* voir dires.[9]

A second problem with the voir dire is one of *effectiveness*. Many lawyers base their peremptory challenges on naive and simple-minded theories about human behavior. Despite an extensive body of research that consistently fails to establish reliable profiles of the biased juror, they continue to adhere to unsubstantiated generalizations. One could argue, of course, that at least some lawyers are skilled in their jury selection strategies. That is true; they vary considerably in that respect. But is that variability better in relation to the impartial-juror ideal, or worse? Paradoxically, we think it is worse. When opposing counsel are not evenly matched, the voir dire serves one side better than another. Under these circumstances, the final jury as a group is probably *less* impartial than the panel of venirepersons that preceded it. Exactly the same argument can be made about the newly conceived science of jury selection. Even though it supplies a more rational, empirically grounded approach to the selection process, ultimately its effect is to turn the voir dire even further to the advantage of a particular party.

Is there a way to modify or restructure the voir dire to meet all desired ends? Perhaps, in a limited way. For example, at least a portion of the voir dire examination can be conducted through written questionnaires. Over the years, psychologists have developed sophisticated techniques of questionnaire construction. Personality inventories and attitude scales have become indispensable tools in the study of how people think, feel, and intend to behave. These instruments are not perfect. But they are probably better than the seat-of-the-pants interviews that judges and lawyers conduct on their own.[10] The use of voir dire questionnaires could serve three additional purposes. First, it would be cost effective. Because an entire panel can be tested at once rather than in small groups, this practice could streamline the voir dire considerably. It would also be possible to accumulate over time a set of carefully written, standardized questions. Second, because questionnaires are administered in written form, prospective jurors would feel free answer sensitive questions more truthfully, without being influenced by what others say and without being afraid of public reaction. Third, there is the benefit of equal access. With prospective jurors' questionnaire responses provided to all parties, lawyers would make their selection decisions on a more equal footing. This proposal is not a panacea for the ills of the voir dire, but it is the kind of innovation that is worth considering.

EVIDENCE AND NONEVIDENCE

It is often said that there is no substitute for common sense when it comes to evaluating the two sides of a dispute. If that is true, then we have reason to place great faith in a system that is dedicated to the use of amateurs. Is that faith well placed?

Jurors are expected to base their verdicts on an accurate appraisal of the evidence to the exclusion of everything else. With that ideal in mind, trials are structured in large part to focus jurors on the evidence, to facilitate their search for the truth, and to shield them from information that is extraneous to the trial record. These objectives are sought through an elaborate network of rules that determine who can testify, how they are to be examined, and what kinds of things they can say. In Chapters 4 and 5, we discussed the psychology of evidence and other temptations. From our analysis of how well jurors assess the credibility of witnesses, and from what we know about their ability, or willingness, to resist the lure of information that is not in evidence, we conclude that there is a good deal of room for improvement.

To begin with, jurors are supposed to distinguish in their memory the evidence, as communicated from the witness stand, from everything else. This is an inherently difficult task, so it would be unrealistic to expect them to perform it flawlessly. As we noted earlier, people very often remember *what* is said, while forgetting *who* said it. The problem with trials is that the task is unnecessarily burdensome because the "everything else" category is larger than it needs to be. The occasional intrusion into the record of inadmissible testimony and objectionable arguments is an inevitable fact of life in an adversarial system. But to add to that, the courts permit cross examiners to impart information through conjecture and innuendo, leaving jurors to confuse in their memory the questions from the answers. The courts also sanction the intrusion of nonevidence through opening statements and closing arguments. And they permit surrogates to read deposition testimony for absentee witnesses, leaving the jury to disentangle the messenger's demeanor from the message he or she is delivering. These are not insoluble problems.

The courts rely heavily on instructions to guide juries through the maze of questions, answers, arguments, objections, and rulings. These instructions serve two distinct purposes. First, they offer advice on how to evaluate the evidence. Judges advise juries how to evaluate witnesses, lineup identifications, and coerced confessions. As we suggested earlier, some of these instructions can be improved in empirically demonstrable ways. From what we know about the nonverbal communication of deception, for example, jurors should be redirected in their attention away from facial-expressive cues and toward body language and vocal cues. And from what we know about eyewitness identifications, jurors should be advised to be wary of assertions of self confidence, and to concentrate instead on the circumstances surrounding the witness's perception, memory, and retrieval.

Instructions are also used to control juries, admonishing them not to make unwarranted inferences. It appears that these directives are not particularly effective, however. They do not deter jurors from entering into their decision-making equation certain confessions that they know to be involuntary, testimony that is relevant but inadmissible, or the fact that a criminal defendant failed to take the stand. It has been suggested that jurors are unresponsive to judicial admonishment because information that is forbidden becomes more salient and seemingly more important. That is surely part of the problem, but there is more. Jurors define their task strictly in terms of the accuracy of their verdict. Not being lawyers, they do not know the underlying reasons for accepting some kinds of evidence and rejecting others. If they think the forbidden information helps them make the right decisions, whether it does or not, then they will not discard it. Assuming the courts want jurors to comply with their cautionary instructions, it might help to explain the reasons for excluding the evidence in question. In our research on confession evidence, described in chapter 4, we were able to mitigate the positive coercion bias by explaining why certain kinds of confessions were excluded as a matter of policy.

One final issue is worth mentioning. Thanks to modern technology, the use of videotaped evidence in court opens an interesting new frontier in trial procedure. The most radical proposal, of course, is to replace the live trial altogether with videotaped testimony as a means of sterilizing the presentation of facts by keeping the jury from hearing inadmissible evidence. There are other, more modest uses of videotape that are worth considering. Most notably, it can be used to preserve evidence in its original form, without the intervention of third parties. That advantage is obvious, we think, when it comes to the presentation of deposition testimony. Through videotape, jurors can watch the testimony of an absentee witness first-hand rather than listen to a clerk or an actor reading from the deponent's transcript. That not only enables jurors to evaluate the witness's demeanor, but also keeps them from having their senses blurred by the appearance of a surrogate. We have also seen that the raw material of evidence can be preserved as well through the use of videotape. A growing number of police departments have begun to record the confessions made by criminal suspects. To the extent that the tapes accurately represent not only the suspects' self-incriminating statements, but the interrogation sessions that elicited them, they should assist juries in their efforts to evaluate the quality of that evidence.

Videotape can be used to record other types of evidence, too. We noted earlier that jurors seem to have trouble evaluating the accuracy of eyewitness identification testimony, in part because they rely heavily on how confident eyewitnesses are, a factor that is not reliably correlated with their accuracy. But what if accuracy and confidence were significantly correlated, as jurors believe they are? In a recent series of experiments, the first author found that when subject-witnesses observed tapes of themselves taken as they made their identifications before indicating their level of certainty, their reported confidence was a more reliable predictor of their accuracy.[11] Put *these* witnesses on the stand, witnesses for whom confidence signals accuracy, and leave jurors to their own devices. It should enable them to more effectively distinguish between those who are correct and those who are mistaken. Better yet, what if jurors were to watch identification tapes for themselves? That is, what if they could see eyewitnesses looking through photographs or a lineup as they identify their suspects? Although additional research is needed on the topic, it is conceivable that jurors' ability to evaluate this type of testimony could be improved through this use of videotape. Indeed, we would suggest the following general principle: the closer people are to the evidence, the better able they are to evaluate it.

INFORMATION PROCESSING

In order for juries to make informed decisions, they must fulfill their role as an information-processing body. In concrete behavioral terms, this means they must acquire, comprehend, store, and retrieve the relevant facts and the law. Nobody expects the jury to function like a high-tech computer. But we do expect it to meet certain minimum standards of human competence.

In Chapter 6 we concluded that in a small number of complex marathon-like civil cases, jurors might have difficulty taking command of the trial facts. Then in Chapter 7, we noted that in an even wider range of cases, they fail to comprehend or apply the law contained in judges' instructions. As we see it, neither of these conclusions is likely to generate much disagreement in the legal community. There is, however, a good deal of controversy over the question, to what or to whom do we attribute this undesirable state of affairs? Former Chief Justice Burger and other jury critics maintain that these problems are the inevitable consequence of a system that is committed to the use of amateurs as decision makers. We emphatically disagree. Before attributing failures to the jury, the courts should take a hard look at their own role in shaping the jury's performance.

What we have seen in these two chapters is that through a variety of archaic methods of trial management, juries are impeded from meeting the information-processing demands of their task. Based on psychologically confused and confusing assumptions about human behavior, the courts treat their juries as passive recipients of information. Consistent with that model, they often deny jurors an opportunity to learn in the courtroom as they do in school, on the job, and in virtually all other areas of life. Many judges thus prohibit jurors from taking notes or asking questions of the witnesses—even though these procedures appear to be useful and nondisruptive. And then, having erected these obstacles, the courts bemoan the jury's inability to overcome them.

Turning from the facts to the law, the ritual of instructing juries reveals the same kind of self-defeating pattern. Over the years, experts have challenged the average person's ability to apply or even understand those instructions. Referring to their "infinite capacity for mischief," Judge Jerome Frank complained that "twelve men can easily misunderstand as much law in a minute than a judge can explain in an hour."[12] After taking a long, hard look at this criticism, we find that, characteristically, the judge's charge is poorly timed and unintelligible. Add to that the fact that juries are rarely provided with a written or taped copy of the instructions and one is led to question why the judiciary is unable to make its laws accessible. When it comes to jury nullification, for example, it appears that because the courts are ambivalent about the jury's power to moderate the law, they prefer not to tell them about it.

With an eye on recent developments in psychology, the judiciary needs to articulate and modify its assumptions about human behavior. If it does, it will discover that, generally speaking, jurors should be woven into the fabric of the trial proceedings as *active*, not passive, participants. Along with clear, well timed instructions, that kind of change would assist the jury in its pursuit of information.

THE DELIBERATION

It is perhaps the greatest asset of a trial by jury that a group of independent citizens, strangers to one another, are thrown together behind the closed door of the jury room and directed to reach a common decision. They are 12 independent minds; they all watch the same trial; and they are equal in their importance to the final outcome. From the diversity of perspectives brought to bear on their task, these jurors share information, compare notes, clash in their values, and argue over interpretations. And somehow, out of all the conflict and tension, 95 percent of all juries succeed in reaching complete agreement on a verdict. As one juror put it, "The thing that struck me the most about jury service was the way twelve strangers were suddenly working together, each person adding a little bit, trying to figure out what happened, what was fair. In the business world, we rarely get this kind of team effort."[13] When it works as it should, jury deliberation is a truly remarkable process.

In Chapter 8 we saw from stories of real juries gone astray, and from controlled observations of mock juries, that they vary in terms of how close they come to fulfilling the ideals of deliberation. We also saw in Chapter 9 that the legal system can exert a substantial amount of control over how juries deliberate, even though they do so in secrecy. Judges can sequester jurors or withhold their identities in order to keep them from feeling pressured by outside sources. Usually, though, the courts offer no guidance on how to deliberate effectively —despite the fact that for most people, it is their first time in the jury room.

What sense does it make for judges to take a hands-off approach on the matter of deliberations, after carefully directing the jury through all other aspects of its task? None, as far as we can tell. And yet custom has it that such guidance is frowned upon and viewed as interference. "You may conduct your deliberations as you choose" is the accepted practice.[14] To be sure, instructions on how to deliberate should be made with caution. Thus, when one judge told his jury to conduct its deliberations like a "board meeting," with never a vote taken, an appeals court had reason for its disapproval.[15] But why not suggest to jurors that they defer an initial vote until they have had a chance to discuss the issues openly and without commitment? And why not recommend to the jury that it begin by going around the table for comments as a way to get everybody speaking? Coupled with the use of a round table rather than a rectangular one, this strategy should mitigate the problem of unequal participation.

It is bad enough that the courts fail to guide juries toward an ideal decision-making process. To make matters worse, they often sanction procedures and structural changes that widen the gap between the ideals and realities of deliberation. In the 1970s the U.S. Supreme Court quietly revolutionized the face of the American jury. It permitted a reduction in its size and then it relaxed its unanimity requirement. Although it is not clear how the size of the group ultimately affects the quality of its decision-making apparatus, it is clear that the nonunanimous jury is unacceptable. It weakens and inhibits jurors who are in the voting minority; it breeds closed-mindedness; it impairs the quality of discussion; and it leaves many jurors unsatisfied with the final verdict. Then there is the *Allen* instruction, otherwise known as the Dynamite Charge. Used to implore the deadlocked jury to return a verdict, it too appears to intimidate members of a voting minority into compliance. And yet, without a potent and vocal dissent, one based on legitimate differences of opinion, what is left of deliberation?

As we have seen in so many other aspects of jury management, the problem is this: Within the legal system there is a fundamental ambivalence that leads the courts to assert an ideal on the one hand, and to sabotage it on the other. In the abstract, they value the kind of exhaustive deliberation that protects litigants against erroneous and unfair verdicts. Justice dictates that no decision is far better than a wrong decision. But in the concrete the system is impatient with lengthy deliberations and intolerant of hung juries. For administrative reasons, a certain measure of accuracy can be sacrificed in order to obtain a verdict. Well, you cannot have it both ways. And when faced with a conflict between a fair trial and a final disposition, the right choice should be clear.

PARTING SHOTS

Ladies and gentlemen of the jury. We conclude by making explicit a point alluded to throughout this book. When trials result in outcomes perceived as just or unjust, we credit or blame the jury for its performance. We hear about prejudice, bleeding hearts, and runaway juries. And we hear former Chief Justice Burger's incessant claim that civil juries are incompetent. These charges are sometimes justified. But juries do not make their decisions in a vacuum. And we do not take enough account of that fact. As attorney Gerry Spence put it, "pity, please, the jury entrapped in a strange and sterile place called a courtroom in which nothing grows and where no sounds can be heard, not the meadowlark's song, not the lilt of a distant boy's whistle, and where the good familiar odors of life are missing."[16] From a psychological perspective, there is substance to that poetry. Trials are very well orchestrated events structured according to a complex network of rules, constraints, and rituals. And what are these rituals based on? They are based on assumptions—often misassumptions—about human behavior. In the end, it is the American jury *trial*, not the jury per se, that should be tried.

NOTES

1. H. Kalven & H. Zeisel, *The American Jury*. Boston: Little, Brown, 1966, p. 3.

2. See R. Stuart (1982), Atlantans' feelings mixed on verdict. *New York Times*, March 1, p. 12.

3. *Batson v. Kentucky*, supra note 1.13.

4. A recent empirical study suggests that jurors are not as candid with judges as with lawyers; see S. E. Jones (1987), Judge-versus attorney-conducted voir dire: An empirical investigation of juror candor. *Law and Human Behavior*, Vol. 11, pp. 131–146.

5. See D. Chmielewski & G. Bermant (1982), Recommendations for the conduct of the voir dire examination and juror challenges. Appearing in G. Bermant's *Jury Selection Procedures in United States District Courts*. Washington, D.C.: Federal Judicial Center.

6. See F. Crosby, S. Bromley, & L. Saxe (1980), Recent unobtrusive studies of black and white discrimination and prejudice: A literature review. *Psychological Bulletin*, Vol. 87, pp. 546–563.

7. *Anatomy of a Jury*. New York: Times Books, pp. 88–89.

8. Personal communication, January 14, 1987.

9. See M. T. Nietzel & R. C. Dillehay (1982), The effects of variations in voir dire procedures in capital murder trials. *Law and Human Behavior*, Vol. 6, pp. 1–13.

10. Questionnaires can be constructed following a number of basic principles of psychometrics. For example, items can be carefully written so as to distinguish between respondents and neutralize social desirability concerns. Central to this enterprise is that because an individual's response to a single inquiry can mean any number of things, a reliable measure of attitudes must consist of several overlapping questions.

11. S. M. Kassin (1985), Eyewitness identification: Retrospective self awareness and the accuracy-confidence correlation. *Journal of Personality and Social Psychology*, Vol. 49, pp. 878–893.

12. *Skidmore v. Baltimore & Ohio R.R.* (1948), 167 F.2d 54, p. 60.

13. Quoted in Wishman, supra note 7, p. 248.

14. *Allis v. U.S.* (1893), 73 F. 165, p. 183.

15. See Note, supra note 8.55, p. 131.

16. G. L. Spence (1986), How to make a complex case come alive for a jury. *American Bar Association Journal*, Vol. 72, pp. 62–66, at p. 65.

COURT CASES

n denotes footnote.

217

NAME INDEX

n denotes footnote.

SUBJECT INDEX